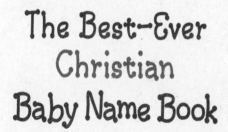

The Best-Ever
Christian
Baby Name Book

The Best-Ever Christian Baby Name Book

Nick Harrison
&
Steve Miller

HARVEST HOUSE PUBLISHERS
EUGENE, OREGON

Cover by Abris, Veneta, Oregon

Cover photos © iStockphoto

THE BEST-EVER CHRISTIAN BABY NAME BOOK
Copyright © 2007 by Nick Harrison and Steve Miller
Published by Harvest House Publishers
Eugene, Oregon 97402

Library of Congress Cataloging-in-Publication Data
Harrison, Nick.
    The best-ever Christian baby name book: Nick Harrison and Steve Miller.
        p. cm.
    Includes bibliographical references.
    ISBN-13: 978-0-7369-1994-4 (pbk.)
    ISBN-10: 0-73
    1. Names, Personal—Religious aspects—Christianity—Dictionaries. 2. Names, Personal—Dictionaries—English. I. Miller, Steve, 1960- II. Title.
    CS2377.H373 2007
    929.4'4—dc22

                                                                2007001237

Printed in the United States of America

07 08 09 10 11 12 13 14 15 / BP-SK / 11 10 9 8 7 6 5 4 3 2 1

For the people in our lives whose names mean the most to us:

Henry, Patricia, Raymond, Joan, Beverly (of course!),
Rachel, Rebecca, Bethany, Winston, Michael, Sean, Joshua, and Emma

Nick Harrison

My wife, Becky; our three sons, Keith, Nathan, and Ryan;
my mother, Betty; and my in-laws, Marty and Pat

Steve Miller

Acknowledgments

Thanks to my family, as always. And to my other family—at Harvest House Publishers...thanks for everything.

—NICK HARRISON

With special appreciation to Priscilla Cameron of the Eugene Bible College library. Thank you for your help with the resources needed to research the information given in this book.

—STEVE MILLER

Contents

• • •

Before You Begin

One of the first important duties new parents face is choosing a name for their baby. Not only does the child usually carry his or her given name throughout life, but studies show that names can have an effect on the child's personality and how others perceive him or her.

For Christians, the selection of a name has yet another dimension. In the Bible we find that God places a high priority on names. There are, for example, many men and women whose names were actually chosen by God, and the meanings of their names carried special significance.

In the very first pages of the Bible we meet Adam ("made from the earth") and Eve ("life-giver"), both names significant. In Adam's case, his name tells us his origin; in Eve's case, we learn about her role in history as the mother of all humankind.

Consider also the best-known patriarch of the Bible, Abraham. At first his name was *Abram*, which means "the father is exalted." But God later entered into a covenant (an agreement) with Abram, part of which included a name change consistent with his future. God gave him the name *Abraham*, which means "the father of a multitude"—a reflection of God's destiny for this great man of faith. The covenant also included a name change for *Sarai*, Abraham's wife, who now became *Sarah*, "a princess."

Another great patriarch of the Bible, Jacob, was born just after his fraternal twin, Esau. Jacob's name means "one who supplants another," as this expresses what happened as Jacob followed Esau out of the womb and as they grew up. Later in his life, after Jacob wrestled with an angel in an effort to receive a blessing, his name became *Israel*, which means "he shall become a prince of God." Again, God's plan for the man was evident in the name given to him.

In the New Testament, the disciple known as Simon was given the new name *Peter* by Christ, because Peter means "rock," and Peter's role in history was to be as a rock of the new Christian faith.

In addition to the names of many characters in the Bible, God was also careful about the revelation of His own name. When God commanded Moses to lead the people of Israel out of Egypt, do you remember God's answer to Moses' question? Moses asked, "Who should I say sent me?" God answered, "I AM WHO I AM. This is what you are to say to the Israelites: I AM has sent me to you....This is my name forever, the name by which I am to be remembered from generation to generation" (Exodus 3:14-15).

God was very protective of His name. He revealed in other places in the Old Testament that He was to be known as *Jehovah-jireh* (the Lord Will Provide), *Jehovah-nissi* (the Lord Our Banner), *Jehovah-shalom* (the Lord Is Peace), *Jehovah-shammah* (the Lord Who Is Present), and *Jehovah-tsidkenu* (the Lord Our Righteousness).

Consider also the importance God put on the name of His Son, Jesus Christ. Before Jesus was born, His name was prophesied to be "Wonderful Counselor, Mighty God, Everlasting Father, Prince of Peace" (Isaiah 9:6).

In the New Testament, it was revealed to the apostle Paul that God had given Jesus Christ "the name that is above every name," and that "at the name of Jesus every knee should bow, in heaven and on earth and under the earth" (Philippians 2:9-10).

Further, consider the power that God invested in the name of Jesus Christ. We're told by Jesus, "I will do whatever you ask in my *name*, so that the Son may bring glory to the Father" (John 14:13). We're also told that the purpose for John's gospel was that "by believing you may have life in his *name*" (John 20:31).

When Peter and John met the lame man at the Gate Beautiful, they prayed for him in the *name* of Christ, and he was healed. When Paul delivered a slave girl from a demon in Acts 16:18, he did so in the *name* of the Lord Jesus.

We're told that there's no other name under heaven by which men can be saved (Acts 4:12). And Jesus said that those of us who are believers should rejoice because our names are written in heaven (Luke 10:20).

Finally, in Revelation, the last book of the Bible, we're told that one day we shall all receive a new name—a name that God Himself chooses for each of us. That's pretty special, isn't it?

As you read through the following pages, we think you'll enjoy discovering the meanings of the many names offered. If you're awaiting the birth of a new baby or that call that tells you you've been chosen to adopt—congratulations! May the many blessings that babies bring to parents be yours in abundance. And may God direct you in this important decision of naming your child.

Practical Suggestions for Choosing Your Baby's Name

When you choose a name for your new baby, there are a number of things you'll want to consider:

Prayer. First, as a Christian, you have the advantage of prayer in selecting a name. Be sure to submit this important choice as well to God as you pray for your baby's health, delivery, and similar concerns.

Heritage. Consider honoring your family's heritage by selecting a grandparent or other ancestor's name. Often a good choice for a middle name, or sometimes even a first name, is the mother's maiden name. Some parents have created interesting names for their baby that are taken from their own names. For instance, a father named Ray and a mother named Jean gave their daughter the created name RaeJean.

Character. If you choose a name with a meaning you hope is eventually evidenced in the child's character, be sure to occasionally remind the growing child of the significance of the name and that it was chosen with great love and care. Don't force your child, however, to assume an attribute or identity that's not truly his or hers. God can mold a child's character His way. Guide, but don't force.

Role models. Many of the names in this book include references to noted Christians with that name. Consider honoring the memory of that person—and at the same time giving your child an excellent role model—by selecting the name of a great Christian man or woman. For instance, a boy might be named Wesley after John Wesley, or a girl might be named Florence after the noted Christian nurse Florence Nightingale. As your child grows, he or she can be told the story of their namesake. A book can be given with the story of the hero or heroine after which they are named. A boy named David might be told not only of King David in the Bible, but also such exemplary Christians as David Brainerd, David Livingston, and David Wilkerson. To call your attention to these possibilities, we've noted some well-known Christian leaders in special sidebars that appear throughout the book.

Dishonorable names. We likewise suggest you don't choose a name that is honoring to false gods or evil men and women from past generations. For example, the name Judas is discouraged...as are the names from pagan religions, such as the name Malini, which, although very melodic, is also the name of the Hindu god of the earth. We have not included such names in this guide, *except when they are also biblical names*. We have, however, made a special effort to select names that *do* have special meaning to Christian believers.

Spelling problems. Beware of choosing names with unusual spellings. These can be creative and unique, but realize that for many years the child will be correcting teachers, friends, and even relatives who may inadvertently spell the name the more traditional way.

Finding balance. Remember that your child will carry the name you choose throughout his or her life. Sometimes parents wanting to mark their child as different do so by picking names that end up becoming troublesome or embarrassing. Think carefully before you give your child an awkward or cumbersome name. An unattractive name, or one that's considered "weird," can become a source of stigma. On the other hand, a name that's abundantly popular may result in a child feeling less unique than peers who have more distinctive, attractive names. Try to find the balance between popularity and uniqueness when choosing a name.

Initials. Keep your child's initials in mind as you consider various names. A child is liable to experience teasing when it's discovered that his or her initials are ICK or DOG or some other undesirable acronym.

Sound. When you've narrowed your choices to a few favorites, say the first, middle, and last names together out loud several times and listen to how they sound. Do the first and middle names fit with your last name? If not, is there a similar name that will work better? Several years ago a friend of mine (Nick) mentioned that she had always dreamed of having a son named Nick...but when she married a man with the last name of Knack, she knew she had to forever abandon that dream.

"Prayer verse." Once you've chosen a name, you might want to consider searching the Bible for a relevant "prayer verse" based on a Bible passage that corresponds to the name's meaning. For example, the name Melinda means "gentle one." An appropriate prayer verse might be Philippians 4:5, which says, "Let your gentleness be evident to all. The Lord is near."

Tips on Creating a Unique Name

One increasingly popular trend among parents today is that of creating a name specially for their child. A name is the first and one of the most important gifts you give to your child, and you may want to gift your newborn with a name that sets him or her apart as a unique individual and provides a special sense of identity. Following are a number of ways to create a new name.

Alter the spelling of an existing name. The vast majority of names today already have a wide range of spelling variations, so this method doesn't guarantee your child will end up with a truly one-of-a-kind name. However, some spelling variations are used so rarely that your son or daughter will still possess an unusual or distinct name. For example...

- Instead of *Danielle*, you can use *Ranielle* (change the first letter to another letter that works well with the rest of the name).

- Instead of *Susan*, you can use *Suzahn* (alter the spelling according to sounds or phonetic elements within the name).

- You can also shorten the syllables of a name such as *Deborah* to create *Debra*, or lengthen the syllables of a name such as *Rosa* to create *Rohsah*.

Combine two existing names to make a new one. As we mentioned earlier, we know of a father and mother named Ray and Jean who combined their names and called their daughter Rae-Jean. Another possibility is to take two names that don't usually appear in combined form and put them together, such as Ray and Anne to create Rayanne. Or, you could use Ron and Ellen to create Ronel or Ronelle.

Use a proper noun (or a variation of it) as a name. The abbreviated form of Texas, which is Tex, is often used as a name or nickname. Boys have been named Tennessee, and girls Montana. Willow (a tree) and Magnolia (a flower) have also been used. What can you come up with?

Turn an English or non-English word into a name. For example, the English word "ocean" can become the girls' name Oceana. Or, the Spanish word *niña,* which means "girl," can become the name Nina, Ninetta, or Ninette.

● ● ●

To help stir your creativity, you'll find on pages 43 and 113 of this book some real-life examples of parents who have created unique names for their children.

Of course, as we've already pointed out, before you finalize your child's name, you'll want to ensure it won't make him or her vulnerable to ridicule. Ask yourself: Does this name lend itself to inadvertent negative associations? Does it look or sound too similar to other names or words that might subject my child to teasing? And, do the initials say or spell something that is potentially embarrassing?

How to Use This Book

In creating *The Best-Ever Christian Baby Name Book,* our goal was not to simply list every conceivable name in existence. Rather, we wanted to equip you, the new parent, with the resources we believe will help you choose the ideal name for your baby.

For that reason, we deliberately selected what we believe are the "cream of the crop" names, with their most popular and reasonable variations and diminutives. Thus, you will find a wide selection of the best names without some of the more outlandish spellings and variations of those names. And for those who are less traditionally inclined, see also the suggestions for creating your own unique name (see pages 15–16).

Also, in our research, we discovered that different sources often give varying meanings and origins for the same name. So, in our effort to create the "best-ever" Christian baby-name book, we've sifted through the many options for these disputable points and have offered what we believe to be the most commonly agreed-upon origins and meanings.

Reading the Entries

Each entry in the book begins with a name that appears in

boldface text. This main entry is then followed by the origin and meaning of the name as well as the variations and diminutives of the name. Below is a sample entry, with the various elements of the entry explained:

ASTERISK INDICATES A BIBLICAL NAME

ENTRY   ORIGIN   MEANING

*Ruth: Hebrew, "friend, companion"

Ruthe, Ruthelle, Ruthi, Ruthie, ⟵——— DIMINUTIVES
Ruthina, Ruthine   AND VARIATIONS

Ruth was a loyal daughter-in- ⟵——— BIBLE CHARACTER
law who moved to Israel with her
mother-in-law, Naomi. Eventually
she became the wife of Boaz. Their
story is told in the book of Ruth.

> **RUTH BELL GRAHAM** ⟵——— NOTABLE CHRISTIAN
> *(1920–)*   WHO BEARS THIS
>   NAME
> was born in Quinjiang, China,
> the daughter of medical
> missionaries. She is the wife
> of evangelist Billy Graham and
> the mother of five children.

For simplicity sake, we use the word *variation* to mean an alternate spelling, a common tweaking, or a foreign version of a name. For example, the name Katherine has *variations* that include Kathryn, Catherine, and even Caitlin. It also has *diminutives* such as Kathy, Kate, and Kay. Some names also have *variations* for the opposite gender. For instance, Charles has *variations* that include Charlton, Carlos (Spanish), and the feminine name Charlene. The diminutives for Charles are names such as Charlie, Chuck, Chip, and Chaz.

If the main entry name has any diminutives or variations (or other forms), those will appear on the subsequent lines. As stated above, we've not attempted to list every possible spelling variation. Rather, we have focused on what are, in general, the more common ones. With this information you can go the extra step, if you wish, to create a more unusual form of a name.

Cross-Referencing the Entries

If you see an entry that reads

Patty: diminutive of Patricia

then you will want to go to the main entry **Patricia** in order to find out the origin, meaning, and various forms of the name Patty.

If you don't find a name you're looking for, consider that it might be a variation or diminutive of another name. Thus, you may find it listed with the name from which it originated.

Finding the Bible Names

Another feature we've included in the book is a significant number of some of the best biblical names. In most instances, we also point you to the references in the Bible where that name is found.

All the Bible names are preceded by an asterisk. In some cases, you will also find, at the end of the Bible name entries, details about the individuals who bore those names.

We did not include every name found in the Bible. Many of these names are simply too unusual, or else they have histories or meanings behind them that may make them less desirable as names for your baby. If, however, you wish to look up every Bible name, there are several resources at your disposal. See "Selected Sources" at the end of this book for some ideas.

Noted Christians

We've also added some short biographical sketches of some

Christians who bore certain names. Many parents like to honor the memory of a noted Christian by naming their child after such a hero of the faith.

Finally, throughout the book we've provided what we believe are some entertaining and insightful insights regarding names.

So go ahead and start your search for the perfect name for your baby...and have fun!

The Ten Most Popular Boys' and Girls' Names

TOP TEN NAMES FOR 2005

Rank	Boys' names	Girls' names
1	Jacob	Emily
2	Michael	Emma
3	Joshua	Madison
4	Matthew	Abigail
5	Ethan	Olivia
6	Andrew	Isabella
7	Daniel	Hannah
8	Anthony	Samantha
9	Christopher	Ava
10	Joseph	Ashley

The above listing comes from the Social Security Administration. Their "baby name" site is extremely interesting. The popularity of names is accessible by year, by decade, or even by state. Check it out at www.ssa.gov/OACT/babynames/.

GIRLS' NAMES
A–Z

A

*Abijah: Hebrew, "God is my father"

Abby, Abi

Abi is mentioned in 2 Kings 18:2 and 2 Chronicles 29:1; 26:5.

Abella: A feminine variation of Abel

Abela, Abelia, Abelle

*Abia: Hebrew, "God is my father"

Abi, Abby, Abiah, Bia

An ancestor of the Lord Jesus Christ. See 1 Chronicles 2:24.

*Abigail: Hebrew, "source of the father's joy"

Abbe, Abbie, Abby, Abbygaile, Abbygale, Abbygayle, Gail, Gale, Galia, Galya, Gayle.

In the Bible, *Abigail* gained favor in King David's sight after imploring the king to spare her family because of her husband Nabal's foolishness. Later, after Nabal's death, Abigail, described as "an intelligent and beautiful woman," became one of David's wives (1 Samuel 25).

*Abihail: Hebrew, "source of strength"

Abby, Abi

Can be both male and female. Queen Esther's father was named Abihail, as were three women in the Bible.

Abra: Hebrew, "mother of a multitude"—a feminine variation of Abraham

Abi, Abby, Abrah

Abriana: Italian, feminine variation of Abraham

Abby, Abrianna, Abrielle, Ana, Anna, Bree

---

* Names preceded by an asterisk are names that appear in the Bible.

Acacia: Greek, "honored one"
Cacia, Cacie, Casey, Cass, Cassia, Cassie, Cayce
Wood from the acacia tree was used in the construction of the ark of the covenant and the tabernacle in the wilderness.

What's in a Name?

One morning my husband woke up from a dream and said, "You're going to have a baby girl and we are going to name her Aavery—with two A's." I said, "What?" He explained to me that while he was dreaming, a little girl came up to him and he started talking to her. When he asked her what her name was, she said it was Aavery, with two A's...and that's how my oldest daughter got her name.

MARCIA FROM OREGON

---

*Achsah: Hebrew, "breaking the veil"
Achsah was the daughter of the Old Testament hero Caleb. Read her story in Joshua 15:16-17, Judges 1:12-13, and 1 Chronicles 4:15.

Ada: Old English, "prosperous"—in some cases, a diminutive of Adelaide
Adda, Addiah, Addie, Addy, Adi

*Adah: Hebrew, "adorned by God"
Adda, Addy, Adiah
Two Adahs are mentioned in Genesis (see 4:19-23 and 26:34; 36:2).

Adia: Swahili, "she is a gift from God"
Addiah, Addie, Addy, Adiah, Ady

Adair: Greek, "she who is beautiful"
Adara, Adare

Adail: German, "she who is noble"
Ada, Adale, Adalia, Addy, Dale

Adama: Hebrew, "made of the earth"—a feminine variation of Adam
Ada, Adamma, Addy

Adelaide: Old German, "she who is noble"
Addie, Addy, Adela, Adele, Adelle, Adella, Adelina, Adeline, Addey, Adellia, Della

Adelpha: Greek, "sisterly"
Addie, Adelle, Adelphia, Dell, Della

Adina: Hebrew, "she who is delicate"
Addy, Adeana, Adeena, Adene, Adina, Adine, Deana, Dena, Dina

Adna: Hebrew, "she who is delightful"
Addie, Addy, Ady

Adnah: Hebrew, "eternal rest"
Addie, Addy, Ady

"The parent's task is not a yoke to be borne; it is a privilege to be enjoyed. If God's design in giving us children is to bless us, the task He calls us to as parents is nothing more than an extension and magnification of that blessing."

—JOHN MACARTHUR

Adora: Latin, "she who is adored"
Addie, Addy, Adoria, Ady, Dora, Dorrie, Dory

Adrian: Greek, "she who is rich"
Addy, Adria, Adriah, Adriana, Adrienne, Anna, Dree

Afra: Hebrew, "doe-like"
Affra, Affrey, Aphra

Afton: Old English, from the town of Afton, England
Aftyn

Agate: Old English, "precious stone"
Aggie, Aggy

Agatha: Greek, "she who is kind"
Agace, Agacia, Agathe, Aggie, Aggy

Agnes: Greek, "she who is pure"
Aggie, Aggy, Agna, Agnella, Agnelle, Agness

Ahava: Hebrew, "essence"
Ahiva, Ahuda

*Ahlai: Hebrew, "she who beseeches"
See 1 Chronicles 2:31,34 and 1 Chronicles 11:41.

Ahn: Asian/Vietnamese, "she who is peaceful"

Aida: Latin, "she who helps"
Aidan (also Gaelic, "fiery one")

Aileen: Scottish/Irish variation of the name Helen

Ailene, Alena, Alene, Alina, Aline, Ally, Alyna, Lena, Lina

Aimee: See Amy

Ainsley: Scottish, "meadow"

Ainslee, Ainsleigh, Ansley

Alana: Irish, "fair one"—also a feminine variation of the male name Alan

Alaina, Alaine, Alainna, Alena, Ally, Laine, Lana, Laney, Lena

Alarice: Old German, "ruler"—a feminine variation of Alaric

Alaricia, Alarise, Alerica, Ally

Alba: Latin, taken from the Italian city of the same name

Albina, Albine, Alva

Alberta: Old German, "she who is brilliant," also a feminine form of Albert

Albertina, Albertine, Ally, Berta, Bertie; also Elberta, Elbertina, Elbertine

Alcina: Greek, "strength of mind"

Alceena, Alcine, Alcy, Ally, Alsina, Alsine, Alsyna

Alda: Old German, "she who is prosperous"

Aldea, Aldina, Aldis, Aldona, Aldys

Aldora: Old German, "gift"

Aldara, Ally, Dora, Dorrie; also Eldora, thus Ella, Ellie

Alea: Arabic, "exalted one"

Aleah, Alia, Ally, Leah, Lia

Aleda: Latin, "winged one"

Alida, Alleda, Ally, Leda

Alena: A Russian variation of Helen

Aleen, Aleena, Alina, Aline

Aleta: Greek, "she who is true"

Aletha, Alethea, Aletta, Leta, Letha, Letta, Lettie, Thea

Alexandra: Greek, from the male Alexander, "he who defends"

Alandra, Alex, Alexa, Alexandria, Alexia, Alexina, Alexine, Alexis, Ally, Landra, Lanny, Lex, Lexa, Lexie, Lexandra, Xandra—many additional variations and diminutives can be created from the name Alexandra

Alfreda: Old English, "she who

is wise"—a feminine variation of Alfred

Alfie, Ally, Elfreda, Freda

Alice: Greek, "she who tells the truth"—also considered by many to be a variation of Adelaide

Alecia, Alicia, Alisa, Alisha, Alison, Allison, Ally, Allysa, Alycia, Alysa, Alyssa, Lecia, Lysa—many additional variations and diminutives can be created from the name Alice

Aliya: Hebrew, "one who ascends"

Aleeya, Aliah, Ally

Allegra: Latin, "she who is full of cheer"

Alegra, Alegria, Allegria, Allie, Legra

Allison: A variation of Alice

Alcy, Alison, Alli, Ally, Allyson

Alma: Latin, "soul"

Almah

Almeta: Latin, "she who reaches for the goal"

Almeda, Elmeda, Elmeta, Meta

Almira: Arabic, "royal one," or a variation of Elmira

Almera, Almyra, Mira, Mirra, Mirrah

Aloysia: Old German, "heroine of war"—also a feminine variation of Aloysius

Ally, Aloys, Aloyse

Alta: Spanish, "high"

Althea: Greek, "healer"

Ally, Altheda, Altheya, Althia, Altheya, Thea

Alva: Spanish, "she who is a fair one"

Albeena, Albena, Albina

Alvina: Old English, "she who is friendly"

Ally, Alveena, Alvine, Alvinia, Vina

Amalia: Hebrew, "the work of God"

Mahlia, Malia, Malie

AMANDA SMITH
(1837–1915)

was born into slavery and, after her conversion as a young woman, became a noted evangelist.

Amanda: Latin, "easy to love"
Amandah, Manda, Mandi, Mandy

Amara: Greek, "she who is beautiful"

Amaris: Hebrew, "promised of God"
Amariah, Maris

Amber: French, from the color amber
Amberlee, Amberleigh, Amberly, Amberlyn, Ambi, Ambur

Amelia: Latin, "she who is ambitious"
Amalia, Amelie, Amylia—this name easily lends itself to many creative variations. Emma and Emily are both considered variants of Amelia.

Amina: Arabic, "she who is worthy of trust"
Amy, Mina

Amity: Latin, "she who is friendly"

Amy: Latin, "she who is beloved," from the same root as the word "amor"
Aimee, Ami, Ammie, Ammy

AMY CARMICHAEL
(1867–1951)
was a determined missionary to the poor of India with a focus on temple prostitutes.
In 1926 she began her Dohnavur Fellowship. She was the author of many popular books, including the classic *If*.

An: Chinese, "she who is peaceful"

Anabel: Latin, "she who is lovable"
Anabella, Annabell, Annabella, Annabelle

*Anah: Hebrew, "she who sings"
See Genesis 36:2,18,25.

Anastasia: Greek, "resurrection"
Ana, Anastacia, Anastasha, Stacey, Stacia, Stacie, Stasha

Andrea: Greek, "she who is full of courage," also a feminine variation of Andrew
Andee, Andi, Andra, Andrah, Andrana, Andreanna, Andri, Andriah, Andriana, Andrina

Angela: Old English, "heavenly being"—literally "angel"

Angel, Angelica, Ange-
lina, Angeline, Angelique
(French), Angelita, Angella,
Angie

What's in a Name?

My parents didn't have a name picked out for me when I was
born. Mom said it was because they thought I would be a boy. Dad's
family always had boys. My only sibling, seven years older than I,
was a boy, so they thought I would be too.

Lest I think a girl wasn't wanted, Mom hastened to add that she
and Dad were delighted that the string of boys had been broken and
they had finally been blessed with a little girl.

At any rate, my parents took their time deciding my name. I often
wonder what they called me during that time—a time that stretched
so long that the doctor finally sent in my birth certificate with
"unnamed O'Barr" in the name field. (I was a teenager before Mom
corrected that with the vital statistics folks.)

A friend of the family had a little girl named Gaylia Mae. My cau-
tious parents finally concluded that my name would be *Ann Gaylia*.

Raised in the South, where double names are common, I was
always called Ann Gaylia by family, friends, and schoolteachers. Only
when I left the South did I notice new friends and acquaintances calling me Ann. It took a while for it to register that folks outside of the
South couldn't be bothered with using two names for anyone, even
close friends.

Having settled in the town where I hope I will remain until God
calls me home, I decided on a new tactic. Anytime I have to give
my name, as on a name card, or for the church roll, I write my two
names together: Anngaylia.

It's now just one name, so people have to call me by that. And it
has worked. Many people meeting me for the first time ask where my
parents came up with the name. Was it Gaelic? Hungarian?

No, just Southern.

ANNGAYLIA FROM WASHINGTON

Ani: Hawaiian, "she who is beautiful"

Anika: Slovak form of Ann, "she who is full of grace"

Anaka, Annika, Anouska

Anita: Spanish, "she who is full of grace"—a Spanish variation of Ann

Aneeta, Anitra, Nita

Ann: English, "she who is full of grace," from Hannah

Ana, Anele, Anna, Anne, Annelle, Annette (French), Annora, Anora. There are many variations and name combinations that can be created using the name Ann. It works well in combination with other proper names (Mary Ann, Bobbi Ann, Sue Ann, Ann Marie, etc.).

ANN JUDSON
(1789–1826)

was the first female American missionary to the Far East. She and her husband, Adoniram, translated the Bible into Burmese, undergoing much suffering and many trials.

---

*Anna: A variation of Ann, from Hannah, "she who is full of grace"

Ana, Annah, Annette (French), Anya (Russian). Many variations of this name occur in combination with other popular names. Examples include Annabelle, Annalisa, Annalysa.

See Luke 2:36-38. Anna (the New Testament form of Hannah) was a widow, a prayer warrior, and one of the first messengers of the good news of a Savior's birth.

*Anah: Hebrew, "God has answered"

See Genesis 36:2,18,25.

Anthea: Greek, "flower"

Anthia, Thea, Thia

Antoinette: French, "she who is praiseworthy"—a feminine variation of Anthony

Antonia (Italian), Antonietta, Netta, Netty, Toni, Tonia

April: Latin, "open"—from the month of April, the seasonal "opening" to spring

Aprila, Aprilette, Aprilina, Avril

Ara: Latin, "altar"

Arah, Ari, Aria, Ariah

Arabella: Arabic, "ornate altar"

Arabelle, Arbelina, Arbeline, Arbella, Arbelle, Bella, Belle

Ardelle: Latin, "enthusiastic"

Arda, Ardeen, Ardella, Ardina, Ardine, Dell, Della

Ardis: Latin, "she who is eager"

Arda, Ardah, Ardie, Ardra, Ardrah, Ardy

Ardith: Hebrew, "field of flowers"—also a feminine variation of Arden

Ardath, Ardys, Ardyth, Aridatha

Areta: Greek, "she who is virtuous"

Aretha, Retha

Ariadne: Greek, "divine"

Aria, Ariadna

Ariana: Welsh, "as valuable as fine silver"

Ariane, Arianna, Arianne

Ariel: Hebrew, "lion of God"—can also be a male name

Ari, Ariella, Arielle, Ella

Arlene: Celtic, "promise"

Arla, Arlana, Arleen, Arlie, Arlinda, Lana

Arva: Latin, "pasture"

Arvilla

Ashley: Old English, "from the ash tree"

Ashlee, Ashleigh, Ashly

Ashira: Hebrew, "rich"

Ashyra

Astra: Greek, "star"

Astrid: Old German, "she who has strength from God"

Athalia: Hebrew, "our God is exalted"

Athalie, Thalia, Thalie

Athena: Greek, "she who is wise"

Athene, Thena

Aubrey: Old German, "she who is noble"

Aubree, Bree

Audrey: Old German, "she who is noble"—a variation of the name Etheldreda

Audie, Audra, Audree, Audreena, Audrina, Audrine

Augusta: Latin, "full of majesty"—a feminine variation of Augustus

Augie, Augustina, Austina, Austine, Gussie

Aurea: Latin, "golden"

Aura, Aurel, Aurelia, Auria, Aurie, Oralia, Oralie

Aurora: Latin, "dawn"

Aurore, Rora, Rori, Rory

Austa: Latin, a feminine variation of Austin

Austina, Austine

Autumn: Latin, from the season

Ava: Latin, "bird"

Avis, Aya, Ayla

Aviva: Hebrew, "youth"

Avi, Viv, Viva

Ayanna: Swahili, "she who is as beautiful as a flower's blossom"

Azaria: Hebrew, "she who hears the Lord"—usually a male name

Azariah, Azzie

Aziza: Arabic/Swahili, "she who is beloved"

Azzie, Azziza, Azzy

B

Babette: French, "she who is foreign"—generally accepted as one of many diminutives for Barbara

Babbie, Babbs, Babe, Babetta, Etta

Bailey: Old English, "bailiff"

Baily, Bay, Bayley

Bambi: from the Disney film of the same name; or possibly from the Italian word for small child, *bambino*

Bambee, Bambie, Bamby

Barbara: Greek, "she who is foreign"—from the same root as the word "barbarian"

Babbie, Babbs, Babbsie, Babs, Barb, Barbie, Barbra, Bebe, Bobbie—many additional variations and diminutives can be created with the name Barbara

Barri: Irish, "excellent spearsman"—also the female variation of the masculine Barry

Bari, Barrie

Basilea: Greek, "royal"—a feminine variation of the masculine name Basil

Basilia

*Bathsheba: Hebrew, "daughter of promise"

See her sad story of adultery with King David in 2 Samuel 11:2-3, 12:24, 1 Kings 1:11-31, 2:13-19.

Beatrice: Latin, "bearer of blessings"

Bea, Beah, Beatrix, Bebe, Bee, Trix, Trixie, Trixy

Becky: See Rebecca

Belicia: Spanish, "she who is devoted to God"

Belice, Belisha

Belinda: Spanish, "attractive serpent"

Bella: Latin, "she who is beautiful"

Belle, Belina, Bellina, Belline

Belva: Latin, "beautiful vista"

Berdine: Old German, "attractive young woman"

Berdie, Berdina, Dina

Bernadette: French, "strong as a bear"—also a feminine variation of the male name Bernard

Bern, Bernadine, Bernetta, Bernette, Bernie, Bernita, Bern

*Bernice: Greek, "she who brings victory"

Berniece, Berenice, Beri, Bern, Bernie, Berri

See Acts 25:13,23; 26:30.

Bertha: Old German, "she who is radiant"

Berta, Bertie, Bertina

Beryl: Greek, from the jewel by the same name

Ber, Berri, Berrie, Berry, Beryle

Bess: Hebrew, a diminutive of Elizabeth, "consecrated to God"

Bessie

Beth: Hebrew—a diminutive for Elizabeth, "consecrated to God"; or Bethany, "house of God"

Bethann, Bethanne

Bethany: Hebrew, "house of God"

Beth, Bethanee, Bethel, Betheny

Bethesda: Hebrew, "house of mercy"

Beth

Betsy: Hebrew—a diminutive for Elizabeth, "consecrated to God"

Betsey, Betsie

Betty: Hebrew—a diminutive for Elizabeth, "consecrated to God"
Bette, Bettie

Bettina: Hebrew—a diminutive for Elizabeth, "consecrated to God"
Betina, Bettine, Tina

*Beulah: Hebrew, "betrothed," a name for the nation of Israel
See Isaiah 62:4.

Beverly: Old English, "meadow of the beaver"
Bev, Beverlee, Beverlie, Bevy

Bevin: Irish, "young woman"
Bev, Bevan, Bevina, Bevinn

Bian: Asian/Vietnamese, "she who will not reveal a secret"

Bianca: Latin, "white, fair"
Blanca

Bibi: Latin, "she who is full of life"
Bebe, Bebee

Billie: Old English, "she who is determined"—usually a diminutive for Wilhemina, Willa, etc. Often used in combination with other names: Billie Jean, Billie Ann, Billie Jo, Billie Sue, etc.

Bindi: East Indian, "a tiny drop"
Bindee, Bindie, Bindy

Bird: English, literally "bird"
Birdie, Birdy

> A good name is more desirable than great riches.
> —PROVERBS 22:1

*Bithia: Hebrew, "daughter of God"
Bithiah, Thea, Thia
See 1 Chronicles 4:18.

Blaine: Irish, "she who is slender"
Blane, Blayne

Blair: Celtic, "field of battle"
Blaire

Blake: Old English, "dark one"
Blakelee, Blakely

Blanche: Latin, "she who is fair"
Belanche, Blanca, Blanch, Blanka

Blenda: Old German, "glorious"

Bliss: Old English, "joyful one"
Blisse, Blyss

Blossom: English, literally a "flower blossom"

Blythe: Old English, "she who is cheerful"
Blithe, Blyth

Bo: Chinese, "dear one"

Bobbi: Usually a diminutive for Barbara (Greek, "foreign one") or Roberta (feminine variation of Robert—Old English, "bright, famous").
Often used in combination with other names, e.g., Bobbi Sue, Bobbi Jo, Bobbi Lynn, Bobbi Ann, etc.
Bobbette, Bobbie, Bobbina

Bonita: Spanish, "she who is pretty"
Bonnie, Nita

Bonnie: Scottish/English, "pretty, attractive, good"
Bonnee, Bonny, Bunny

Bopha: Asian/Cambodian, "she who is like unto a flower"

Brandi: Dutch, from the strong drink, brandy
Brandee, Brandie, Brandilyn, Brandy

Breanna: Irish, "she who is strong"—also a feminine variation of Brian (Irish, "powerful one")
Breanne, Bree, Breena, Briana, Brianna, Brianne, Brinna, Bryana, Brynna

Breck: Irish, "freckled one"

Brenda: Irish, "raven"—also a feminine variation of Brendan
Bren, Brenn, Brenna, Bryn, Brynn

Brett: Latin, "she who is from Britain"
Bretta, Britt

Briana: See Breanna.

Bridget: Celtic, "she who is strong"
Birget, Birgette, Birgit, Bridgett, Brigetta, Brigette, Brigitte

Brittany: Irish, "she who is strong"
Britt, Britney, Brittin, Brittney

Bronwyn: Welsh, "she who is full-figured"
Bronny, Bronwynn

Brooke: Old English, literally, a brook of running water
Brook, Brooks

Brunhilde: Old German, "she who is a warrior"
Brunhilda, Hilda, Hilde, Hildy

Bryn: Gaelic, "she who is honorable"
Brynn, Brynna, Brynne

Buffy: English, nickname possibly derived from the American buffalo

Bunny: English, a synonym for rabbit—or a variation of Bonnie. Often a nickname that begins as an endearment in early childhood.
Bunni, Bunnie

C

Note: Many "C" names may also be spelled with "K" or sometimes "S" (Catherine/Katherine, Cheryl/Sheryl). You may wish to experiment and see what creative variations you can come up with.

Cadence: Latin, "to fall," as used in music terminology—the "cadence" or rising and falling of the melody
Cadda, Caddie, Cadena, Kadena, Kadence

Cailyn: A variation of Catherine
Cailin, Caylin, Kay, Kaylee, Kaylyn

Caitlin: Irish variation of Catherine
Cate, Catelin, Catelynn, Kaitlin, Katelin, Katelynn

Calandra: Greek, "lark"
Cal, Callia, Callie, Cally

Calantha: Greek, "flower"
Cal, Callie, Cally

Calista: Greek, "astonishly attractive, most beautiful"
Cala, Calesta, Calla, Callie, Callista, Cally, Lista

Callie: A variation of Calandra, Calanth, Callista, but occasionally a proper name in its own right

Calvina: A feminine variation of Calvin
Cal, Callie, Cally, Vina

Camilla: Latin, "religious attendant"
Cam, Camille, Cammie, Cammy

*Candace: Latin, "bright white"

Candee, Candice, Candis, Candiss, Candy

See Acts 8:27.

Candida: Latin, "white, without blemish"

Candi, Candide, Candy

Caprice: Italian "she who is impulsive, capricious"

Cara: Italian, "she who is dear"

Carah, Carra, Kara

Carilla: Spanish form of Carillo, a Spanish variation of Charles

Carrie, Corilla

Carissa: Greek, "she who is dear"

Carisa, Charisa, Charissa

Carita: Latin, "charity"

Karita

Carla: A feminine variation of Charles

Carlie, Karla, Karlie

Carlene: A feminine variation of Charles

Car, Carleen, Carlina, Carline, Carlita

Carly: Usually a diminutive for any of several names,

including Carlene, Charlotte, Caroline, Carolyn, and others; often used as a proper name on its own

Carlie, Karlee, Karli, Karlie

Carlotta: Italian, feminine variation of Charles

Car, Carrie, Lotta, Lottie

Carmel: Hebrew, "garden"

Carm, Carmela, Carmelina, Carmie

Carmen: Latin, "song"

Carm, Carma, Carmie

Carol: French, "song"

Carole, Carola, Carroll

Caroline: A feminine variation of Charles

Carolina, Carrie, Lina

Carolyn: A feminine variation of Charles

Many additional variations and diminutives can be created for the name Carolyn. Some may prefer the use of "K" in creating many of these names.

Caralyn, Carolin, Carrie, Lyn

Carrie: Often a diminutive for Carol, Carolyn, Caroline

Cari, Cary, Kari, Karrie, Kary

Caryn: A variation of Karen

Carina (Danish), Carine (Swedish)

Casey: Irish, "she who is full of courage"

Casie, K.C., Kaycee

Cassandra: Greek, "temptress"

Cass, Cassaundra, Cassie, Kassandra, Sandra, Sandy

Cassia: Greek, from a seasoning akin to cinnamon

Cassidy: Irish, "she who is clever"

Cass, Cassie, Kassidy

Casta: Latin, "she who is modest"

Cass, Cassie

Catalina: Spanish variation of Catherine

Cat, Cata, Cataline, Lina

Catherine: Greek, "untainted, pure"

There are many variations and diminutives possible for Catherine, including many alternate spellings beginning with the letter "K." Some of the more popular variations include Cath, Catharine, Cate (Italian), Caterina, Cathleen, Cathrine, Cathryn, Cathy, Katharine, Katherine, Kathrine, etc.

CATHERINE BOOTH
(1829–1890)

was, along with her husband, William, a founder of the Salvation Army, one of the most effective ministries in modern times.

CATHERINE MARSHALL
(1915–1983)

was one of the most popular Christian authors of the last half of the twentieth century. Her best-known book is the novel *Christy,* based on the life of her mother, Leonora Wood.

Cathleen: An Irish variation of Catherine

Cathy, Kathleen, Kathy

Catia: Japanese, "she who is precious"

Cat, Tia

Cecile: Latin, a feminine variation of Cecil ("blind one")

Cec, Cecilia, Cecily, Ceil, Celia, Cicel, Cicely, Cilla

Celeste: Greek, "of the heavens"

Celesta, Celestina, Celestine

Celine: Latin, "heavenly"

Celina, Celinda, Celindra, Selina, Seline, Selindra

Chantel: French, "song"

Chantelle, Chantele, Shantel, Shantele, Shantelle

Charity: Greek, "grace"

From the same root, "charis" (meaning "gift"), from which we get "charismatic," or "charisma" referring to the "gift" or charisma. In many Christian circles, charity also refers to love as manifested by good deeds toward others. In the King James version of the Bible, 1 Corinthians 13 uses the word "charity" where more modern versions use the word "love."

Char, Charis

Charlotte: A feminine variation of Charles

Char, Charleen, Charlene, Lottie, Lena

Charmain: Greek, "she who is joyful"

Char, Charmaine, Charmian

Chastity: Latin, "pure, undiluted"

Chas, Chaz

Chelsea: Old English, from a seaport in Britain

Chelsey, Chelsie

What's in a Name?

My dad was in the Air Force and stationed in Okinawa, Japan. And, of course, my mom and my brothers were all there with him. I came along in the third year of Dad's tour there. My mom would go a few times a week to one of the local schools to just speak English. The students knew the language but needed to hear someone speaking it so they could get the inflections right. As my mother's pregnancy neared its end, one of the students mentioned that if the baby was a girl she needed a Japanese name and suggested *Catia* (pronounced "kah-**tee**-ah"), which means "my precious little one." And that is the name that was given to me.

CATIA FROM TEXAS

Chenda: Asian/Cambodian, "she who is wise"

Cherise: French, "she who is cherished"

Cher, Cherry, Sherise

Cheryl: French, "she who is beloved"
Cher, Cherie, Cherilyn, Sheryl

Chita: English, "kitten"

*Chloe: Greek, "verdant"
Clo, Cloe
See 1 Corinthians 10:11.

Christiann: Greek, "anointed one"
Chris, Christiana, Christianna, Christianne, Christy, Christyann

Christabel: Latin, "beautiful Christian"
Belle, Bella, Chris, Christabella, Christabelle, Christy

Christine: Old English, a feminine variation of Christian
Chris, Chrissie, Chrissy, Christa, Christiana, Christin, Christina, Christy, Cristina, Chris (all of these variations may also be spelled with a "K")

CHRISTINA ROSSETTI
(1830–1894)
was an English Christian and widely respected poet. Her work remains popular today.

Cindy: A diminutive for Cynthia

Clara: Latin, "clear"
French variations include Clair, Claire, Clare, Claretta, Clarette, Clarita; other variations include Clarice, Clarina, Clarinda, Clarine, Clarissa, Clarita (Spanish), Clorinda

Clarise: A variation of Clare
Clarice, Clarissa

*Claudia: Latin, "she who is lame"—also a feminine variation of Claude
Claudella, Claudelle, Claudette, Claudina, and Claudine
See 2 Timothy 4:21.

Clementine: Latin, "full of mercy"—from the same root as the word "clemency"
Clem, Clementina, Clemmy, Tina

Cleopatra: Greek, "daughter of the reknowned one"
Cleo, Pat, Patty

Clio: Greek, "praise"
Cleo

Cloris: Greek, "floral"
Chloris, Clo

Clover: Old English, "to cling," also from the blossom of the clover
Clo

Cody: English, "pillow"
Codee, Codi, Codie

Colby: Old English, a British regional name

Colette: French, "necklace"
Coletta

Colleen: Irish, "girl"
Coleen, Colene, Colline

Connie: Usually a diminutive for Constance

Constance: Latin, "unchanging"—from the same root as the word "constant"
Conna, Connie

Consuelo: Spanish, "consolation"
Connie

Cora: Greek, "young woman"
Coralee, Coralie, Coraline, Coralina, Coretta, Corette, Corey, Corrie, Cory

Coral: A name derived from the sea coral
Coralie, Koral, Koralie

Cordelia: Latin, "tenderhearted"
Corrie, Cory, Delia, Della

CORRIE TEN BOOM
(1892–1983)

was a Dutch woman who worked in her family business and was rounded up by the Nazis and taken to the Ravensbruck death camp with her sister, Betsie. Their crime was being part of a Christian family who hid Jews in their attic, rather than see them exterminated by the Nazis. Betsie died in the camp, but Corrie was eventually released and began a worldwide ministry telling her dramatic story to whoever would listen. Her bestselling book, *The Hiding Place,* was made into a successful movie.

Corine: Greek, "maiden"
Coreen, Corina, Corinna

Corinthia: A place name, from Corinth in ancient Greece.
Paul's two letters to the Corinthian church are part of the New Testament.

Cornelia: Latin, a feminine
variation of Cornelius
Cora, Corrie, Cory

Corona: Spanish, "crown"

Cosette: French, "the people's
victory"
Cosetta

Courtney: Old English, "court"
Court, Cortney, Kourtney

Crystal: Latin, "clarity, clear-
ness, purity"
Christal, Chrystal, Krystal

Cybil: See Sybil
Cybele, Cybelle

Cynthia: Greek, "luminous one,
moonlike"
Cinda, Cindee, Cindi, Cindie,
Cindy, Cynda, Cyndra,
Cynthea

D

Dacey: Usually a diminutive of
Candace
Dacie, Dacy

Dacia: Latin, an Italian regional
name

Dada: Yoruba (Nigeria), "she
with the hair of curls"

Dagmar: Danish, "the Dane's joy"
Dar

Dahlia: From the flower by the
same name, named for the
Swedish botanist Andrew
Dahl
Dalia, Dally

Daisy: Old English, "day's eye"
Daisey, Daisie

Dakota: A Native American
tribal name

Dale: Old English, "valley"
Daile, Dayle

DALE EVANS [ROGERS]
(1912–2001)

was the stage name of the
woman born Frances
Octavia Smith. She
changed her name to Dale
Evans when she embarked
on a successful singing
career. She later married
cowboy star Roy Rogers.
Her bestselling books
include *The Woman at the
Well* and *Angel Unaware*,
the story of Robin Eliza-
beth, the Down syndrome
daughter of Dale and Roy,
who died shortly before her
second birthday.

Dallas: Irish, "she who is wise"

*Damaris: Greek, "heifer"
Damara
See Acts 17:34.

Dana: Old English, "she who is from Denmark"
Dania, Danna, Dayna

Danica: Slavic, "dawn star"
Danika

Danielle: A feminine variation of Daniel
Danella, Danessa, Danette, Danila, Danita, Danna, Dannie, Danny

Daphne: Greek, "laurel tree"
Dafna, Dafne, Daphna

Dara: Hebrew, "she who is wise"
Daragh, Darah, Darragh

Daralis: Old English, "she who is beloved"
Daralice, Daraliss, Daralyce

Darby: Irish, "at liberty," "unfettered, free one"
Darbie

Darcy: French, "dark"
Darce, Darcee, Darcey

Daria: Greek, "prosperous"—also a feminine variation of Darius, "kingly"
Darian, Darice, Darien, Darrie

Darlene: English, "she who is beloved"
Darla, Darlah, Darleene

Davida: A feminine variation of David, "beloved"
Davena, Davene, Davina, Davita

Dawn: Old English, "daybreak"
Dawna

Deanna: Old English "valley"—also a variation of Diana and the feminine variation of Dean
Deana, Deanne, Dee, Deena, Dina

*Deborah: Hebrew, "bee"
Deb, Debbie, Debby, Debra, Debrah, Debs
There are two noted Deborahs in the Bible. The first was Rebekah's nurse (see Genesis 24:59, 35:8). The second and more commonly recognized Deborah was the faithful woman who became a judge of the Hebrew people. See Judges 4 and 5 and Hebrews 11:32-34.

What's in a Name?

My maternal grandfather had a college buddy named Dana who became very dear to the family. Thus, my grandfather named his firstborn son (my uncle) Dana. When the next generation of children were born among the siblings (who had all since moved thousands of miles apart), three of my grandfather's seven children (my mother, her sister, and her brother Dana) all chose the name Dana for their daughters.

After remaining separated across the country for over three decades, we finally had a family reunion where ALL of the Danas met in the same room for the first time! We called it the Dana convergence! We were a group of related strangers finally meeting, with our common name serving as a wonderful icebreaker. What fun we had as the Danas posed for photos together, compared stories about why each parent had chosen the name Dana, what it was like to have a unisex name, and so on. That reunion was the beginning of warm relationships developing between cousins who had previously been strangers, and a time of renewal for the siblings who had not been in the same room since the death of their mother 30 years prior.

In the 15 years since that reunion, my mother has passed away and my eldest cousin Dana's mother has passed away, but the Danas converged again last year for my Uncle Dana's 80th birthday. He was not in the best of health, but was delighted to have us all together, and garnered strength for his celebration. We earned hearty laughs from the birthday party guests when we all launched into our various versions of the Bob Newhart show routine, "Hi, I'm *Dana,* and this is my cousin *Dana* and my other cousin *Dana*...and my Uncle *Dana!*" I am so thankful for a name that has become a precious tie that binds!

DANA THE LESSER, OREGON DANA, LI'L DANA, AND
DANA #4 (ALL NAMES I USE TO IDENTIFY MYSELF WHEN
CORRESPONDING WITH THE OTHERS!) FROM OREGON

Dee: Usually a diminutive for many names such as Deirdre, Delores
DeeDee, Didi

Deirdre: Irish, "sorrowful one"
Dee, DeeDee, Deidra, Deidre

Delaney: Irish, "she who is born of the challenger"

Delcine: Latin, "sweet one"
Delcy, Dulcine, Dulcy

Delia: A diminutive of Cordelia

*Delilah: Hebrew, "yearning with desire"
See Judges 16:4-21.

Della: A diminutive of Adelle

Delma: Spanish, "from the sea"

Delores: Spanish, "lady of sorrows"
Dee, Deloris, Dolores, Lorie, Loris

Delta: Greek, "entryway"

Dena: Often a diminutive for Dinah, Diana, or Deanna
Deana, Deena, Dina

Denise: A feminine variation of Dennis
Deniece, Denys

Dep: Asian/Vietnamese, "she who is beautiful"
Depp, Deppa

Derry: Irish, "redheaded one"
Deri, Derri

Deryn: Welsh, "birdlike"

Desdemona: Greek, "she who needs the blessing of God"
Des, Desi, Mona

Desiree: French, "she who is fondly desired"
Des, Desi, Desiri

Desma: Greek, "pledge, oath"
Des, Dessie

Destiny: Old French, "future" or literally "destiny"
Des, Dessie

Diana: Latin, "divine one"
Deana, Dena, Di, Dian, Diane, Dianna, Dyana, Dyanne

Diella: Latin, "she who worships God"
Dyella

Dina: See Deana

*Dinah: Hebrew, "vindicated one"

Dyna, Dynah
Dinah was the daughter of Jacob and Leah. See her story in Genesis 34.

Dionne: Greek, "source of love"
Diona, Dione Dionna

> "Love should be the golden thread that runs through all your actions in dealing with the child. Kindness, gentleness, tolerance, patience, sympathy, a willingness to enter into childish troubles, a readiness to take part in childish joys—these are the cords by which a child may be led most easily."
>
> —J.C. Ryle (1816–1900)

Dixie: English, "wall"
Dixee, Dixy

Docilla: Latin, "she who is calm"—from the same root as the word "docile"
Dosilla

Dodie: Hebrew, "she who is beloved"
Dody

Dolly: Usually a diminutive for Dorothy
Doll, Dolley, Dollie

Dolores: Latin, "lady of sorrows"—see Delores
Delora, Delores, Dolora

Dominique: Latin, "she who belongs to God"—also a feminine form of Dominic
Doma, Domini, Dominica

Donata: Latin, "she who is worthy"

Donica: Latin, "gift"

Donna: Italian, "lady"
Dona, Donella, Donelle, Donetta, Donita

Dora: Greek, "gift"
Often a diminutive for Dorothea, Dorothy, Theodora, Eudora, etc.
Doralia, Doralyn

*Dorcas: Greek, "gazelle"
Dor, Dorcia, Dorrie
Dorcas was a generous New Testament believer in Christ and benefactress of the early church. See Acts 9:36-43.

Doreen: Greek
Dor, Dorena, Dorene, Dorine, Dorrie

Doris: Greek, "one from the sea"
Do, Dorea, Doria, Dorie, Dorinda

Dorit: Hebrew, "generation"
Dorita, Dorrit

Dorothy: Greek, "gift of God"
Dorette, Doretta, Doro, Dorothea, Dory, Dottie, Dotty, Thea

DOROTHY SAYERS
(1893–1957)

was an influential Christian thinker, an associate of C.S. Lewis, and the author of the popular Lord Peter Wimsey mysteries and several Christian works, including *The Man Born to Be King.*

Dova: English, "dove"
Dove, Dovie

*Drusilla: Latin, "watered by the dew"
Drew, Dru, Drucilla
See Acts 24:10-27.

Dulcie: Latin, "sweet"
Dulcia, Dulcine, Dulcy, Dulsea

Dusty: German, "she who contends"—also sometimes a diminutive for Dustin

Duyen: Asian/Vietnamese, "she who is full of grace"

Earlene: Irish, "oath"
Earla, Earleen, Earletta, Earlette, Earline

Eartha: English, "from the earth"
Erda, Herta, Hertha

Ebony: Greek, "dark one"
Eb, Ebonie

Edana: Celtic, "passionate"

Edeline: Old German, "she who is cheerful"—sometimes a variation of Adeline
Eddy, Edelene, Edy

Eden: Hebrew, "pleasantness"
Edena, Edin

Edina: English, "she who prospers"

Adina, Dina, Edie

Edith: English, "valuable gift"

Dita, Edita, Edie, Edithe, Edy, Edyth

EDITH SCHAEFFER

(1914–)

along with her husband, Francis, started the L'Abri Fellowship in Switzerland in 1955. The influence of L'Abri reached far and wide, affecting many young searchers who found Christ through this unique and powerful ministry.

Edna: Hebrew, "pleasant"—from the same root word as Eden

Edra: Hebrew, "she who is strong"

Edwina: English, "treasured friend"—also a feminine variation of Edwin

Edie, Edina, Wina

Eileen: An Irish variation of Helen

Ailene, Alene, Ayleen, Ilene

Elaine: Greek, "light"—a variation of Helen

Alain, Alaina, Alaine, Elaina, Elayne, Ellie, Lainie, Laney

Elana: Hebrew, "tree"

Elberta: Old German, "exceedingly brilliant"

Berta, Bertie, Ellie

Eleanor: a variation of Helen

Eleanora, Elinor, Elinore, Ellie, Nora

Eldora: Spanish, "as precious as gold"

Eldoria

Electra: Greek, "shining one"

Elena: An Italian variation of Helen

Elfrida: Old German, "she who is wise"—a feminine variation of Alfred

Elfreda, Ellie, Freda

Eliana: Hebrew, "God has answered my prayer"

Anna, Elianna, Ellie

*Elizabeth: Hebrew, "consecrated to God"

Beth, Betha, Bethy, Bess, Bessie, Betsy, Bette, Bettina,

Betts, Betty, Elisabeth, Elisa, Elise, Elisheba (see Exodus 6:23), Elissa, Eliza, Lisette, Liz, Liza, Lizabeth, Lizzie

Read the story of Elizabeth, the mother of John the Baptist, in Luke 1:5-80.

ELISABETH ELLIOT
(1926–)

was married to Jim Elliot, one of the five missionaries martyred in 1956 by the Huaorani (Auca) people. She wrote about his life in several of her many books, which include *Shadow of the Almighty* and *Through Gates of Splendor.*

ELIZABETH FRY
(1780–1845)

was a pioneer of prison reform in nineteenth-century England.

Elke: German, "she who is noble"
Elka

Ella: Greek, "elf-like"—also a variation of Helen
Ellie, Elly

Ellen: A Scottish variation of Helen
Ellie, Ellyn

Elma: Greek, "she who is easy to please"—also a feminine variation of Elmo

Elmira: Arabic, "noble lady"
Ellie, Mira

Eloise: French, "great in battle"—a variation of Louise
Aloysia, Ellie, Eloisa, Elouisa

Elora: a diminutive of Eleanora and variation of Helen

Elsa: German, "noble young woman"
Elsie, Elsy

Elspeth: Hebrew, "dedicated to God"
Ellie

Elvira: Latin, "fair"
Ellie, Elva, Vira

Elysia: Greek, "fully satisfied"
Elicia, Elisha, Elysa

Elza: Hebrew, "God is the source of my joy"

Emelda: A variation of Emily
Emeline, Emmy, Imelda

Emerald: From the gem, which is the birthstone for May

Emily: Latin, "she who is industrious"—also a variation of Amelia
Amalie, Ameline, Em, Ema, Emilyn, Emlyn, Emmalee, Emmi, Emmy, Emylee

Emma: Old German, "all-encompassing"—also can be a diminutive of Emily
Em, Emmy

Emmanuelle: Hebrew, "God with us"
Emmy

Emmylou: A combination of Emily and Louise

Enid: Latin, "of the soul"

Erica: Old German, "one of great strength"—a feminine variation of Eric
Erika, Ricki

Erin: Irish, the old name given to Ireland
Errin, Eryn

Erma: A variation of Irma

Ernestine: Old German, "purposeful one"
Ern, Erna, Ernesta

Esme: English, "guardian"
Es, Essie

Esmeralda: Spanish, from the gemstone emerald
Es, Essie

Esperanza: Spanish, "hope"

Estelle: French, "starlike"—also a variation of Esther
Es, Essie, Estee, Estella, Estrella, Stella

*Esther: Persian, "starlike"
Es, Essie, Esta, Estra, Hester
Read the compelling story of the Bible heroine Esther in the book that bears her name.

Ethel: Old German, "she who is noble"
Ethelinda, Ethelyn, Ethlyn

ETHEL WATERS
(1900–1977)
was a popular singer and movie star when she was converted to Christ. She worked with the Billy Graham Crusades, and her signature song was "His Eye Is on the Sparrow," which became the title of her bestselling autobiography.

Etta: Usually a diminutive for Georgetta, Henrietta, Marietta, etc., but also used as a proper name in its own right

Eudora: Greek, "pleasant gift"
Dora

Eugenia: Greek, "of noble birth"—also a feminine variation of Eugene
Eugenie, Genie, Jean, Jeanie

EUGENIA PRICE
(1916–1996)
was an extremely successful Christian writer of both nonficton and fiction.

Eula: Greek, "well-spoken"

*Eunice: Greek, "glorious victory"
The mother of Timothy. See Acts 16:1-3, 1 Timothy 1:5, 3:14; 4:5.

Eurydice: Greek, "large one"

Evangeline: Greek, "messenger of good news," as in "evangelist"
Eva, Evangelina, Vannie

*Eve: Hebrew, "life-giver"
Eva, Evie, Evita
The mother of all living, Eve's story is found in Genesis 2 and 3.

EVANGELINE BOOTH
(1865–1950)
was the daughter of William and Catherine Booth, founders of the Salvation Army. She continued their work well into the twentieth century.

Evelyn: English, "hazelnut"
Avelyn, Evie

Faith: Middle English, "she who believes"

Fanny: Usually a diminutive for Frances
Fannie

Farrah: Middle English, "attractive"
Fara, Farra

Fausta: Latin, "she who is blessed"
Faustina, Faustine

Fawn: Old French, "young deer"
Faunia, Fawna, Fawnia

Fay: Old French, "fairy" or "elf-like"—or sometimes a

diminutive for Frances or Faith

Fae, Falina, Faline, Faye, Fayetta, Fayette, Faylena, Faylina, Fayline (the latter four variations may also be traced to the word *feline*, meaning "catlike")

Fedora: Russian, "gift of God"

Felice: Latin, "happy, merry, gay"—also a female variation of Felix

Felicia, Felise, Felita, Licia, Lise, Lita, Phelicia, Phylicia

Fern: Old English, name derived from the fern plant

Fernanda: A feminine variation of Ferdinand

Anda, Fern, Nan, Nana, Nanda

Fifi: Usually a diminutive or nickname; very rarely used as a proper name

Fiona: Irish, "she who is a fair one"

Fionna, Fionne

Flannery: Irish, "redheaded one"

Flan, Flanna, Flannary

Flavia: Latin, "golden one"

Fleur: A French variation of Florence

Fleurette

Florence: Latin, "flower"

Flo, Flora, Floria, Florice, Florida, Florinda, Floris, Florrie, Flory, Flossie, Flossy

---

FLORENCE NIGHTINGALE
(1820–1910)
was the mother of modern nursing. She declared that "Christ is the author of our profession."

Foluke: Yoruba (Nigerian), "she who is protected by God"—can be male or female

Frances: Old German, "free one"—also a female variation of Francis

Fanny, Fran, Francesca, Francine, Francisca, Francoise, Franny

---

FRANCES "FANNY" CROSBY
(1820–1915)
was one of Christianity's most famous and beloved hymn-writers. Among her 9000 hymns are "Blessed Assurance," "To God Be the Glory," and "Rescue the Perishing."

FRANCES RIDLEY HAVERGAL
(1836–1879)
was an English poet, author, and hymn composer. Among her most memorable hymns is "Take My Life and Let It Be."

Frederica: A feminine variation of Frederick, German, "peaceful ruler"

Freda (often a diminutive for Winifred), Freddie, Freddy, Fredia, Fredrika, Frieda, Rica, Ricca

Fritzi: German, a female variation of Fritz, which is a diminuative for Frederick

Fritzie

G

Gabrielle: A female variation of Gabriel, "God is my strength"

Gabbi, Gabbie, Gabriella, Gaby, Gavrielle

Gail: Hebrew, usually a diminutive for Abigail

Gael, Gale, Gayla, Gayle

Galina: A Russian variation of Helen

Galeen, Galena, Galene, Gay, Gaylene, Gayline

Gana: Hebrew, "garden"

Garnet: Middle English, a precious jewel, the gemstone garnet

Garnett, Garnette, Garney

Gay: Old French, "merry one"

Gaye

Galyn: Hebrew, "the Lord is a redeemer"

Galia, Gaylia

Gemma: Latin, "precious stone"—from the same root as "gem"

Jemma

Geneva: Old French, "juniper tree"

Gen, Genny, Gin, Ginny

Genevieve: Old French, "white wave"

Gena, Genny, Gin, Ginny, Jenny

Genna: Arabic, "little bird"

Jenn, Jenna, Jenny

Georgia: Greek, "one who farms or works with the land"

Georgette, Georgiana, Georgina, Georgine, Georgy. Many more combinations are possible.

Geraldine: German, "spear warrior"—a feminine variation of Gerald

Geralda, Geri, Gerilyn, Gerri, Jeri, Jerri

Germaine: French, "from Germany"

Germane, Jermaine

Gertrude: Old German, "spear maiden"

Gerda, Gert, Gerta, Gertie, Trudy

Gianna: Italian, "God is gracious"

Gigi: Usually a diminutive; no known independent meaning

Gila: Hebrew, "she who is joyful"

Gilana

Gilda: Old English, "gilded" (with gold)

Gildy

Gillian: Latin, "she who is youthful"

Gilliana, Gilliann, Gillie, Jill, Jillian, Jilly

Gina: Usually a diminutive for Angelina, Eugenia, Regina, Virginia, etc.

Geena, Gena, Ginna

Ginger: Latin, "spice"—also a common diminutive for Virginia

Giselle: Old German, "promise"

Gisella, Gizella, Gizelle

Gladys: Irish, "princess"

Gladdis, Glady

GLADYS AYLWARD
(1902–1970)

was a very successful missionary to China. Her story is told in the Alan Burgess biography *The Small Woman.* Her story inspired the popular movie *The Inn of the Sixth Happiness.*

Glenna: Welsh, "valley" or "glen"—a feminine variation of Glen

Glena, Glenda, Glenice, Glennis, Glinda, Glynis

Gloria: Latin, "glory, praise, adulation"

Glorianna, Glorianne, Glory, Glorya, Gloryanna

Golda: Old English, "gold"

Goldia, Goldie, Goldy

Grace: Latin, "full of grace"

Gracia, Gracie, Gratiana

Greer: Scottish, "watchful one"

Greta: A common diminutive for Margaret, but also commonly used as a proper name

Gretchen, Grete, Gretel, Gretha

Griselda: Old German, "gray warrior"

Griesella, Grishilda, Zelda

Guadalupe: Spanish, "valley of the earth"

Lupe, Lupita

Guinevere: Welsh, "white lady"

Guinna, Gwen, Gwenna, Gwenny

Gwendolyn: Irish, "white browed one"

Gwen, Gwenn, Gwenna, Gwenyth, Gwyn, Gwynne

H

*Hadassah: Hebrew, "myrtle tree" or the Hebrew version of Esther

*Hagar: Hebrew, "one who flees"

Hagar was Sarah's handmaiden and mother of Abraham's first son, Ishmael.

Read Hagar's story in Genesis 16, 21, and Galatians 4:24-25.

Halcyon: Greek, "kingfisher"

This name has come to be associated with happy memories. Thus, a more meaningful definition in keeping with the current usage of the word might be "she who brings pleasant memories."

Haley: Norse, "heroine"

Hailey, Halley, Hallie, Hally, Hayley

Halle: African, "unexpected delight"

Halla

Hana: Japanese, "flower"—also a variation of Hannah

*Hannah: Hebrew, "favored one of God"

Hana, Hanna, Hanne, Hanni

Hannah was the barren wife of Elkanah. In desperation, she cried out to God and, in faith, she received the blessing she sought. Samuel was the firstborn of her six children. In gratitude and in keeping with a pledge she made to God,

Hannah dedicated Samuel to God's service. See the story of Hannah, the mother of Samuel, in 1 Samuel 1 and 2.

HANNAH WHITALL SMITH
(1832–1911)

was a noted speaker at the popular Keswick conventions in nineteenth-century England. Her classic book *The Christian's Secret of a Happy Life* is still a perennial bestseller and a "must read" for every Christian.

Harley: Old English, "meadow"
Harlee, Harleigh, Harlene

Harmony: Greek, "harmony" or "in accord"
Harmonia, Harmonie

Harper: Old English, one who plays the harp

Harriet: Old German, "mistress of the home"—also a feminine variation of Henry (as in Henrietta) and Harry
Harrietta, Harriette, Hattie

Hasia: Hebrew, "she who is protected by the power of God"

Hattie: Usually a diminutive for Harriet.

Haviva: Hebrew, "beloved daughter"

Hazel: Old German, "victory"
Hazell, Hazelle

Heather: Middle English, from the plant of the same name

Hedda: Old German, "warrior"
Heda, Heddi, Heddy, Hedy, Hetta

HARRIET BEECHER STOWE
(1811–1896)

was an abolitionist whose bestselling novel, *Uncle Tom's Cabin* (1852), has been suggested as a contributing factor to the American Civil War.

Heidi: German, "she who is cheerful"—also a diminutive of Adelaide
Heide, Heidy

Hein: Asian/Vietnamese, "she who is gentle"—can be either male or female

*Helah: Hebrew, "sickly"
See 1 Chronicles 4:5-7.

What's in a Name?

"Honey...I had a positive pregnancy test," I said weakly into the phone. I then waited for my beloved spouse to say something profound that would stop my rising hysteria and explain to me how a 45-year-old woman and a 51-year-old man, who were already the weary parents of three nearly grown children, could be having this conversation.

I was sadly disappointed in my husband's response, which was mostly silence, interrupted by mutters and prayers. At least I think they were prayers—I heard "Oh God" several times. We then did the math: My husband would be 70 when this one graduated from high school.

I had an odd sort of denial about this child, which the ultrasound had revealed would be a girl. She didn't seem real to me and, perhaps for this reason, I couldn't think of a name for her. I read baby-name books. I obsessively read the names in movie credits. I wrote lists of names on the pages of a yellow legal-sized pad. Nothing clicked.

Nearing the end of my pregnancy, knowing I would soon be bringing home a bundle of joy named Baby Girl, I turned to the Lord in prayer. "Lord, give me a name for my baby," I prayed desperately, half afraid that this was just too trivial a request to lay before the God of the Universe.

A day or so later, as I was waking from sleep, I heard a voice that was warm and filled with a smile say, "Gillian Blythe." Something clicked. I resisted grabbing my baby-name book—partly because I was afraid this name would mean "goat herder" or "village liar," and also because I wanted to live with just the sound of this name for a while.

I finally braced myself and picked up my tattered baby-name book. There I discovered that Gillian Blythe means "young and happy." My God was giving me a promise for this child. I would live to see her raised, I would survive her teen years, and she would bring me joy.

When my husband and I look at our "Gillybean," we know our God is faithful to keep all of His promises, praise Him. He gives wonderful surprises and, occasionally, a full night's sleep.

CANDI FROM NEW MEXICO

Helen: Greek, "light"

Has many variations, including the following names and their variations and diminutives:

Aileen, Eileen, Elaina, Eleanor, Elena, Ellen, Helena, Helene, Helyn, Lenore

---

HELEN ROSEVEARE
(1925–)

is a British doctor and was a medical missionary to the Congo.

Helga: Old German, "godly one"

Heloise: A French variation of Louise, "strong warrior"

Eloisa, Eloise, Heloisa

Henrietta: A feminine variation of Henry

Etta, Ettie, Hen, Henny, Henriette, Hettie, Hetty

Hermione: Greek, "daughter of the earth"

Herma, Hermia, Herminia

Hester: A variation of Esther

Hess, Hestia, Hestina, Hestine

Hila: Hebrew, "worthy of praise"—also a female variation of Hillel

Hilary: Greek, "she who has a merry heart"

Hil, Hillarie, Hillary, Hilly

HENRIETTA MEARS
(1890–1963)

was an educator and important figure in Christian ministry in the mid-twentieth century. In 1933, she founded Gospel Light, a successful Christian publishing house that is still producing many excellent Christian resources.

Hilda: Old German, "she who is a warrior"—can be a diminiuative for the German Brunhilde

Hilde, Hildy

Hildegard: Old German, "one who protects"

Hildegarde, Hildy, Hilly

Hinda: Hebrew, "doe"

Hynda

Holly: Old English, from the plant of the same name

Hollie, Hollis

Honey: Old English, from the "honey" of the bee; often used as an endearment

Honora: Latin, "she who is honorable, worthy of praise"
Honorah, Honore, Honoria, Nora, Norah

> You created my inmost being; you knit me together in my mother's womb. I praise you because I am fearfully and wonderfully made; your works are wonderful, I know that full well.
>
> —PSALM 139:13-14

Hope: Old English, "expectancy"
Hope is one of the Christian virtues.

Hortense: Latin, "gardener"—from the same root as the word *horticulture*
Hortensia

Hosanna: Greek, "Praise the Lord!"

*Huldah: Greek, "weasel"
Hulda
See 2 Kings 22:14-20 and 2 Chronicles 34:22-33.

Hyacinth: Latin, from the plant of the same name
Hyacintha, Hyacinthia

I

Ianthe: Greek, "flower"
Iantha, Ianthia

Ida: Old German, "she who is joyful"
Idella, Idelle

Ilene: A variant spelling of Eileen, a variation of Helen
Ileene

Ilka: Slavic, "she who aspires"
Ilke

Ilsa: An Old German diminutive for Elizabeth
Ilse

Imelda: Latin, "image"—also a variation of Imogene

Imogene: Latin, "imaginative one"—from the same root as the English word "imagination"
Emogene, Gene, Genie, Imogenia

Ina: Latin
Originally a diminutive for names in "ine" or "ina" such as Clementine, Clementina, Albertine, Albertina, Bernadine, Bernadina. More

recently, Ina has become a proper name in its own right.

Inez: Greek, "she who is gentle"—also a Spanish variation of Agnes
Ines, Ynes, Ynez

Ingrid: Scandinavian, "daughter"
Inga, Inge, Inger, Ingmar

Iola: Greek, "dawn"

Iona: A Scottish place name from an island off the coast of Scotland

Ione: Greek, "beautiful flower"

Irene: Greek, "peaceful one"
Erina, Ireen, Irina (Russian), Irine

Iris: Greek, "rainbow"
Irisa, Irissa

Irma: Old German, "warrior"
Erma, Irmina, Irmine

Isabel: Hebrew, "she who is consecrated to God"—a variation of Elizabeth
Bella, Belle, Isabella, Isabelle, Isobel, Izabel, Izabela, Izzy, Ysabel, Ysabella, Ysabelle

Isadora: Greek, "gift"
Dora, Dorrie, Isadore, Izzy

Isolde: Celtic, "fair daughter"
Isolda, Isolte

Ivana: Greek, "gift of God"—also a feminine variation of Ivan, which is a Russian version of John
Iva, Ivah, Ivanna, Yvanna

Ivory: English, from the desirable substance derived from the tusks of elephants and other tusked animals

Ivy: Old English, from the plant of the same name
Ivie

Jacinda: A Spanish variation of the Greek Hyacinth, named for the flower
Jacenda, Jacenta, Jacinta, Jacinth, Jacinthia

Jacoba: A feminine variation of the male Hebrew name Jacob, "one who supplants"
Jacobina, Jacobine

Jacqueline: An Old French variation of the male names Jacob and James, meaning "one who supplants."

Many variations include
Jacke, Jackee, Jackie, Jacklyn,
Jacklynn, Jacklynne, Jaclyn

Jade: English, from the gemstone jade
Jada, Jayda, Jayde

*Jael: Hebrew, "one who climbs"
(as a goat)
Yael
See Judges 4:17-22, 5:6, 24-
27.

Jaime: French, "beloved one"

Jamie: Hebrew—a feminine
variation of the male James,
a variation of the Hebrew
Jacob, "one who supplants"
Jama, Jami, Jayme

Jamila: Arabic, "she who is
lovely"—also a female variation of the male name Jamil
Jamilla, Jamille

Jane: Hebrew, usually a female
variation of the male John,
"God's gracious gift"
Jan, Jana, Janae Janella,
Janelle, Janessa, Janet,
Janice, Janine, Janis, Janna,
Jayne, and Jeanette are
among the numerious varia-
tions for this name

JAN (JANICE) KARON
(1937–)
is the author the
bestselling Mitford
series of novels.

Jardena: Hebrew, "flowing
downward"—a female varia-
tion of Jordan

Jasmine: Persian, from the
flower of the same name
Jasmin, Jasmina Jaz,
Jazmynne

MADAME JEANNE GUYON
(1648–1717)
was a French mystic much
persecuted for her faith.
Her autobiography is
still in print and con-
sidered by many to be a
Christian classic. Other
books of her writings also
remain popular.

Jayleen: American, usually a
combinative name of Jay and
Lynn
Jay, Jaylene, Jaylynn

Jean: A Scottish form of Jane
Gean, Genie, Jeana, Jeane,
Jeanna, Jeananne, Jeanette
(French), Jeanice, Jeanie,
Jeanine, Jeanne

*Jedidah: Hebrew, "beloved of Jehovah"

Jedida

See 2 Kings 22.

*Jehosheba: Hebrew, "promise of God"

See 2 Kings 11:2 and 2 Chronicles 22:11.

*Jemima: Hebrew, "dove"

Jem, Jema, Jemimah, Jemma, Jemmy

Jemima was the eldest of Job's daughters born to Job and his wife after the tragic loss of their first family. See Job 42:14.

Jennifer: Celtic, "white wave"

Genna, Gennie, Gennifer, Jen, Jenn, Jenna, Jennie, Jenny, Jinny

Jerri: American, usually a diminutive for Geraldine

Geri, Gerri, Jera, Jeri, Jerilyn, Jerrie, Jerry

*Jerusha: Hebrew, "a goodly inheritance"

Geri, Gerri, Jeri, Jerri

See 2 Kings 15:33, 1 Chronicles 6:12, 2 Chronicles 27:1-6.

Jessamyn: A French variation of Jasmine

Jess, Jessie, Jessy

Jessica: Hebrew, "rich"

Jess, Jessa, Jessalyn, Jessie, Jessika, Jessy

Jessie: a Hebrew, female variation of the male name Jesse

Jessy

JESSIE PENN-LEWIS
(1861–1927)

was a forceful presence in Christian work during the early part of the twentieth century, largely associated with the Welsh revival. She wrote widely and was editor of *The Overcomer,* one of the early deeper-life magazines.

Jestine: A varation of Justine

Jess, Jessie, Jesstina, Jessy

Jewel: English, literally a precious stone

Jewelle

*Jezebel: Hebrew, "unworthy"

See her tragic story in 1 Kings 16:31, 18:4-19, 21:5-25, 2 Kings 9.

Jillian: Latin, "young one"— also a variation of Julia

Gill, Gillian, Gilly, Jill, Jilli-
anne, Jilly, Jillyanna

Joakima: Hebrew, "God is my
judge"
Joachima

Joan: Hebrew, "God is gra-
cious"—often a variation of
Jane (a female variation of
John)
Joane, Joanie

*Joanna: Hebrew: "God is gra-
cious"—a variation of Jane
Joanne, Johanna, Johna,
Jone, Jonna
See Luke 8:1-3, 23:55, 24:10.

Jobeth: American, usually a
combination name of Jo and
Beth
Jobie, Joby

Jobina: Hebrew, "afflicted
one"—a female variation of
Job
Jobie, Jobina, Joby

Jocelyn: Latin, "she who is
joyful"
Joceline, Joseline, Joselyn

*Jochebed: Hebrew, "the glory
of God"
See Exodus 2:1-11, Hebrews
11:23.

Jodi: American, usually a
diminutive for Joan, Joanna,
Jocelyn, Judith, etc.
Jodee, Jodie, Jody

Joelle: Hebrew, "Jehovah is
God"—a female variation of
Joel
Jo, Joela, Joella, Joellen,
Joelyn

Joleen: Hebrew, "God, our
increase"
Jo, Jolena, Jolene, Joline,
Jolynn

Jolie: French, "beautiful"
Jolee, Joli, Joly

Joni: American variation of
Joan (a variation of John,
"God's gracious gift")

JONI EARECKSON TADA
(1949–)
is the author of many
books, including her
bestselling autobiography,
Joni, which tells the dramatic story of the 1967
diving accident that left
her a quadriplegic.

Jonina: Hebrew, "like a dove"—
a female variation of Jonah
Jo, Nina

Jora: Hebrew, "autumn rain"
Jorah

Jordan: Hebrew, "flowing downward" (as does the Jordan River)
Jorda, Jordana, Jorden, Jordi, Jordine, Jordy, Jorie, Jorrie, Jory

Josephine: A French female variation of Joseph, "God shall add"
Jo, Josefina, Josephina, Josetta, Josette, Josie

Jovana: Possibly a variation of the Italian Giovanna, a female variation of John
Jo, Jovanna, Jovannah

Joy: English, "she who is joyful"
Joi, Joye

Joyce: Latin, "she who is joyful"
Joice, Joyse

Juanita: A Spanish variation of Jane/Joan/John, "God's gracious gift"
Juana, Wanita

*Judith: Hebrew, "praiseworthy"
Jude, Judi, Judy, Judye
See Genesis 26:34.

*Julia: Greek, "youthful one"

Julian, Juliana, Julianna, Julianne, Julienne, Juliet, Juliette (French)
See Romans 16:15.

JULIA WARD HOWE
(1819–1910)

was an American poet, author, and ardent abolitionist. Her stirring "Battle Hymn of the Republic" is still one of the most beloved of American songs.

JULIAN OF NORWICH
(1342–1413)

was an English Christian mystic whose writings remain popular today.

June: English, after the month of the same name, also "young one"
Juna, Junetta, Junette, Junia

Justine: Latin, "she who is just"—a feminine variation of Justin
Justa, Justina, Tina

"K" names have much in common with "C" names. Many popular

names beginning with either letter are simply variations of the spelling of the name. Some of these names include Candace, Kandace; Carla, Karla; Carolyn, Karolyn; Casey, Kasey; Catherine, Katherine; Cathleen, Kathleen; Cody, Kody; and so on. When you see a "K" name you like, consider that it might also be spelled with a "C."

Kai: Native American, "willow"

Kaitlin: Irish, "pure"—a spelling variation of Caitlin
Kaitlyn, Katelyn, Kathlynn

Kale: Possibly a variation of Carl/Charles, so originally a boy's name, currently appropriate for either sex
Cale, Kaley, Kalie, Kayleigh

Kalena: Hawaiian, "she who is pure"
Kalina, Kalinda

Kanya: Asian/Thai, "a young woman of grace"
Kania

Kara: Greek, a variation of Katherine
Cara, Karah, Karrah

Karen: Greek, a variation of Katherine
Caren, Carin, Caron, Caryn,

Karin (Scandanavian), Karina (Russian), Karon, Karyn

Kari: A diminutive for Carolyn, but increasingly a proper name in its own right
Carrie, Carey, Karie, Karilyn, Karrie, Kerry

Karla: A German variation of Carla, which is a variation of the male name Charles

Kassia: A Polish variation of Katherine
Cassia, Cassie, Kasia, Kass, Kassie

Kate: Greek, a diminutive for Katherine
Cate, Kati, Katie, Katy

Katharine: Greek, "pure one"
Many variations exist for this name, including spelling variations and diminutives.
Catherine, Cathy, Kate, Katherine, Kathryn, Katie, Kathy, Kit, Kitty

---

KATHERINE VON BORA
(1499–1552)
was the beloved wife of
Martin Luther.
As an endearment, he
called her "Kitty."

Kathleen: An Irish variation of Katherine

Cathleen, Kate, Kathlyn, Kathy, Katy

Kathryn: See Katharine

Cathryn

Kathy: Usually a diminutive for Katharine

Katrina: German variation of Katharine

Kate, Katrine, Katy, Trina, Trinie, Triny

Kay: Greek, "she who rejoices"— in some cases, a diminutive for Katharine

Kaye

Kayla: Hebrew, "crown of laurels"

Cayla, Kala, Kalah

Keara: Celtic, "dark one"

Kiera, Kierra

Keely: Irish variation of Kelly ("courageous warrior")

Keena, Kina, Kyna

Kelila: Hebrew, "laurel-crowned one"

Kelly: Irish, "victorious warrior"

Kelley, Kelli, Kellie, Kellina

Kelsey: A Scandinavian variation of Chelsea

Kelcy, Kelsi, Kelsy

Kendall: Old English, "she who is from the bright valley"

Kenda

Kendra: Old English, "she who is learned or knowledgeable"

Kenda, Kendry

Kenna: Irish, "she who knows"—also a female variation of Kenneth

Kenzie: Scottish, a variation of MacKenzie

Kerry: Irish, "dark one"

Carrie, Kari, Keri, Kerri, Kerrie, Kiera

Keshia: African, "she who is favored"

Kesia

*Keturah: Hebrew, "sweet smelling incense"

Ketura

Keturah became Abraham's wife after the death of his beloved Sarah and bore him six sons. See her story in Genesis 25:1-6.

Kevyn: An Irish feminine variation of Kevin

*Kezia: Hebrew, from the sweet-smelling herb cassia

Kez, Keziah, Kezzie

See the story of this second daughter of Job (after Jemima, see above) in Job 42:14.

Kiana: Irish, "ancient one"

Kia, Kianna, Kianne

Kiara: Possibly a variation of the Italian Chiara, a variation of Claire.

Kimberly: An English place name

Kim, Kimberley, Kimberli Kimmie, Kimmy, Kym

Kirby: Old English, "she (or he) who is from the village church"

Both girls and boys are named Kirby.

Kiri: Asian/Cambodian, "she who comes from the mountains"

Kirsten: Greek, "anointed one"

Kiersten, Kierstin, Kirsta (Scandinavian), Kirstie, Kirsty

Kitty: Greek, usually a diminutive of Katherine or an endearment

Ketty, Kit

Koren: Greek, "young woman"

Kristin: Greek, "anointed one"

Kris, Krista, Kristi, Kristia, Kristie, Kristina, Kristine, Kristy

Kyle: Irish, "she who is pretty"

Kyla, Kylie, Kylyn

Kyra: Greek, a feminine variation of Cyrus

Kira

L

Labonya: Asian, "she who is beautiful"

Lacey: Latin, "she who is happy"—often a diminutive for Larissa, Alicia, and similar names

Lacie, Lacy

LaDonna: American, "the pretty one"

Ladonna

Lae: Laotian, "she who is dark"

Lael: Arabic, "she who was born at night"

Laela, Leila, Layla

Laine: French, often a diminutive for Elaine

Laina, Lainey, Lane

Laini: Swahili, "she who is tenderhearted"

Lan: Asian/Vietnamese, for the Vietnamese word for "flower"

Lana: Latin, "soft"—also a female variation of Alan or a diminutive for Alana

Lanetta, Lanette, Lanna

Lane: American, see Laine

Lani: Greek, "sent from heaven"—also a diminutive for Leilani

Lanni, Lanny

Lara: Latin, "well-known, loved"—also a diminutive for Larisa, Russian version of Larissa

Larra

LaRae: Possibly a variation of Laura or Rae ("doe")

Larine: Latin, a name derived from a bird from the gull family

Larina

Larissa: Latin, "she who is playful"

Larisa

Lark: Middle English, from the bird of the same name

Latifah: Arabic, "she who is gentle"

Latiffah

Laura: See Laurel

Laurel: Latin, from the laurel plant, a crown made from which signifies victory.

Many variations and diminutives (often used as proper names) include LaRae, Larina, Larine, Laura, Laurella, Laurelle, Lauren, Laureen, Laurena, Laurene, Lauretta, Laurette, Laurie, Loraine, Loretta, Lorinda, Loree, Lori, Lorice, Loricia, Loree, Lorna, Lorraine, Lory

Laverne: Latin, "of springtime"

Lavern, Laverna

Lavinia: Latin, "she who is pure"

Lavina, Vin, Vina, Vinny

Layla: Swahili, "she who is born at night"

*Leah: Hebrew, "she who is weary"

Lea, Leia

Leah was the wife of Jacob, given to him in place of her sister, Rachel, whom Jacob worked seven years to marry. After marrying Leah, he worked another seven years for Rachel. See the story in Genesis 29–30.

Leandra: Latin, a feminine variation of the male name Leander ("he who is as fierce as a lion")
Andie, Leanda, Lee

Leanne: English, a combination name of Lee and Anne
Leann, Leanna, Lee Ann

Lee: Irish, "meadow"
Leigh

Leila: Hebrew, "one with dark beauty"
Layla, Leilah, Lela, Lelah

Leilani: Hawaiian, "daughter from heaven"

Lemuela: Hebrew, "dedicated to God"—a feminine variation of Lemuel

Lena: Greek, "light"
Lenetta, Lenette, Lynette, Lina

Lenore: Greek, "light"
Leonora, Leanore, Lenny, Lenora, Lyn, Nora

Leona: Latin, "lioness"—also a female variation of Leo
Leola, Leontine, Leontyne

"Our children are not born with Bibles in their heads or hearts. And who ought to be the instructor, if not the parent? Yea, who will do it with such natural affection? As I have heard sometimes a mother say in other respects, Who can take such pains with my child, and be so careful as myself that am its mother?"

—**WILLIAM GURNALL (1617–1679)**

Leonora: Greek, "she who is from the light"—a variation of Eleanor/Eleanora
Lenora, Lenore, Leonore

Lesley: Scottish, "meadow"
Leslee, Leslie

Leta: Latin, "she who is joyful"
Lita

Letha: Greek, "she who forgets"
Lethia

Letitia: Latin, "she who is joyful"

Leticia, Letta, Lettie, Letty, Tish, Tisha, Letta

LETTIE COWMAN
(1870–1960)

along with her husband, Charles, was a missionary, but is best remembered for her work in compiling several devotional books, including the classic *Streams in the Desert*.

Levia: Hebrew, usually a female variation of Levi

Lewanna: Hebrew, "moonlike"

Levana, Lewana, Lou, Lu, Luanna

Lexine: Greek, "she who helps others"—often a diminutive of Alexandra

Lexia, Lexy

Liana: French, "vinelike"

Lian, Liane, Lianne

Libby: Usually a diminutive for Elizabeth or Olivia

Libbie, Livvie

Liesl: A German diminutive for Elizabeth

Lilith: Arabic, "she who is of the night"

Lillian: Latin, taken from the lily, a flower popular at Easter

Lil, Lila, Lilah, Lilia, Lilias, Lilis, Lilla, Lillia, Lillis, Lilly, Lily

---

LILIAS TROTTER
(1853–1928)

was a talented artist who set her natural gift aside to pursue the life of a missionary to the Muslims of North Africa.

Linda: Latin, "she who is pretty"

Lindi, Lindie, Lynda, Lynde

Lindsay: Old English, "from the island of the linden trees"

Lindsey, Lindsy, Linsey

Linnea: Scandinavian, "lime tree"

Linea, Lynea, Lynnea

Lisa: Hebrew, often a diminutive for Elizabeth, but increasingly a proper name in its own right

Leeza, Lise, Liset, Lisetta, Lissa, Lysa

Lisabeth: Hebrew, usually a variation of Elizabeth

Beth, Liz, Liza

Livia: Latin, usually a diminutive for Olivia
Livie, Livvie, Livvey, Livy

Liz: Usually a diminutive for Elizabeth
Liza, Lizetta, Lizette, Lizzie, Lizzy

*Lois: Greek, "she who is desirable"
Lois was the mother of Timothy. See 2 Timothy 1:5.

Lola: Spanish, usually a diminutive for names such as Dolores, Laurel, and Louise, but increasingly a proper name in its own right

Lolita: Spanish, "little sad one"
Lita, Lolo, Lulita

Lona: Latin, "lioness"
Lonee, Loni, Lonna, Lonni

Lora: Latin, one of the many diminutives of Laurel

Lorelei: Old German, "temptress"
Laralei, Loralei

Lorena: English, one of the many variations of Laurel

Loretta: English, one of the many variations of Laurel
Lauretta, Lorella, Lorelle

Lori: English, one of the many variations of Laurel
Loree, Lorie, Lory

Lorine: English, one of the many variations of Laurel
Loreen, Lorinda

Loris: Greek, often a diminutive for Chloris
Lorice, Lorisa

Lorna: Latin, one of the many variations of Laurel

Lorraine: Latin, "she who sorrows"
Lo, Loraine, Lorinda, Rainie

Lottie: Usually a diminutive of Charlotte
Lotti, Lotty

LOTTIE MOON
(1840–1912)
gave her life in service to Christ as a missionary to China.

Louella: A combination name of Lou and Ella
Luella

Louise: Old German, "strong warrior"
Aloise, Lou, Louisa, Lu, Luisa (Spanish variation), Luise

Luann: Hebrew, "strong warrior"

Lu, Luana, Lu Ann, Luanna

Lucia: An Italian variation of Lucille

Luciana

Lucille: Latin, "she who brings light"

Lucilla, Lucinda, Lucie, Lucy

Lucretia: Latin, "worthy of praise"

Lulu: Usually a diminutive for names such as Louise, Luann, Lucinda, etc.

Lupe: Spanish, usually a diminutive for Guadalupe

Lurleen: A modern variation of Lorelei

Lurlene, Lurline

***Lydia:** Greek, "she who comes from Lydia" (a former country in Asia Minor)

Lyda, Lidia

Lydia's story can be read in Acts 16:12-15 and Philippians 1:1-10.

Lyla: English, a female variation of Lyle

Lynn: A diminutive for Linda, but more recently a proper name in its own right

Lin, Lyn, Lynna, Lynella, Lynelle

Lynette: A variation of Lynn—the "ette" ending is usually a diminutive for "little"

Linetta, Linette, Lynetta, Lynette

Lyris: Greek, "she who plays the lyre"

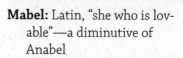

Mabel: Latin, "she who is lovable"—a diminutive of Anabel

Amabel, Amable, Amaybelle, Mabelle (French), Mable, Maybel, Maybelle, Mayble

---

MABEL SHAW
(1889–1973)
The first single woman missionary sent by the London Missionary Society to Central Africa. She was also an author.

Mackenzie: Scottish Gaelic, "son of the wise ruler"—a name for both boys and girls

MacKensie, McKenzie, McKensie

Madeline: Hebrew, "tower of strength," Greek, "woman from Magdala" (a town on the Sea of Galilee)

Mada, Madaleine, Madalena (Spanish), Madalyn, Maddie, Maddy, Madelaine, Madeleine, Madelena, Madelene, Madelina, Madge, Magdala, Magdalee, Magdalena, Magdalene

Madge: A diminutive of Madeline, Margaret

Madison: Old English, "son of the mighty warrior"—a boy's name also used for girls

Mae: A variation of May

Madonna: Latin, "my lady"

Madona

Madra: Spanish, "mother"

Madre

*Magdala: Hebrew "a tower"— see Madeline

*Magdalene: Hebrew, "a tower"—see Madeline

Magdalena

Mary Magdalene was a demon-possessed woman who became a Christian and was the first to see the resurrected Jesus (John 20:1-18).

MAGDALENA HERBERT
(1878–1938)

was a missionary to the Comanche Indians in Oklahoma.

Maggie: A diminutive of Margaret

Maggi, Maggy

Magnilda: Old German, "strong in warfare"

Magnolia: A flower named after the French botanist Pierre Magnol

Mahalia: Hebrew, "tender one"

Mahala, Mahalah, Mahalee, Mahali, Mahaliah, Mahalla, Mehalia

MAHALIA JACKSON
(1911–1972)

Was one of America's foremost gospel singers. The granddaughter of a slave, she was awarded with a Lifetime Achievement Grammy Award.

Mahogony: Spanish, "rich, strong," also the name of a kind of wood

Mahagony, Mahogani, Mohogany

What Does It Mean to Anglicize a Name?

Anglicization is the process by which non-English names, words, or phrases are made English in character or changed into English equivalents. Some of the sounds in English do not have equivalent pronunciations in foreign languages, and vice versa. So to make a name pronounceable or familiar to English speakers, names of non-English origin are often altered. Here are some examples of anglicization:

- The French *Aimée* becomes the anglicized *Amy*
- The Old Irish *Bairre* becomes the anglicized *Barry*
- The Gaelic *Conchobhar* becomes the anglicized *Connor*
- The German *Raghnaid* becomes the anglicized *Rhona*
- The Irish *Sean* (which is the Gaelicization of *John*) becomes the anglicized *Shawn*

During the nineteenth and twentieth centuries, large numbers of immigrants to America anglicized their names to make them more accessible to their new English-speaking neighbors. That trend, however, has slowed considerably as various nationalities have become more protective about preserving key elements of their native culture.

This process of altering names can work in a different direction as well. A great example is most of the Hawaiian names that appear in this book. The Hawaiian alphabet has only 13 letters, while English has 26. And many of the sounds in English have no equivalent sounds in Hawaiian. Thus, names such as *Daniel* are "Hawaiianized" by becoming *Kaniela,* or *Michelle* becomes *Mikala.* These are not true Hawaiian names, but simply Hawaiian forms, or Hawaiianizations, of these names. An example of a true Hawaiian name is *Moana,* which comes from the Hawaiian word *moana,* which means "ocean, open sea."

Maila: Hawaiianized variation of Myra

Maimuna: Swahili, "she who is blessed"

Maire: Scottish variation of Mary

Maisie: A diminutive of Margaret, a Scottish variation of Margery and Margaret
Maisey, Maizie, Mazey, Mazie

Majesta: Latin, "majesty"

Makaleka: Hawaiianized variation of Margaret

Makela: Hawaiianized variation of Marcella

Malaika: Swahili, "angel"

Malaka: Hawaiianized variation of Martha

Maliana: Hawaiianized variation of Marian

Mallory: Old German, "army counselor"
Mal, Mallorie, Malori, Malorie, Malory

Malvina: Gaelic, "refined, polished"
Mal, Malva, Mavina, Melvina, Melvine

Mandisa: South Africa/Xhosa, "sweet"

Mandy: A diminutive of Amanda
Manda, Mandee, Mandie, Mandy

Manuela: Hebrew, "God is with us"—a Spanish feminine variation of Emmanuel
Manuelita

*Mara: A variation of Mary
Marah
Mara is the name given to the Israelite's first campsite after the Red Sea crossing because of the bitter water found there (Exodus 15:22-27).

Marcella: Latin, "belonging to Mars, warlike"—a feminine variation of Marcel, Marcus
Marcela (Spanish), Marcele, Marcelle (French), Marcha, Marcia, Marcie, Marcille, Marcy, Marsha, Marshe

Marcenya: A modern name, origin and meaning uncertain

Marcia: Latin "fearless, brave,

warlike," feminine variation of Mark

Marcella, Marci, Marcille, Marcina, Marcy, Marsiella

Marcy: A diminutive of Marcella

Marcey, Marci, Marcie, Marsie

Mare: Irish variation of Mary

Mair, Maire

Your eyes saw my unformed body. All the days ordained for me were written in your book before one of them came to be.

—PSALM 139:16

Margaret: Greek, "pearl"

Greta, Gretchen (German), Gretel, Gretta, Madge, Mag, Maggi, Maggie, Maggy, Marga, Margareta, Margarete, Margarette, Margarita (Italian, Spanish), Margarite, Marge, Margaretta, Margarie, Margerita, Margery, Marget, Margette, Margie, Margita, Margorie, Margory, Margret, Margy, Marje, Marji, Marjie, Marjorey,

Marjorie (Scottish), Marjy, Meg, Megan (Irish), Meggi, Meggy, Meghan, Peg, Peggi, Peggie, Peggy—additional variations are possible to create with this name

MARGARET OF NAVARRE
(1492–1549)

was a supporter of the Reformation in France and sister of King Francis I.

MARGARET BAXTER
(1615–1691)

was the wife of Puritan preacher and writer Richard Baxter.

Margarita: A variation of Margaret

Margery: A diminutive of Margaret

Marge, Margi, Margie, Margy, Marje, Marji, Marjorey, Marjorie, Marjy

Marguerite: French variation of Margaret

Margarite, Marguerita

Maria: Latin and Spanish variation of Mary

Mariah, Marie, Mariya,

Marja, Marya (Slavic), Mayra, Mayria

MARIA ASPDEN
(d. 1900)
joined the China Inland Mission in 1891 and died a martyr in the Boxer Rebellion on July 12, 1900.

MARIA TAYLOR
(1832–1905)
was the wife of James Hudson Taylor. Together, they served as missionaries in China and founded the China Inland Mission.

Mariam: Greek variation of Mary

Marian: French combination of Mary and Ann, variation of Mary
Mariam, Mariana, Mariane, Marianne, Marion, Maryann, Maryanne

Marianne: French combination of Marie and Ann
Mariana (Spanish), Mariane, Mariann, Marianna (Italian), Marianne, Maryann, Maryanna, Maryanne

Maribel: A combination of Mary and Belle

Maribelle, Marybelle, Meribel, Meribella, Meribelle

Maridel: A variation of Mary

Marie: French variant of Mary
Maree, Marrie, Maretta (Italian)

Mariel: French variation of Mary

Marietta: Italian variation of Mary

Marigold: The name of a flower

Marilyn: A combination of Mary and Lynn
Maralin, Maralynn, Marilin, Marillyn, Marilynne, Marrilyn, Marylin

Marina: Latin, "from the sea"
Marena, Marinna, Marna, Marne, Marni, Marnie

Marion: French variation of Mary—also a name given to boys
Marian, Maryan, Maryonn, Maryonne

MARION HARVEY
(d. 1681)
was a young woman martyr of the Scottish Reformation.

MARION SCOTT STEVENSON
was a Scottish missionary
to Gikuyu, Kenya, in the
early 1900s.

Maris: Latin, "of the sea"

Marisa, Marise, Marisea,
Marisee

Marisa: A variation of Maris

Mari, Marissa Mareesa,
Marissa, Marisa (Russian),
Maryse (Dutch)

Marisol: A combination of Mary
and Sol

Marissa: A variation of Maris

Maressa, Marisa, Marisse,
Merissa, Morissa

Marjorie: A variation of Margery, diminutive of Margaret

Marge, Margerey, Margerie,
Margery, Margey, Margi,
Margie, Margy, Marje, Mar-
jerie, Marjerey, Marji, Marjie,
Marjori, Marjory, Marjy

Marla: A variation of Marlene

Marlah

Marlene: A combined variation
of Mary and Magdalene

Marla, Marlane, Marlayne,
Marlea, Marlee, Marleen,
Marlena (German), Marley,
Marlie, Marline, Marlyn,
Marlynn, Marylynne

Marlo: A possible variation
of the masculine name
Marlow—also sometimes a
diminutive of Marlene

Marloe, Marlow, Marlowe

Marsha: A variation of Marcia

Marta: Spanish variation of
Martha

*Martha: Aramaic, "lady,
woman"

Marta, Marth, Marthe, Mar-
thena (Spanish), Marthine,
Marti, Martie, Marty, Mattie

Martha was the sister of
Mary and Lazarus (see John
11:20,30).

MARJORY BONAR
(1808–1889)
was the mother of Scottish
minister and hymn-writer
Horatius Bonar.

MARTHA BROOKS
(1608–1680)
was the first wife of Puritan preacher and writer
Thomas Brooks.

Martina: Latin, "warlike"—a feminine variation of Martin

Marta, Marteena, Martie, Martine (French), Marty

Marva: Hebrew, "sage"

MARY SLESSOR
(1848–1915)

was a Scottish missionary to Africa who was affectionately known as "Ma" Slessor. In addition to winning Africans to Christ, she helped found an institute that offered training in trades and medical work.

---

*Mary: Hebrew, "bitter"

Mae, Maira (Irish), Mara (Slavic), Marabel, Marabelle, Mare, Maree (French), Mari, Maria, Mariam, Marian, Mariann, Marianna, Marianne, Maridel, Marie, Mariel, Mariella, Marielle, Marietta, Mariette, Marilee, Marilyn, Marion, Marita, Marja (Swedish), Marjorie (Scottish), Marya, Maryann, Maryanne, Marylin—additional variations are possible to create with this name

There are six Marys in the New Testament: 1. Mary the mother of Jesus (Luke 1–2); 2. Mary Magdalene (John 20); 3. Mary, the mother of James and Joseph (Mark 15:40); 4. Mary, the sister of Martha and Lazarus (John 11); 5. Mary, the mother of John Mark (Acts 12:12); and 6. Mary of Rome (Romans 16:6).

MARY MULLER
(1805–1898)

was the wife of preacher and orphanage founder George Muller.

Maryann: A combination of Mary and Ann

Mariahn, Marianne, Maryanna, Maryanne

MARY ANN ALDERSEY
(1797–1868)

was the first woman missionary to China.

Marybeth: A combination of Mary and Beth (a diminutive of Elizabeth)

Maribeth

Maryellen: A combination of Mary and Ellen (a diminutive of Helen)

Mariellen

Marylou: A combination of Mary and Louise
Marilou, Maryl, Meryl

Mathna: Swahili, "praise"

Matilda: Old German, "she who is a battle maiden"
Matilde (French), Mathilda, Matilde, Matti, Mattie, Matty, Tilda, Tildie, Tildy

Mattea: Hebrew, "gift of God"—a feminine variation of Matthew
Mathea, Mathia, Matthea, Matthia

Maud: A variation of Matilda
Maude, Maudie

MAUDE CARY
(1808–1889)
was a missionary who went to Morocco in 1901 and worked with the Muslims there for 50 years, learning Arabic as well as the difficult Berber language.

Maura: Irish variation of Mary
Moira, Mora, Morah

Maureen: Irish Gaelic, "little Mary"
Maura, Maurene, Maurine, Moreen, Morena (Spanish), Morene, Moria

Mawuli: Ewe (Ghana), "there is a God"

Mawusi: Ewe (Ghana), "in the hands of God"

Maxine: Latin, "greatest, renowned"—a feminine variation of Maximilian
Max, Maxeen, Maxena, Maxene, Maxi, Maxie, Maxina, Maxine, Maxy

Maxy: A feminine variation of Max
Maxi, Maxie

May: Latin, "month of May"
Mae, Maia, Maye, Mei

MAY ROSE NATHAN
(d. 1900)
was a missionary martyred during the Boxer Rebellion in China.

Mead: Old English, "meadow"
Meade, Meide

Meara: Irish Gaelic, "mirth, joy"
Mira, Meera

Megan: Irish Gaelic variation of Margaret

Meg, Meagan, Meaghan
(Welsh), Meg, Meghan,
Meghanna, Meghanne

Meira: Hebrew, "light"—a feminine variation of Meir

Melanie: Greek, "dark, black"

Mel, Mela (Polish), Melaine,
Melana (Russian), Melani,
Melania, Melannie, Melany,
Mellanie, Melli, Mellie, Melly

Melanctha: Greek, "dark
flower"

Melba: Greek, "soft"

Malva, Mellba, Melva

Melelina: Hawaiianized variation of Marilyn

Melika: Hawaiianized variation
of Melissa

Melina: Greek, "she who is
beautiful"

Malina, Mallina, Meleana,
Meleena, Mellina

Melinda: Latin, "mild, gentle
one"

Linda, Lindy, Lynda,
Malinda, Malinde, Malynda,
Melinde, Mellinda, Melynda

Melissa: Greek, "honeybee"

Lissa, Mel, Melesa, Meleesa,

Melicia, Melisa, Melise, Mel-
isha, Melisse, Mellie, Mellisa,
Melly, Milli, Millie, Milly

Melody: Greek, "song"

Melodee, Melodey, Melodie,
Melodye

Melosa: Spanish, "sweet as
honey"

Melvina: Celtic, "like a chief-
tain"—a feminine variation
of Melvin

Malva, Malvinda, Melveen,
Melvene, Melvine

Mercedes: Spanish, "mercies"

Mercede, Mercedez

Mercy: Middle English, "compassion, mercy"

Mercey, Merci, Mercia,
Mercie

Meredith: Old Welsh, "protector
of the sea"

Meradith, Meredithe, Meri,
Merry

Merry: Old English, "joyful,
lighthearted, happy"

Marylee, Merie, Merrilee,
Merri, Merrie, Merrielle,
Merrilee, Merrily

Merryanne: A combination of
Merry and Anne

Meryl: A variation of Muriel

Merrell, Merril, Merryl, Meryle

Meyya: Swahili, "Mary"

Mia: Italian, "mine"

Mea, Meya

*Michal: Hebrew, "Who is like the Lord?"—a feminine variation of Michael

Micah, Michal, Michael, Michaela, Michaeline, Michele, Micheline, Michelle

Michal was King Saul's youngest daughter and King David's first wife (see 1 Samuel 14:49, 18:27).

Michaela: See Michal

Michelle: Hebrew, "Who is like the Lord?"—a feminine variation of Michael

Chelle, Macelle, Machelle, Mechelle, Meshella, Micaela, Michaela, Michaeline, Michele, Michelina, Micheline, Michell, Mishaelle, Mishella, Mychelle, Myshell, Myshella

Miguela: Spanish, feminine variation of Miguel

Mikala: Hawaiianized variation of Michelle

*Milcah: Hebrew, "queen, counsel"

There are two Milcahs in the Old Testament—see Genesis 24:15 and Numbers 26:33.

Mildred: Old English, "gentle counselor"

Mil, Milda, Mildrid, Milli, Millie, Milly

MILDRED CABLE
(1878–1952)

served as a missionary in China and the Gobi Desert for 36 years, then worked for the British and Foreign Bible Society.

Milena: Hawaiianized variation of Myrna

Mimi: French variation of Miriam

Mina: German, "love"

Mena, Minette, Minna, Minnette, Minnie

MINA S. EVERETT
(1857–1936)

spent most of her life as a Southern Baptist missionary in the frontier regions of the American West, establishing churches and schools. She also served in Brazil and Mexico.

Mindy: Latin, "mild, gentle one"—a diminutive of Melinda

Minda, Mindee, Mindi, Mindie

Minerva: Greek, "she who is wise"

Minnie, Minny, Myna

Minna: Old German, "Will-helmet"—a diminutive of Wilhelmina

Mina, Minda, Minetta, Minette, Minne, Minnie, Minny

Minnie: A diminutive of Mary and Wilhelmina

Minnee, Minny

MINNIE SUE ANDERSON
(1892–1967)
was an author and a missionary to Nigeria.

Mira: A diminutive of Miranda

Mirella, Mirelle, Mirielle, Mirra, Myra

Mirabel: Latin, "great beauty"

Meribel, Meribell, Meribelle, Mira, Mirabella, Mirabelle

Miranda: Latin, "she who is extraordinary"

Maranda, Meranda, Mira, Miran, Mirandala, Mirra, Mirranda, Myra, Myranda, Randa, Randi, Randie, Randy

*Miriam: Hebrew, "bitter, strong"

Mariam, Meriam, Mimi (French), Mirriam, Myriam

Miriam, the sister of Moses, watched over his safety as he floated in the Nile River in a basket (Exodus 2:4). A second Miriam is found in 1 Chronicles 4:17, a daughter of Ezra.

Mishaela: A modern variation of Michelle

Missy: A diminutive of Melissa

Missie

Misty: Old English, "mist"

Mysti

Moana: Hawaiian, "ocean"

Moani: Hawaiian, "gentle breeze"

Moira: Irish variation of Mary

Maura, Moyra

Molly: Irish variation of Mary

Mollee, Molley, Molli, Mollie

Mona: Irish Gaelic, "noble one"—also a diminutive of Ramona

Moina, Monah, Monica, Monique, Monna, Moyna

Monica: Latin, "adviser, counselor"

Mona, Monika, Moniqua, Monique, Monnica

MONICA
(c. 331–387)

was the mother of early church theologian and writer Augustine of Hippo.

Monique: French variation of Monica

Montana: Latin, "mountainous"

Morgan: Welsh, "dweller by the sea"

Morgana, Morgane, Morganica, Morganne, Morgen, Morgin

Moriah: Hebrew, "God is my teacher"

Mariah, Moraiah, Moria, Moryah

Morna: Irish, "beloved, affection"

Myrna

Morrow: Origin and meaning unknown

MORROW COFFEY GRAHAM
(1892–1981)

was the mother of evangelist Billy Graham.

Moselle: A feminine variation of Moses

Mosella, Mozelle

Mudiwa: Shona (Zimbabwe), "beloved"

Muna: Swahili, "hope"

Muriel: Irish Gaelic, "sea-bright"

Merial, Meriel, Merryl, Meryl, Meryle, Murial, Muriella, Murielle

Myra: Latin, "wonderful"—a feminine variation of Myron

Maira, Mira, Myree

Myrna: Irish Gaelic, "she who is polite, gentle"

Meirna, Merna, Mirna, Mirne, Morna, Moyna

Myrtle: Greek, "myrtle"—a flowering shrub

Mertle, Mirtle, Myrta, Myrtia, Myrtie

N

*Naamah: Hebrew, "pleasant, sweetness"

Naava, Naavah, Nama, Nava

See Genesis 4:22 and 1 Kings 14:21.

Nabila: Swahili, "noble"

Nada: diminutive of Russian Nadezhda, "hope"

Nada, Nadia, Nadie, Nadja, Nady, Nadya

Nadine: Slavic, "hope"—a variation of Nada

Nada, Nadean, Nadeen, Nadena, Nadene, Nadia, Nadie, Nadina, Nadiya, Nadya, Nadyna, Nadyne

Nadiya: Swahili, "generous"

Nafia: Swahili, "gift"

Nafisa: Swahili, "precious gem"

Naima: Swahili, "she who is graceful"

Nakawa: Swahili, "she who is beautiful"

Nan: A diminutive of Nancy

Nan, Nana, Nance, Nancee, Nancey, Nanci, Nancie, Nancy, Nanella, Nanelle, Nanette (French), Nania, Nanine, Nanna, Nannette (French), Nannie, Nanny

Nancy: Hebrew, "graceful"—a variation of Ann

Nance, Nancee, Nanci, Nancie, Nanice, Nanncy, Nannie, Nanny, Nansee, Nansey

Naneki: Hawaiianized variation of Nancy

Nanette: French diminutive of Nan

Nannette

Nani: Hawaiian, "beautiful"

Nanyanika: Ewe (Ghana), "God's gift"

*Naomi: Hebrew, "pleasant"

Naoma, Naome, Naomia, Naomie, Noami

Naomi was the mother-in-law of Ruth. Her story can be read in the Bible book of Ruth.

Nariko: Japanese, "gentle child"

Nastasia: Greek, "resurrection"—a diminutive of Anastasia

Nastassia, Nastassya

Nasya: Hebrew, "miracle of God"

Nasia

Natalie: Latin, "child born at Christmas"

Nat, Nata, Natala, Natalee, Natalene, Natalia (Russian), Natalina (Polish), Nataline, Natalya, Natilie, Nattie, Natty, Talia, Talya

Natasha: Russian diminutive of Natalie

Nastassia, Natacha, Natascha, Natasha

Nathania: Hebrew, "a gift, or given of God"—a feminine variation of Nathan

Nataniella, Natanielle, Nathaniella, Nathanielle, Netania, Netanya

Nayo: Yoruba (Nigeria), "we have joy"

Neala: Irish Gaelic, "champion"—a feminine variation of Neal

Neale, Nealla, Neila, Neile, Neilla, Neille

Neida: A modern name, possibly a variation of Nita

Nell: A diminutive of Helen

Neila, Neilla, Nel, Nella, Nellene, Nellie, Nelly

Nellie: See Nell, Helen

Nell, Nelley

Nellwyn: Old English, "friend of Nell"

Nell, Nellwynn

Nessie: Greek, "pure"—a diminutive of Agnes

Nessa, Nessi, Nessy

Nettie: A diminutive of -ette in names such as Annette

Netta, Netty

NETTIE FOWLER MCCORMICK
(1835–1923)

was a Christian philanthropist who helped many become trained for ministry and mission work.

Neva: Spanish, "covered in snow, snowy"

Nevada, Nevara, Neve, Nevia

Ngina: Kikuyu (Kenya), "a servant"

Ngozi: Ibo (Nigeria), "blessing"

Nicole: Greek, "victorious people"—a feminine variation of Nicholas

Nichelle, Nicholle, Nichola, Nichole, Nicholette, Nicholle, Nicia, Nicki, Nickie, Nickola, Nicky, Nicola (Italian), Nicole, Nicolea, Nicolli, Nicolla, Nicolle, Niki, Nikita (Russian), Nikki, Nikky, Nikola, Nikole, Nycole, Nykole—additional variations are possible to create with this name; some of the spelling variations above are used for both boys and girls

Nike: Greek, "victory"
Nika

Nikita: Russian variation of Nicole

Nikki: A variation of Nicole
Nickie, Nicky, Niki, Nikkey, Nikky

Nina: Spanish, "girl"
Neena, Nena, Ninette, Ninnette, Ninya, Nyna

Nisi: Hebrew, "emblem"
Nissi

Nissa: A modern name, origin and meaning uncertain

Nita: Spanish, "grace"—a diminutive of names such as Anita, Juanita
Anita

Nkechi: Ibo (Nigeria), "this is for God"

*Noah: Hebrew, "rest, comfort"
Noa, Noë
One of the five daughters of Zelophehad (Numbers 26:33).

Noel: French, "Christmas"—a name for both boys and girls
Noela, Noeleen, Noelene, Noeline, Noell, Noella, Noelle (French), Noleen

Noelani: Hawaiian, "heavenly mist"

Nollie: see Olive

Nomble: Xhosa (South Africa), "beautiful"

Nona: Latin, "the ninth"
Nonah, Noni, Nonie, Nonna, Nonnah

Noni: Swahili, "she who is a gift of God"

Nora: Latin, "woman of honor"—also a diminutive of Eleanor
Norah, Norella, Norelle

Noreen: Irish variation of Norma
Norina, Norine

Norma: Latin, "pattern, precept"

Noreen, Normie, Normina

Nura: Swahili, "brightness"

Nurisha: Swahili, "shine light upon"

Nyameke: Akan (Ghana), "gift from God"

Nydia: Latin, "from the nest"

Neda, Nedda, Nidia, Needia

Nyimbo: Swahili, "song"

Nysa: Latin, "goal, aim"

Nissa, Nisse, Nyssa

O

Oceana: A modern name that means "ocean, sea"

Oceanna

Octavia: Latin, "eighth"—a feminine variation of Octavius

Octaviana, Octavianne, Octavie (French), Ottavia (Italian), Tavi, Tavia, Tavie, Tavy

Odele: Possibly German, "rich," or Greek, "song"

Odela, Odelet, Odellette, Odelina, Odeline, Odella, Odelle

Odelia: Hebrew, "praise God"

Odele, Odella, Odellia, Odilia, Otha, Othelia, Othilia

Odessa: Greek, "long voyage"

Odissa, Odyesa, Odyssia

Olabisi: Yoruba (Nigeria), "multiplied joy"

Olena: Russian version of Helen

Alena, Elena, Lena, Lenya, Olinia, Olenya, Olina, Olinia

Olethea: A variation of Alethea—Latin, "truth"

Oleta

Olga: Russian, "peace," or Scandinavian, "holy"

Elga, Helga, Olva

PRINCESS OLGA OF KIEV
(c. 902–969)

was a Russian ruler who is credited with promoting Christianity. She was the grandmother of Vladimir I, who Christianized what is now Ukraine and southern Russia.

Oliana: Polynesian, "Oleander"
Oleana, Olianna

Olinda: Old English, "holly"

> "At the birth of my children, I will resolve to do all I can that they may be the Lord's. I will now actually give them up by faith to God; entreating that each child may be a child of God the Father, a subject of God the Son, a temple of God the Spirit, and be rescued from the condition of a child of wrath, and be possessed and employed by the Lord as an everlasting instrument of His glory."
>
> **—COTTON MATHER (1663–1728)**

Olivia: Latin, "olive tree, olive branch"
Liva, Livia (Hebrew), Nola, Nollie, Olia, Oliva, Olive, Olivet, Olivete, Olivette (French), Olivya, Olva

Olive: See Olivia

Olubayo: Yoruba (Nigeria), "greatest joy"

Oluremi: Yoruba (Nigeria), "God consoles me"

Olympia: Greek, "from Mount Olympus"
Olimpia, Olympias, Olympie

Omorose: Fon (Benin), "beautiful child"

Oneida: Iroquois (American Indian), "standing rock"

NOLLIE TEN BOOM
(1892–1983)
The sister of Corrie ten Boom, a Dutch Christian Holocaust survivor whose family helped many Jews escape from the Nazis during World War II.

Onella: Greek, "light"

Opal: Sanskrit, "a precious stone"
Opali, Opalina, Opaline

Ophelia: Greek, "help"
Also a famous character in Shakespeare's *Hamlet*.
Ofelia, Ofilia, Ophelie

Oralia: Latin, "golden"
Aurelie, Oralee, Oralie, Orelle, Oriel, Orielle, Orlena, Orlene

Oriana: Latin, "dawn"
Oria, Oriane, Orianna, Orlanna

Orlanda: Old German, "fame of the land," feminine variation of Orlando

*Orpah: Hebrew, "fawn"

Ophra, Ophrah, Oprah, Orpa, Orpha

Orpah was the daughter-in-law of Naomi in the book of Ruth (1:4-14).

Orsa: Latin, "bear"—a variation of Ursula

Orsalina, Orsaline, Orselina, Orseline, Orssa, Ursa

Ortensia: An Italian variation of Hortense

Ortensa

Oseye: Fon (Benin), "she who is happy"

Ovelia: A Spanish variation of Ophelia

P

Pacifica: Latin, "to pacify, to make peace"

Page: French, "young attendant"

Padget, Padgett, Paget, Pagett, Paige

Palma: Latin, "palm tree"

Palmeda, Palmer, Palmira, Palmyra, Pelmira

Paloma: Spanish, "dove"

Palloma, Palometa, Palomita, Peloma

Pamela: Greek, "loving, kind, all honey"

Pam, Pama, Pamala, Pamalla, Pamelia, Pamelina, Pamella, Pamelyn, Pamilla, Pammi, Pammie, Pammy, Pamyla

Pansy: French, "thought," also the name of a flower

Pansey, Pansie

Paola: Italian, a feminine variation of Paolo

Paris: The place name of the capital of France

Parris, Parrish

Pat: A diminutive of Patricia

Patience: Latin, "to suffer"

A virtue name popular among the Puritans.

Patia, Patsy, Patty

Patricia: Latin, "noble one"—a feminine variation of Patrick

Pat, Patrica, Patrice (French),

Patrizia (Italian), Patsy,
Patte, Pattee, Pattey, Patti,
Pattie, Patty, Tricia, Trish,
Trisha

PATIENCE BROOKS
(1608–1680)

was the second wife of
Puritan preacher and
writer Thomas Brooks.

Paula: Latin, "petite"—a feminine variation of Paul

Paola (Italian/Spanish), Pao-
lina, Paule, Pauleen, Pauletta,
Paulette, Paulina, Pauline,
Paulyne

Paulette: See Paula

Peace: Latin, "peace"

A virtue name used by the
Puritans.

Pearl: Latin, "pearl, a jewel"

Pearla, Pearle, Pearleen, Pear-
lette, Pearlie, Pearline, Perl,
Perla, Perle, Perlette

Peggy: A diminutive of Margaret

Peg, Peggie

Peleka: Hawaiianized variation
of Bertha

Pelekila: Hawaiianized variation of Priscilla

PATRICIA MARY ST. JOHN
(1919–1993)

was a missionary who
served in Morocco for 27
years and founded a school
for nurses. She was also
a beloved and successful
writer of children's books,
including the best-selling
Tanglewoods' Secret (1948).

Penelope: Greek, "weaver"

Pen, Penalopa, Penna,
Penney, Pennie, Penny

Peninah: Hebrew, "pearl"

Penina

Penny: Greek, "weaver"—a
diminutive of Penelope

Penee, Pennee, Penney,
Pennie

Pepita: Spanish, "she shall add"

Pepa, Pepi, Peppie, Peppy,
Peta

Pernella: French variation of
the Greek word for "rock,"
and a feminine variation of
Peter

Perpetua: Latin, "perpetual"

Perry: French, "pear tree"

Perrey, Perri, Perrie

Petra: Greek, "rock"—a feminine variation of Peter

Pet, Peta, Peterina, Petria, Petrina, Patrine, Pietra (Italian)—additional variations are possible to create with this name

---

PETRA MALENA MALLA MOE
(1863–1953)
was a Norwegian who was influenced by American evangelist Dwight L. Moody and became an evangelist in Africa.

Petunia: North American Indian, "petunia flower"

Phares: Hebrew, "bursting forth"—derived from the biblical name Perez

Pheodora: Russian from the Greek for "gift of God"—a feminine variation of Theodore

Fedora, Feodora, Fyedora

Philana: Greek, "adoring"

Filania, Filanna, Phila, Philena, Philene, Philina, Philine, Phillina

Philantha: Greek, "lover of flowers"

Filanthia, Philanthia, Philanthie

Philene: A feminine variation of Phil or Phillip

Philiberta: Old English, "very brilliant"—a feminine variation of Filbert

Filberta, Filiberta, Philberta, Philberthe

Philippa: Greek, "lover of horses"—a feminine variation of Philip

Felipa (Spanish), Filipa, Filipia, Filippa (Italian), Pelipa, Pelippa, Philipa, Philippe, Phillipa

Philomena: Greek, "she who is friendly, loving"

Filomena, Mena

Philyra: Greek, "lover of music"

*Phoebe: Greek, "pure, shining, radiant"

Febe, Pheabe, Phebe, Pheby, Phoeboe

Phoebe was a deaconess who carried Paul's epistle to the Romans to the church at Rome (see Romans 16:1-2).

Phyllida: Greek, "leafy branch"—a variation of Phyllis

Fillida, Phillida, Phyllyda

Phyllis: Greek, "leafy branch"
Filis, Fillis, Fillys, Fyllis,
Philis, Phillis, Philys, Phylis,
Phylliss

PHYLLIS THOMPSON
(1906–2000)

served in remote inland
China as a missionary
for 15 years, then went on
to write 44 books, including biographies.

Pippa: Greek, "lover of horses,"
a diminutive of Philippa
Pippy

Placidia: Latin, "she who is
serene"
Placida

Poleke: Hawaiianized variation
of Paulette

Polly: A variation of Molly and a
diminutive of Mary
Pollee, Polley, Polli, Pollie,
Pollyanna

Pomona: Latin, "fruit"

Poppy: Latin, "poppy flower"

Preciosa: Spanish, "she who is
precious"

Preye: Ibo (Nigeria), "God's gift
or blessing"

Prima: Latin, "first"
Primalia, Primetta, Primina,
Priminia

Primrose: Latin, "first rose"
Primarosa, Primorosa

What's in a Name?

After two ultrasounds had con-
firmed it, my husband and I
were excited about our second
baby boy—to be born on April
2, 2000, and to be named Nicholas. However, we got a late
April Fool's joke when our boy
decided to be born a girl. Prior
to the ultrasound we couldn't
agree on a girl's name—I had
wanted Olivia and my husband
wanted another name. When
I saw that our new baby was a
girl and not a boy, I exclaimed,
"Olivia!" Well, after I had
just gone through the rigors
of giving birth, my husband
wasn't about to disagree! That
was the easiest argument I've
ever won.

LISA FROM OREGON

*Priscilla: Latin, "ancient,
worthy"
Cilla, Cyla, Prisca, Priscella,
Priscille, Prisilla, Prysilla

Priscilla and her husband, Aquila, encouraged the apostle Paul. See Acts 18:26.

Prisciliana: Spanish variation of Priscilla

Prudence: Latin, "good sense, foresight"

A virtue name used by the Puritans.

Pru, Prudenca, Prudi, Prue

Pualani: Hawaiian, "royal flower"

Pulika: Swahili, "obedience"

Purity: Middle English, "purity"

A virtue name popular with the Puritans.

Queen: Old English, "queen"

Quanda, Queena, Queene, Queenette, Queenie

Querida: Spanish, "dear, beloved"

Quinn: Irish Gaelic, "she who is wise"

Quin

Quintessa: Latin, "essence"

Quintie, Tess, Tessa, Tessie

Quintina: Latin, "fifth"

Quenta, Quentina, Quinta, Quintana, Quintessa

*Rachel: Hebrew, "ewe, little lamb"

Rachael, Racheal, Rachele (Italian), Rachelle (French), Rae, Rahel (German), Raquel, Raquela, Ray, Raychel, Shell, Shelley, Shellie, Shelly

Rachel was the wife of Jacob, and the mother of Joseph and Benjamin (Genesis 25:16-20; 29:18; 30:23-24).

RACHEL SAINT
(1914–1994)

was an evangelical Christian missionary to Ecuador. Her brother, Nate, was among the missionaries killed along with Jim Elliot (Elisabeth Elliot's husband) by the Huaorani (Auca) people in South America in 1956.

Radhi: Swahili, "forgiveness"

Radhiya: Swahili, "she who is content"

Rae: Old English, "doe"
LaRae, Raeann, Ray, Raye, Rayna

Rafaela: Spanish, a feminine variation of Rafael

Rahima: Swahili, "compassionate"

Rahimu: Swahili, "mercy"

Raina: A variation of Regina
Rainah, Raine, Rainey, Rainelle, Rana, Rane, Ranelle, Raya, Rayana, Rayna, Reyna

Raissa: Old French, "thinker"
Raisa, Razel

Ramona: Spanish, "wise protector"—a feminine variation of Raymond
Mona, Ramonda, Ramonna, Romona, Romonda

Ran: Japanese, "water lily"

Randy: Latin, "admirable"—a diminutive of Miranda
Randa, Randee, Randelle, Randene, Randi, Randie

Ranielle: A modern name, possibly a variation of Danielle

Ranita: Hebrew, "song"

Ranice, Ranit, Ranite, Ranitra, Ranitta

Raphaela: Hebrew, "God heals"—a feminine variation of Raphael
Rafa, Rafaela, Rafaele, Rafaelia, Rafaella, Rafella, Rafelle, Raphaella, Raphaelle

Raquel: A Spanish variation of Rachel
Raquelle

Rashida: Swahili, "righteous"

Raven: Old English, "raven"—a large black bird
Ravenna, Ravenne, Rayven

Raya: Hebrew, "she who is a friend"

Rayanne: A combination of Ray and Anne

Razina: Swahili, "strong, patient"

Reba: A diminutive of Rebecca
Reyba, Rheba

*Rebecca: Hebrew, "bound"
Becca, Becka, Beka, Beckee, Beckey, Beckie, Becky, Beka, Bekka, Bekki, Bekkie, Raba, Rebeca (Spanish), Rebecka, Rebeka, Rebekah, Rebekkah,

Rebeque (French), **Reveka** (Slavic), **Revekah**, **Revekka**, **Riva**, **Rivi**, **Rivkah**

Rebekah was the wife of Isaac, and the mother of Jacob and Esau (see Genesis 22:23, 24:67, 25:26).

REBECCA ST. JAMES
(1977–)

is a Christian pop rock singer, songwriter, speaker, and author. She has won multiple Dove Awards and a Grammy.

Regina: Latin, "queen, noble woman"

Gina, Raina, Raine, Rani, Rayna, Reggi, Reggie, Régine (French), Reina, Reine, Reinetta, Reinette, Reyna, Rina

Rehani: Swahili, "promise"

Rehema: Swahili, "compassion"

Remedios: Spanish, "help, remedy"

Rena: Hebrew, "joy, song"

Reena, Reneta, Rene, Renee, Renette, Renita, Rina

Renata: Latin, "reborn"—the

Latin variation of Renée (French)

Ranae, Ranay, Renae, René, Renée, Renelle, Renetta, Renette, Renie, Renisa, Renise, Renita, Rennae, Rennay, Rennie

René: Greek, "peace"—a diminutive of Irene; also a name for both boys and girls

Reney, Renie, Rennie

Renée: French, "reborn"

Ranae, Ranay, Ranée, Renae, René, Renelle, Renie, Rennie, Renny

---

RENÉE OF FRANCE
(1510–1575)

was a Christian noblewoman who helped Protestants who were being persecuted during the Reformation, including John Calvin.

Renita: Latin, "resistant"

Reneeta, Renyta

Reubena: Hebrew, "behold, a son"—a feminine variation of Reuben

Reuvena

Rhea: Greek, "motherly"

Rea, Rhia, Ria

Rheanna: A modern name of which the origin and meaning are uncertain
Reann, Reanna, Rheana, Rheanne

Rheta: Greek, "well-spoken"

***Rhoda:** Greek, "a rose, from Rhodes"
See Acts 12:14.

Rhona: Old Norse, "rough island"
Rhona, Roana

Rhonda: Greek, possibly "grand"
Rhodeia, Rhodia, Rhodie, Rhody, Roda, Rodi, Rodie, Ronda, Rodina

Ria: A diminutive of Victoria
Rea

Ricarda: Old German, "powerful ruler"—a feminine variation of Richard
Rica, Ricarda, Richarda, Richardella, Richardene, Richardette, Richardina, Richardyne, Richel, Richela, Richelle, Richette, Ricki, Riki

Richelle: A feminine variation of Richard

Rickie: a diminutive of Frederica

Ricki, Ricky, Rika, Riki, Rikki, Rikky

Rilla: Low German, "small brook"
Rella, Rilletta, Rillette

Risa: Latin, "laughter"
Riesa, Rise, Rysa

Rissa: A diminutive of names such as Clarissa and Marissa

Rita: A diminutive of Margarita
Reeta, Reida, Reita, Rheeta, Rheta, Rieta, Ritta

Riva: Hebrew, "bound"—see Rebecca
Reba, Reeva, Reva, Rifka, Rivi, Rivka, Rivke, Rivkah

***Rizpah:** Hebrew, "hot stone"
See 2 Samuel 21:8-14.

Roanna: A variation of Rosanne
Ranna, Roanne, Ronni, Ronnie, Ronny

Roberta: Old English, "bright, famous"—a feminine variation of Robert
This popular name has many variations.
Berta, Bertie, Berty, Bobbe, Bobbee, Bobette, Bobbie, Bobby, Bobbye, Bobette,

Bobi, Reberta, Roba, Robbee, Robbey, Robbi, Robbie, Robby, Robeena, Robella, Robelle, Robena, Robetta, Robette, Robin, Robina, Robinette, Robinia, Robyn, Robyna, Robynna, Ruperta (Spanish)

Robin: Old English, "shining with fame"—a diminutive of Robert; also a name for both boys and girls

Robee, Robbey, Robbi, Robbie, Robbin, Robby, Robbyn, Robena, Robene, Robenia, Robi, Robina, Robine, Robinia, Robyn, Robyna, Robynette

Rochelle: French, "the little rock"

Roch, Rochell, Rochella, Rochette, Roschella, Roschelle, Roshelle, Shell, Shelley, Shelly

Roderica: Old German, "renowned ruler"—feminine variation of Roderick

Rica, Roderiga, Roderiqua, Roderique, Rodriga

Rolanda: Old German, "fame of the land"—a feminine variation of Roland

Orlanda, Orlande, Rolande, Rollande

Roline: Old German, "man"—a diminutive of Caroline

Rolene, Rollene, Rolleen, Rollina, Rolline, Rolyne, Rolynne

Roma: Latin, "eternal city"

Romelle, Romilda, Romina, Romma

Romaine: French, "from Rome"—a feminine variation of Romain

Romane, Romayne, Romeine, Romene

Romola: Latin, "she who is from Rome"

Roman, Romala, Romana, Romella, Romelle, Rommola, Romolla

Rona: Old Norse, "rough island"

Rhona, Ronalda, Ronella, Ronel, Ronnelle, Ronna

Ronnell: A feminine variation of Ron and Ronald

Ronelle, Ronel, Ronnel

Ronni: A feminine variation of Ronald

Ronalda, Ronee, Ronette, Roni, Ronna, Ronnee, Ronnelle, Ronnella, Ronney, Ronnie, Ronny

Rory: Irish Gaelic, "red king"— a name used for both boys and girls

Rori

Rosa: A Spanish variation of Rose

Rosabel: A combined variation of Rose and Belle, "beautiful rose"

Rosabella, Rosabelle

Rosalie: An Irish variation of Rose

Rosalee, Rosaleen, Rosaley, Rosalia, Rosalina, Rosaline, Rosalyne, Roselia, Rosella, Roselle, Rozalia, Rozalie, Rozele, Rozelie

Rosalind: Spanish, "beautiful rose"

Ros, Rosalen, Rosalin, Rosalina, Rosalinda, Rosalinde, Rosaline, Rosalinn, Rosalyn, Roselin, Roselina, Roselinda, Roselinde, Roseline, Roselyn, Roslyn, Roz, Rozali, Rozalia, Rozalin—additional variations are possible to create with this name

Rosalyn: A combined variation of Rose (Latin, "rose") and Lynn (Spanish, "pretty")

Rosalin, Rosalynn, Roselynn, Roslyn, Rozlynn

Rosamond: Old German, "famous protector"

Ros, Rosamonde, Rosemonde (French), Rosemonda, Roz, Rozamond, Rozamonda

---

ROSALIND GOFORTH
(1864–1942)

was the wife of Jonathan Goforth. Together they served as missionaries in China and Manchuria. She wrote the classic *How I Know God Answers Prayer.*

Rosana: A combination of Rose and Ana

Rose: From "rosa," the Latin name for the flower

Rhonda, Rhodes, Rhodia, Rhody, Rosa (Italian/Spanish), Rosaleen, Rosalia, Rosalie, Rosalin, Rosalina, Rosaline, Rosanie, Rosario, Roselia, Roselina, Roseline, Rosella, Roselle, Rosena, Rosene, Rosetta (Italian/Spanish), Rosette (French), Rosey, Rosi, Rosie, Rosina, Rosita, Roslyn, Rosy, Roza, Rozalie, Roze, Rozella, Rozelle, Rozy—additional variations are possible to create with this name

What's in a Name?

My son Harlan was diagnosed with leukemia when he was ten months old. For the next 27 months, he underwent treatment for his disease. During this time I became pregnant again. I was pretty scared to be having a baby while my other child was going through cancer treatment. I'd seen two other women who had gotten pregnant during their child's treatment, and their children had died. One of them wasn't taking it well and was shunning her newborn. It was a tense time for me.

Harlan's treatment ended in April, just after his third birthday. Our daughter was due a month later in May. Going through Harlan's illness had truly been a storm for us. He'd almost died twice—once from septicemia and another time from grand mal seizures.

When naming our newborn daughter, I considered the name Rainbow because I thought it was beautiful and I wanted a really special name for her (I had three boys already). At first, I just didn't know if I could really name a child that. I thought she might be teased a lot, but one of my friends said that even if I named her Jane Doe, other kids would still find a way to make fun of it!

Surprisingly, my mom liked the name Rainbow too. To celebrate the end of my son's treatment, she had sent us a card that said, "After every storm is a rainbow." At that moment, I knew this daughter was our Rainbow after the storm, and we felt she was God's promise that Harlan was completely healed and that the storm was past.

At the time of this writing, Harlan is 14 years old, has virtually *no* effects from his cancer or the treatment, and is excelling in school and orchestra.

And that is the story of how our Rainbow Noelle was named!

SUSANNE FROM TEXAS

Roseanne: A combined variation of Rose and Anne

Roanna, Roanne, Rosanna, Rosannah, Rosanne, Roseann, Roseanna, Rozanna, Rozanne

---

ROSE PATIENCE GRENFELL
(1849–1906)

was the wife of George Grenfell. Together they served as missionaries in Africa.

Rosemary: Latin, "dew of the sea"

Rosemaree, Rosemarey, Rosemaria, Rosemarie, Rosmarie, Rozemary

Rowena: Old English, "well-known friend"

Ranna, Rena, Ronni, Ronnie, Ronny, Rowe

Roxanne: Persian, "dawn, brilliant one"

Rox, Roxana, Roxane, Roxann, Roxanna, Roxene, Roxey, Roxiane, Roxianne, Roxie, Roxine, Roxy, Roxyann, Roxyanna

Ruby: Latin, "red"—a red gemstone

Rubee, Rubetta, Rubette, Rubey, Rubi, Rubia, Rubie, Rubina, Rubya

Rufina: Latin, "red-haired"—a feminine variation of Rufus

Rufeena, Rufeine, Ruffina, Ruphyna

Rukiya: Swahili, "she who rises high"

*Ruth: Hebrew, "friend, companion"

Ruthe, Ruthelle, Ruthi, Ruthie, Ruthina, Ruthine

Ruth was a loyal daughter-in-law who moved to Israel with her mother-in-law, Naomi. Eventually she became the wife of Boaz. You can read their story in the Bible book of Ruth.

Ruthann: A combined variation Ruth and Ann

Ruthanna, Ruthanne

RUTH BELL GRAHAM
(1920–)

was born in Quinjiang, China, the daughter of medical missionaries. She is the wife of evangelist Billy Graham and the mother of five children.

Ruzuna: Swahili, "calm"

Sabina: Latin, "Sabine woman (Italy), woman from Sheba"
Sabine, Sabinna, Sabyna, Savina, Savine, Sebina, Sebinah, Zabinah

Sabiha: Swahili, "she who is graceful"

Sabra: Hebrew, "to rest"
Sabrah, Sebra

Sabrina: Latin, "from the border"
Brina, Sabreena, Sabrinna, Sabryna, Sebreena, Sebrina, Zabrina

Saburi: Swahili, "patience"

Sadie: Hebrew, "princess"—a diminutive of Sarah
Sada, Sadah, Sadelle, Sadye, Saida, Saidee, Saidey, Saidie, Saydie, Sydell, Sydella, Sydelle

Safiya: Swahili, "pure"
Safiyah

Sage: Latin, "wise, healthy"
Saige, Sayge

Saida: Swahili, "happy"

Saiha: Swahili, "good"

Sakina: Swahili, "she who is calm"

Sala: Swahili, "prayer"

Salama: Swahili, "peace"

Salina: Latin, "by the salt water"
Saleena

Sally: Hebrew, "princess"—a diminutive of Sarah
Sal, Saletta, Sallee, Salletta, Sallette, Salley, Sallianne, Sallie, Sallyann

> Sons are a heritage from the Lord, children a reward from him. Like arrows in the hands of a warrior are sons born in one's youth. Blessed is the man whose quiver is full of them.
>
> —Psalm 127:3-5

***Salome:** Hebrew, "peaceful"
Sahlma, Salima, Salma, Salmah, Saloma, Salomea, Salomey, Salomi, Selima, Selma, Selmah, Solome, Solomea

There are two Salomes in the New Testament: one was

the daughter of Herodias, who requested that John the Baptist be put to death (Matthew 14:6-11). The other was the mother of James and John, who were asked by Jesus to become His disciples (Matthew 10:2).

Salvia: Latin, "whole, healthy"

Sallvia, Salvina

Samala: Hebrew, "requested of God"

Samale, Sammala

Samantha: Aramaic, "she who listens"—a feminine variation of Samuel

Sam, Samey, Sami, Samantha, Sammee, Sammey, Sammie, Sammy, Simantha, Symantha

Samara: Hebrew, "guarded by God"

Sam, Samaria, Samarie, Sammara, Sammy, Semara

Samuela: Hebrew, "heard by God"—a feminine variation of Samuel

Samella, Samelle, Samuella, Samuelle

Sandra: Greek, "helper, defender of mankind"—a diminutive of Alexandra

Sandee, Sandi, Sandie, Sandrea, Sandrella, Sandrelle, Sandria, Sandrina, Sandrine, Sandy, Sondra, Sonndra, Zandra, Zondra

Sandy: A diminutive of Sandra—also a name for both boys and girls

Sandee, Sandi, Sandie

*Sapphira: Greek, "sapphire"—a deep blue gemstone

Safira, Saphira, Sapir, Sapira, Sapphira, Sephira

Sapphira was the wife of Ananias. The couple, unfortunately, chose to act deceptively when they sold some land and gave only part of the money to the Lord. They were punished with death. See Acts 5:1-10.

SARAH EDWARDS
(1703–1758)
was the wife of Jonathan Edwards, an eminent American preacher, theologian, and missionary.

SARAH GWYNNE WESLEY
(1726–1822)
was the wife of English hymn-writer and preacher Charles Wesley.

*Sarah: Hebrew, "princess"

Sara, Sarai, Saraia, Sarena, Sarette, Sari, Sarina, Sarine, Sarita, Saritia, Sarra, Sarrah, Sera, Serah, Serita, Shara, Zara, Zarah, Zaria, Zarita (Spanish)

Sarah was the wife of Abraham and the mother of Isaac (see Genesis 11:29, 21:1-7).

Sasha: A Russian diminutive of Alexandra

Sacha, Sascha

Savannah: Spanish, "treeless plain, meadow"

Savana, Savanna, Sevanna

Scarlett: Middle English, "deep red"

Scarlet, Scarletta, Scarlette

Seba: Greek, "from Sheba"

Sabah, Sheba, Shebah

Sebastiane: Latin, "honorable, respected"—a feminine variation of Sebastian

Sebastiana, Sebastianne

Seema: Hebrew, "precious, treasure"

Cima, Cyma, Seemah, Sima, Simah

Sekelaga: Nyakyusa (Tanzania), "rejoice"

Selena: Greek, "the moon"

Celene, Celie, Celina, Celinda, Celine, Salena, Salina, Sela, Selena, Selina, Selinda

Selma: Celtic, "fair"

Anselma, Sellma, Selmah, Zelma, Zelmah

Selwyn: Old English, "friend of the family"

Selwin, Win, Winnie, Winny, Wyn, Wynn

Senalda: Spanish, "a sign"

September: The name of the ninth month of the year

Septima: Latin, "seventh"

*Serah: Hebrew, "abundance"

Sera

See Genesis 46:17.

Seraphia: A variation of Seraphim

Seraphim: Hebrew, "burning, ardent"

Sarafina, Serafina, Seraphine

Serena: Latin, "she who is calm, serene"

Cerena, Reena, Rena, Sarina, Saryna, Serene, Serenna,

Serina, Serenity, Seryna, Sirena

SERAPHIA
(d. c. AD 125)

Was a slave girl of Antioch who shared the gospel with her mistress, Sambine. Both women were later martyred for their faith.

Serwa: Ewe (Ghana), "noble woman"

Shaina: Hebrew, "she who is beautiful"
Shaine, Shana, Shanee, Shani, Shanie, Shanya, Shayne

Shaleen: A modern name whose origin and meaning are uncertain
Shalene, Shaline, Shelene

Shalom: Hebrew, "peace"—a greeting sometimes used as a name
Shalome, Shalva, Shalvah, Shelom, Shilom, Sholome

Shana: Hebrew, "the Lord is gracious"—a feminine variation of Sean
Sean, Seana, Seanna, Shana, Shanna, Shannah, Shaun, Shauna, Shaunee, Shaunie, Shawn, Shawna

Shandra: modern variation of Sandra

Shani: Swahili, "marvelous"

Shannon: Irish Gaelic, "wise one"—a name for both boys and girls
Channa, Shana, Shane, Shani, Shanna, Shanon

Sharee: A variation of Sherry.

Shari: A Hungarian variation of Sarah

Sharlene: Old Gaelic, "man"—a feminine variation of Charles
Sharleen, Sharlina, Sharline, Sharlyne

Sharon: Hebrew, "princess, of the plain"
Shara, Sharan, Sharen, Sharene, Shari, Sharie, Sharla Sharyn, Sheran, Sherri, Sherry

Shasta: A name whose origin and meaning are uncertain; the name of a mountain in northern California

Shea: Irish Gaelic, "majestic"—also a name for both boys and girls
Shae, Shay, Shaye, Shayla, Shealyn, Shealynn

Sheba: Hebrew, "from Sheba"—also a variation of Bathsheba (Hebrew, "daughter of promise")

Saba, Sabah, Scheba, Shebah, Sheeba, Shieba

Sheena: Hebrew, "the Lord is gracious"

Sheenah, Sheina, Shena

Sheila: An Irish variation of Cecilia

Seila, Selia, Shayla, Sheilah, Shela, Sheila, Shelia, Shiela

Shelby: Old English, "estate on the ledge"

Shel, Shelbea, Shelbee, Shelbey, Shelbi, Shelbie, Shellby

Shelley: Old English, "sloping meadow"

Schelley, Shell, Shellee, Shelli, Shellie, Shelly

*Sherah: Hebrew, "female relative"

Sheerah

See 1 Chronicles 7:24.

Sherry: French, "dear, cherished"

Sharee, Shari, Sharie, Sharrie, Sheree, Sherey, Sheri, Sherie, Sherina, Sherree, Sherrey, Sherri, Sherye

Sheryl: A variation of Shirley

Cheralyn, Cheralynn, Cherilyn, Cherilynn, Cheryl, Sheralyn, Sheralin, Sherileen, Sherill, Sherilyn, Sherrell, Sherrill, Sherryl, Sheryll

Shifra: Hebrew, "she who is beautiful"

Schifra, Shifrah

Shina: Japanese, "faithful"

Shiri: Hebrew, "my song"

Shira, Shirah, Shirit

Shirley: Old English, "from the bright meadow"

Sher, Sheree, Sheri, Sherlee, Sherli, Sherlie, Sheryl, Shirlee, Shirlene, Shirline

Shona: A feminine variation of Sean

Shaina, Shaine, Shana, Shanie, Shonah, Shone, Shoni, Shonie, Shuna

Shoshana: Hebrew, "rose"

Shosha, Shoshanah, Sosaana, Sosannah

*Shua: Hebrew, "rich, noble"

See 1 Chronicles 7:32.

Shukura: Swahili, "she who is grateful"

Shulamith: Hebrew, "peace"
Shula, Shulamit, Sula, Sulamith

Sibyl: Greek, "prophetess, oracle"
Cybele, Cybil, Cybilla, Sabilla, Sabylla, Sibel, Sibell, Sibella, Sibelle, Sibil, Sibilla, Sibyll, Sybel, Sybella, Sybill, Sybilla, Sybille

Sidonie: Latin, "fine cloth"—*Sidon* is a place name in the Middle East
Sidaine, Sidonia, Sidony, Sydona, Sydonah, Sydonia

Sierra: Spanish, "saw" (for cutting), "mountain range"
Ciera, Cierra, Siera, Sierah, Sierrah, Sierre

Sigfreda: Old German, "peaceful victory"
Sigfreida, Sigfrida, Sigfrieda, Sigfryda

Sigourney: A name whose origin and meaning are unknown
Sigornee, Sigournee, Sigournie

Sikia: Swahili, "harmony"

Silvia: Latin, "from the forest"—a variation of Sylvia
Silva, Silvann, Silvanna, Silvie, Silvy, Silvya, Sylvia, Sylvie

Simcha: Hebrew, "joy"
Simchah

Simone: Hebrew, "one who hears"—a feminine variation of Simon
Shimona, Shimonah, Simeona, Simona, Simonia, Symona

Sivia: Hebrew, "deer"
Sivya

Socorra: Spanish, "aid, help"
Secorra, Socaria, Succora

Sofia: See Sophia

Solane: Spanish, "sunshine"
Solenne

Soledad: Spanish, "solitude"

Sondra: A variation of Sandra, which is a diminutive of Alexandra
Saundra, Sohndra, Zaundra, Zohndra, Zondra

Sonia: The Russian diminutive of Sophia
Sohnia, Sonja, Sonje, Sonya

Sophia: Greek, "she who is wise"

Sofia, Sofie, Sofiya (Russian), Sofy, Sofya, Sonia, Sonja, Sonya, Sophey, Sophie, Sophy, Zofia (Polish)

Sorcha: Irish Gaelic, "bright, shining"

Sorrel: A botanical name

Sorel, Sorelle, Sorrell, Sorrelle

Spring: Old English, "springtime"

Ssanyu: Uganda, "happiness"

Stacy: Irish variation of Anastasia—Greek, "resurrection"

Stace, Stacee, Stacey, Staci, Stacia, Stacie, Stasey, Stasia, Stasie, Stasey, Stasha, Stasy, Stasya (Russian), Taci, Tacie, Tacy

Star: Old English, "star"

Starla, Starlene, Starletta, Starlette, Starr

Stella: Latin, "star"

Estella, Estelle, Stela, Stelle

Stephanie: Greek, "crowned one"—a feminine variation of Stephen

Fania, Fanya, Stefa, Stefana, Stefania, Stefanie, Steffa, Steffanie, Steffenie, Stepfanie, Stepha, Stephana, Stephania, Stephene, Stephine, Stevana, Stevena, Stevie, Stevey—additional variations are possible to create with this name

Stevie: A feminine variation of Steve and diminutive of Stephanie

---

SUSANNAH SPURGEON
(1832–1903)

was the wife of English preacher C.H. Spurgeon. She started and ran the Book Fund, a ministry that supplied books to poor ministers.

Stina: Greek, "anointed, Christian"—a diminutive of Christina

Stine

Stormy: Old English, "tempest"

Stormie, Stormey

Subria: Swahili, "patience rewarded"

Sue: See Susan

Summer: Old English, the name of one of the four seasons

Somer, Sommers, Sumer, Summers

Sunny: English "bright, cheerful"

Sunnee, Sunnie, Sunshine

Surayya: Swahili, "she who is noble"

Susan: Hebrew, "graceful lily"

Sue, Sueann, Susana, Susanetta, Susann, Susanna, Susannah, Susanne, Suse, Susee, Susette (French), Susi, Susie, Susy, Suzan, Suzana, Suzane, Suzanna, Suzanne, Suze, Suzee, Suzetta, Suzette (French), Suzie, Suzy, Zanna, Zannie

---

SUSANNA ANSLEY WESLEY
(1669–1742)

was an author, teacher, and mother of 19 children, including John Wesley and Charles Wesley.

---

*Susannah: Hebrew, "graceful lily"

Suesanna, Susana, Susanna, Suzanna, Zanna, Zannah, Zanne, Zannie

Susanna was among the women whom Christ healed. She showed her appreciation by joining the other women who followed Christ and the disciples and helped with their sustenance. See Luke 8:2-3.

What's in a Name?

When my mother was in the hospital to give birth to her third child (there would eventually be two more), she just couldn't decide on a name. She turned to my father for suggestions, but he was no help at all. Finally, in frustration, she threatened, "If you don't come up with a name, I'm going to name this baby after the next person I see!"

It was shortly thereafter that a nurse walked in the room. Her name badge read "Susan K." True to Mom's word, my little sister was named Susan K. We were all just glad she was a girl and not a boy!

KIM FROM OREGON

Suzanne: French variation of Susan

Susanna, Susanne, Suzane, Suzannah, Suzette, Suzzanne, Zanne, Zannie

Suzette: See Susan

Swana: Old English, "swan"

Sybil: A variation of Sibyl

Sibyl, Sibylla, Sybel, Sybella, Sybelle, Sybill, Sybilla

Sydney: Old French, "Saint Denis"

Cydney, Sidney, Sidnie, Sydnie

Sylvia: Latin, "from the forest"

Silva, Silvana, Silvania, Silvanna, Silvia, Silviana, Silvianne, Silvie, Sylva, Sylvana, Sylvanna, Sylviana, Sylvianne, Zilvia, Zylvia

Syntyche: Hebrew, "fortunate"

Syntyche was among the women in the church at Philippi (Philippians 4:2).

T

Tabita: Swahili, "graceful"

*Tabitha: Aramaic, "a gazelle"

Tabatha, Tabbee, Tabbey, Tabbi, Tabbie, Tabby, Tabita, Tabytha

Tabitha (also known as Dorcas) was raised from the dead by the apostle Peter. See Acts 9.

Tacita: Latin, "silent one"

Tacey, Tacia, Tacie, Tacye

Taffy: Welsh, "beloved"

Tavi, Tavita, Tevita

Talia: Hebrew, "dew from heaven"

Tali, Tallie, Tally, Talya, Thalia

*Talitha: Aramaic, "maiden, little girl"

Taleetha, Taletha, Talicia, Talisha, Talita

See Mark 5:41.

*Tamar: Hebrew, "palm tree"

Tama, Tamara, Tamarah, Tamera, Tamma, Tammara, Tammi, Tammy, Tamora, Tamra, Tamrah, Thamar, Thamara, Thamera

Tamar was Judah's daughter-in-law, who is part of the lineage of David and Christ (see Genesis 38:12-30, Matthew 1:3). A second Tamar was the daughter of King David (2 Samuel 13:1-19), and a third Tamar was the daughter of David's son Absalom (2 Samuel 14:27).

Tamara: See Tamar

Tammey, Tammi, Tammie, Tammy

Tamika: A modern name of which the origin and meaning are uncertain

Tameka, Tamieka, Tamike, Tamique, Temika, Tomika, Tonica, Tonique

Tammy: A diminutive of Tamara

Tami, Tamie, Tammee, Tammey, Tammi, Tammie

Tamsin: Hebrew, "twin"—a variation of Thomasina

Tamasin, Tamasine, Tamsine, Tamsinne, Tamsyn, Tamsynne, Tamzen, Tamzin

Tamu: Swahili, "she who is sweet"

Tanisha: A modern name of which the origin and meaning are uncertain

Taneesha, Taniesha, Tanitia, Tannicia, Tannisha, Teneesha, Tinecia, Tynisha

Tansy: Greek, "immortality"

Tansee, Tansey, Tansia, Tanzey, Tanzie

Tanya: Russian, "fairy princess"

Tana, Tahnya, Tania, Tanita, Tanja, Tonya

*Taphath: Hebrew, "a drop of myrrh"

Taphath was one of the daughters of King Solomon (1 Kings 4:11).

Tara: Irish Gaelic, "rocky hill"

Tarah, Tari, Taria, Tarra, Tarrah, Taryn, Terra

Taraji: Swahili, "faith"

Taralynn: A combination of Tara and Lynn

Taralyn, Taralynne

Tari: See Tara

Taryn: A variation of Tara

Taran, Tarin, Tarina, Tarnia, Tarryn, Taryna

Tasha: Russian, "Christmas child"—also a diminutive of Natasha

Tahsha, Tashey, Tashi (Slavic), Tashina, Tasia, Taska, Tasya

Tatum: Old English, "cheerful"—a feminine variation of Tate

Tata, Tate

Tauna: A modern name of which the origin and meaning are uncertain

Taylor: Middle English, "tailor"

Tailor, Tayler

Teague: Irish Gaelic, "poet"

Teagan, Tegan, Teigan, Teigen, Teigue

Tecia: Greek, "fame, of God"

Teccia, Tekia, Tekli, Telca, Telka, Thekla

Telisa: A modern name, possibly based on Lisa

Temira: Hebrew, "tall"

Temora, Timora

Temperance: Latin, "moderation"

A virtue name popular with the Puritans.

Tendayi: Shona (Zimbabwe), "give thanks"

Teodora: Spanish, a feminine form of Teodoro (Theodore)

Terema: Swahili, "cheerful"

Terena: A feminine variation of Terence

Tareena, Tarena, Tarina, Tereena, Terenia, Terenne, Terriell, Terriella, Terina, Terrena, Terrene, Terrin, Terrina, Teryl, Teryll

Teresa: See also Theresa

Terasa, Terasina, Terasita, Terecena, Teresia (Spanish), Teresina, Teresita (Spanish), Teresse, Tereza, Terezita, Terosina, Terrie, Terry, Tersa, Tersia, Tesa, Tesia, Tess, Tessa, Tessie, Tessy

---

TERESA OF AVILA
(1515–1582)

was a mystic, writer, and monastic reformer of the Middle Ages.

Terra: Latin, "earth"

Tera, Terah, Terrah

Terri: A diminutive of Theresa

Terea, Teree, Terell, Terella, Teri, Terie, Terree, Terrey, Terry (this variation also for boys), Terrye

Tertia: Latin, "third"

Tercia, Tersia, Tersha

Tess: A variation of Tessa and a diminutive of Teresa

Tessa: A diminutive of Teresa

Tess, Tessie, Tessy, Teza

Tessie: See Teresa

Thaddea: A feminine variation of Thaddeus, Greek, "courageous, tender"

Tada, Taddie, Thada, Thadda, Thadee, Thaddie

Thalassa: Greek, "from the sea"
Talassa

Thalia: Greek, "to flourish"
Talia, Thaleia, Thalie, Thalya

Thelma: Greek, "nursing"
Telma, Thellma

Themba: Zulu (South Africa), "trusted"

Theodora: Greek, "gift of God"—a feminine variation of Theodore
Dora, Fedora, Feodora (Russian), Fyodora, Tedda, Teddey, Teddi, Teddie, Teodora, (Spanish), Teodosia (Italian), Theda, Theo, Theodosi, Theodosia, Todora

---

THEODORA
was a woman martyred in AD 249 under the Roman emperor Decius for refusing to offer sacrifices to Roman idols.

Theophania: Greek, "God's appearance"
Theofania, Theophanie, Teofanie, Teophania, Teophanie

Theophila: Greek, "God-loving"
Teofila, Teophila, Theofila

Theresa: Greek, "harvester"
Resa, Taresa, Tera, Terasa, Teresa, Terese, Teresia, Tereza, Teri, Terri, Terrie, Terry, Tess, Tessa, Tessi, Tessie, Tessy, Therese, Tresa, Treza, Zita—additional variations are possible to create with this name

---

THEODOSIA ALLEINE
(1634–1668)
was the wife of Puritan minister Joseph Alleine.

Thomasa: Greek, "twin"—a feminine variation of Thomas
Thomasina, Thomasine, Toma, Tomasa, Tomasina, Tomasine, Tommi, Tommie, Tommy

Thora: Old Norse, "thunder"—a feminine variation of Thor
Thordia, Thordis, Tyra

Tia: Spanish, "aunt"
Thia, Tiana, Tiara

Tiara: Latin, "headdress"
Tyara

Tiberia: Latin, "the River Tiber"
Tibbie, Tibby, Tyberia

Tierra: Spanish, "earth"

Tiffany: Old French, "appearance of God," from Greek, Theophania
Teffan, Teffany, Thefania, Theophania, Tifara, Tiff, Tiffan, Tiffaney, Tiffani, Tiffanie, Tiffie, Tiffney, Tiffy, Tiphani, Tiphanie, Tiphara, Tyffany

Tilda: A diminutive of Matilda
Thilda, Thilde, Tildie, Tildy, Tilley, Tillie, Tilly

Timothea: Greek, "honoring God"—a feminine variation of Timothy
Thea, Tim, Timi, Timmey, Timmi, Timmie, Timotheya

Tina: A diminutive of names ending with -tina or -tine, but increasingly a proper name in its own right
Teena, Teenie, Teina, Tena, Tine, Tiny

Tira: Hebrew, "enclosure"

*Tirzah: Hebrew, "pleasantness"
Thersa, Thirsa, Thirza, Thirzah, Thursa, Thurza, Thyrza, Tierza, Tirza, Tyrzah
See Numbers 26:33.

Tisha: A diminutive of names ending with -ticia
Ticia, Tish

Tita: Greek, "of the giants"—possibly a feminine variation of Titus
Teeta, Tyta

Tivona: Hebrew, "fond of nature"
Tibona, Tiboni, Tivoni

Toby: Hebrew, "God is good"
Thobie, Thoby, Toba, Tobe, Tobee, Tobelle, Tobey, Tobi, Tobiah, Tobye

Tomasa: Spanish, feminine variation of Tomas (Thomas)
Tamasa, Tomana, Tomasena, Tomasina, Tomaza, Tomeseta

Toni: Latin, "priceless"—a diminutive of Antoinette
Tona, Tonee, Toney, Tonia, Tonie, Tony, Tonya

Topaz: Latin, a gemstone that is found in various colors—blue, brown, and yellow
Topaza

Tori: Latin, "victory"—a diminutive of Victoria
Torey, Toria, Torie, Torrey, Torrye, Tory

Tosan: Shekiri (Nigeria), "God knows the best"

Tracy: A diminutive of Theresa—also a name for both boys and girls
Trace, Tracee, Tracey, Traci, Tracie, Trasey

Tricia: A diminutive of Patricia
Trichia, Tris, Trisa, Trish, Trisha, Trisia, Trissina

Trina: A diminutive of Katrina
Treena, Treina, Trenna, Trinette, Trinnette

Trinity: Latin, "triad"
Tini, Trini, Trinidad, Trinidade, Trinita, Trinitee, Trinitey

Trisha: See Patricia

Trixie: Latin, "bringer of gladness"—a diminutive of Beatrice
Trix, Trixee, Trixey

Trudy: Old German, "beloved"—a diminutive of Gertrude
Truda, Trude, Trudey, Trudi, Trudie, Trudye

*Tryphena: Greek, "delicate"
Tryphena was one of two women whom the apostle Paul commended for devoted service to the church (Romans 16:12).

> "Only God Himself fully appreciates the influence of a Christian mother in the molding of the character of her children.... If we had more Christian mothers we would have less delinquency, less immorality, less ungodliness and fewer broken homes. The influence of a mother in her home upon the lives of her children cannot be measured."
>
> —BILLY GRAHAM

*Tryphosa: Greek, "delicate"
Tryphosa may have been a twin sister of Tryphena. Paul praised her for her wonderful labors for the Lord (Romans 16:12).

Tsifira: Hebrew, "crown"

Tumaini: Swahili, "hope"

Twyla: Middle English, "woven of double thread"
Tuwyla, Twila, Twilla

Tyana: A modern name of which the origin and meaning are uncertain; possibly a variation of Dana, Dyana

Tyler: Old English, "maker of tiles"—also a name for both boys and girls
Tyller

Udele: Old English, "prosperous"
Uda, Udella, Udelle, Yudella, Yudelle

Ula: Celtic, "sea jewel"
Eula, Ulla, Yulla

Ulrica: Old German, "power of the home"—a feminine variation of Ulric
Rica, Ricka, Ula, Ulka, Ullrica, Ulrika, Ulrike

Una: Latin, "one, unity"
Euna, Ona, Oona, Unah

Unity: Middle English, "unity"
A word as a name, used by the Puritans.
Unita, Unite, Unitey

Urania: Greek, "heaven"

Ourania, Ouranie, Urainia, Uraniya, Uranya

Urbana: Latin, "of the city"—a feminine variation of Urban
Urbanna

Ursula: Latin, "little bear"
Orsa, Orsala, Orsola (Italian), Ulla, Ursa, Ursala, Ursel, Urselina (Spanish), Ursella, Ursina, Ursine, Ursola, Ursule, Ursulette, Ursulina, Ursuline

Uzuri: Swahili, "beauty"

Val: A diminutive of names such as Valentina and Valerie

Valentina: A feminine variation of Valentine
Teena, Teina, Tena, Tina, Val, Vale, Valentia, Valentine, Valida, Valina Vallatina, Valli, Vallie, Vally

Valerie: Latin, "strong"
Val, Valeree, Valerey, Valari, Valaria, Valarie, Vale, Valeree, Valeria (Italian), Valeriana (Spanish), Valery, Vallarie, Valleree, Vallerie, Vallery, Vallie, Vallorie,

Vallory, Valorie—additional variations are possible to create with this name

Valonia: Latin, "shallow valley"

Vallonia, Vallonya, Valonya

Valora: Latin, "courageous"

Vallora, Valloria, Vallorie, Vallory, Valoria, Valorie, Valory, Valorya, Valoura, Valouria

Vanessa: A name invented by Jonathan Swift for his poem "Cadenus and Vanessa" (1713)

Nessa, Nessi, Nessie, Nessy, Van, Vanesa, Vanesse, Vanetta, Vannessa, Vanna, Vannie, Vanny, Venesa, Venessa, Venetta, Vinessa

Vania: A feminine variation of Ivan, Russian version of John, "gift of God"

Vanya

What's in a Name?

When my wife and I named our children, we decided to create names from words in the Bible so that our children would have "different" names but not so different that they would struggle with them. Rather, we wanted the names to be unusual so people would ask about their origin and our children would be able to naturally talk about Christ. Here are the names we created:

Tiffera: From the Hebrew word *tip'ara* or *tipharah*, meaning "beauty" and "glory," found in Isaiah 43:7 and 62:3. We wanted our daughter to be a beauty (spiritually) and to reflect the glory of God.

Cabe: From the Hebrew word *kabed* meaning to "be heavy, weighty." A person "weighty" in society is someone with influence who has honor or is honorable, impressive, and worthy of respect. This word is found in Proverbs 21:21; 29:23, and 1 Samuel 9:6. We wanted our son to have "weight" for Christ in society.

Tamin: From the Hebrew word *tamim* meaning to be "complete, perfect, upright, blameless," and full of "integrity." This word is found in Psalm 15:1-2; 37:18; 84:11. We wanted this daughter's name to reflect her completeness and perfection in Christ.

BARD FROM OREGON

Varda: Hebrew, "rose"

Vardia, Vardina, Vardis

*Vashti: Persian, "beautiful"

Vashti was the wife of King Ahasuerus of Persia, but after falling out of favor with the king, she was replaced by Esther. This fascinating story is found in Esther 1–2.

Velma: A diminutive of Wilhelmina

Vehlma, Bellma

Venetia: Latin, "kindness, forgiveness"

Vanecia, Vanetia, Venecia, Veneta, Venetta, Venezia, Venice, Venise, Venita

Venus: Latin, "love, loveliness"

Venusa, Venusina, Venusita

Vera: A diminutive of Veronica

Veradis, Verasha, Veira, Verena, Verene, Veria, Verita

Verena: Old German, "defender"

Varena, Varina, Vera, Veradis, Vereena, Verene, Verina, Verine, Verna, Veryna

Verna: Latin, "springtime, springlike"

Verda, Verne, Verneta, Vernetta, Vernette, Vernice, Vernie, Vernise, Vernisse, Vernita, Virna, Vyrna

Verona: A diminutive of Veronica

Verona, Verone

Veronica: Latin, "true likeness"

Roni, Ronica, Ronika, Ronne, Ronnee, Ronni, Ronnie, Veira, Vera (Slavic), Veronice, Veronicka, Veronika, Veroniqua

Vespera: Latin, "evening star"

Vesperina

Vicky: A diminutive of Victoria

Vicci, Vickie, Vickey, Vicki, Vicky, Vikkey, Vikki, Vikky

Victoria: Latin "the victorious"—a feminine variation of Victor

Toria, Torie, Toya, Vic, Vici, Vicci, Vickee, Vickey, Vicki, Vickie, Vicky, Victoire (French), Victoriana, Victorie, Victorina, Viktoria, Viktoria, Viktorina, Vitoria (Spanish), Vittoria (Italian)

Vida: Hebrew, "loved one"—a diminutive of Davida

Veda, Vidette, Vieda, Vita, Vitia

Vienna: A modern name whose origin and meaning are uncertain—possibly a place name

Vigilia: Latin, "wakefulness"

Vilhelmina: A variation of Wilhelmina
Vilhelmine, Villhelmina

Vilma: Russian diminutive of Vilhelmina
Wilma

Vina: A diminutive of Davina
Vena, Veina, Vinetta, Vinette, Vinia, Vinica, Vinita, Vinya

Vincentia: A feminine variation of Vincent
Vicenta, Vicentia, Vincenta, Vincetta, Vinette

Vinette: A feminine variation of Vinny (Vincent)

Viola: A variation of Violet

Violet: Latin, "a violet flower"
Vi, Viola, Viole, Violetta, Violette, Viollet, Voilletta, Vyolet

Virginia: Latin, "maiden, virgin"
Genia, Genya, Gigi, Gina

(Italian), Ginger, Ginia, Ginni, Ginnie, Ginny, Ginya, Jinia, Jinnie, Jinny, Virgie, Virginie (French), Virgy, Virgye—additional variations are possible to create with this name

Vita: Latin, "life"
Vitas, Vitia, Vitella

Viva: Latin, "full of life"
Vivca, Vivva, Vyva

Vivian: Latin, "living"
Vi, Viv, Vivia, Viviana, Viviane, Vivianna, Vivianne, Vivie, Vivien, Vivina, Vivyan, Vivyana

Vonette: A variation of Yvonne

VONETTE ZACHARY BRIGHT
(c. 1921–)
was the cofounder of Campus Crusade for Christ with her husband, Bill Bright, in 1951.

Vonna: A variation of Yvonne

Vynn: A variation of Vina
Vynetta, Vynette

W

Walanika: Hawaiianized variation of Veronica

Walda: Old German, "powerful warrior"—a feminine variation of Walter

Wallis: Old English, "from Wales"—a feminine variation of Wallace
Walless, Wallie, Walliss, Wally, Wallys

Wambui: Kikuyu (Kenya), "singer"

Wanaka: Hawaiianized variation of Wanda

Wainika: Hawaiianized variation of Juanita

Wanda: Old German, "wanderer"
Vanda (Czech), Vonda, Wahnda, Wandy, Wenda, Wendaline, Wendi, Wendy, Wendye

Wangai: Kikuyu (Kenya), "born from God"

Wendy: From *Peter Pan* by James Barrie (1880–1937)—also a diminutive of Gwendolyn

Wenda, Wendee, Wendey, Wendi, Wendie, Wendye

Wenona: Old English, "provider of bliss"
Wenonah, Winona, Wynona

Whitney: Old English, "from the white island"
Whitnea, Whitnee, Whitni, Whitnie, Whitny

Wilhelmina: A feminine variation of William
Billie, Elma, Helma, Helmina, Mina, Minnie, Minny, Valma, Velma, Vilhelmina, Vilma, Wilene, Wilhemine (Danish), Willa, Willamina, Willamine, Willandra, Willemina, Willetta, Willette, Williamina, Wilmette, Willmina, Wilma, Wilmena, Wilmette, Wilmina, Wylma—additional variations are possible to create with this name

Willow: Middle English, "willow tree"

Wilma: A diminutive of Wilhelmina
Valma, Vilma, Willma, Wilmina, Wylma

Wilona: Old English, "desired"
Wilone

Winifred: Old English, "friend of peace"
Freda, Freddi, Freddie, Freddy, Fredi, Fredy, Wenefreda, Wina, Winafred, Winefred, Winefreda, Winfrieda, Winifryd, Winnie, Winnifred, Wyn, Wynelle, Wynette, Wynifred, Wynn, Wynne, Wynnifred

Winnie: A diminutive of Winifred

Winona: Native American Indian (Sioux), "firstborn daughter"
Wenona, Wenonah, Winnie, Winoena, Winonah, Wynona

Wren: Old English, "wren"

Wyetta: A feminine variation of Wyatt

Wynelle: A variation of Wynne

Wynne: Old Welsh, "she who is fair, pure"
Win, Winne, Winnie, Winny, Wyn, Wynelle, Wynn

X

Xanthe: Greek, "golden yellow"
Xantha

Xaviera: Basque, "new house"—a feminine variation of Xavier

Xenia: Greek, "hospitable"
Cena, Xeenia, Xena, Xene, Ximena, Zeena, Zena, Zenia, Zina, Zyna

Xin: Chinese, "elegant"

Xylia: Greek, "of the woods"
Xylina, Xylona, Zylina

Y

Yaffa: Hebrew, "she who is lovely"
Jaffa, Yaffah

Yakira: Hebrew, "precious"
Yakirah

Yancey: A name whose meaning and origin are uncertain—possibly a Native American word meaning "Englishman"
Yancee, Yancie, Yancy

Yedida: Hebrew, "dear friend"
Yedidah

Yelena: Latin, "lily"

Yemina: A feminine variation

of Benjamin, Hebrew, "son of the right hand"

Yetta: Old English, "to give, giver"—a diminutive of Henrietta
Yette

Ynez: Greek "pure"—a Spanish variation of Agnes
Ines, Inez, Ynes, Ynesita

Yolanda: Greek, "violet flower"
Iola, Iolanda, Iolande, Jolanna, Jolanne, Yalinda, Yalonda, Yola, Yolande, Yolane, Yolantha, Yolanthe, Yolette, Yollande

Yonina: Hebrew, "dove"
Jona, Jonina, Yona, Yonah, Yonina, Yoninah, Yonita

Yosepha: Hebrew, "Jehovah increases"—a feminine variation of Joseph
Josefa, Josepha, Yosefa

Yoshe: Japanese, "lovely"

Yoshi: Japanese, "good"

Ysabel: Hebrew, "pledged to God"—a variation of Elizabeth
Yabella, Yabelle, Ysabell, Ysabella, Ysabelle, Ysbel

Ysanne: A modern combination of Ysabel and Anne
Ysande, Ysanna

Yvette: A diminutive of Yvonne
Ivett, Ivetta, Ivette, Yevette, Yvedt, Yvetta

Yvonne: French, "knight of the lion"
Evona, Evonne, Ivetta, Ivona (Russian), Ivone (Portuguese), Ivonne, Vonna, Yevette, Yve, Yvetta, Yvette

Z

Zabina: A variation of Sabina

Zahavah: Hebrew, "gilded"
Zachava, Zachavah, Zahava, Zachava, Zehavah, Zehavit

Zahra: Swahili, "blossom"

Zaina: Swahili, "she who is beautiful"

Zakiya: Swahili, "she who is smart"

Zalira: Swahili, "flower"

Zandra: A variation of Sandra and a diminutive of Alexandra

Zahndra, Zandie, Zandy,
Zanndra, Zohndra, Zondra

Zanna: A diminutive of
Susanna
Zana, Zanne, Zannie

Zara: Hebrew, "dawn"
Zaira, Zarah, Zaria, Zarina,
Zarinda

Zarifa: Swahili, "graceful"

Zawadi: Swahili, "a gift has
come"

Zelda: A diminutive of Griselda
Selda, Zelde, Zeilda

Zelia: Hebrew, "she who is zealous"
Zele, Zelie, Zelina

Zelma: A diminutive of
Anselma
Zellma

Zena: Greek, "welcoming"—a
variation of Xenia
Zeena, Zeenia, Zeenya,
Zenia, Zenya, Zina

Zephyr: Greek, "west wind"
Sefira, Sefarina, Sephira,
Zefir, Zefiryn, Zephira,
Zephirine, Zephyra, Zeph-
rine

Zera: Swahili, "dawn"

*Zeruiah: Hebrew, "balsam
from Jehovah"
See 1 Chronicles 2:16.

Zetta: Hebrew, "olive"
Zayit, Zeta, Zetana

Zevida: Hebrew, "gift"
Zevuda

Zhane: A modern name of
which the origin and meaning are uncertain

Zhi: Chinese, "character"

Zhin: Chinese, "treasure"

Zhuo: Chinese, "brilliant"

Zia: Latin, "grain"
Zea

*Zibiah: Hebrew, "a female
gazelle"
See 2 Kings 12:1.

*Zillah: Hebrew, "shadow"
Zila, Zilla, Zylla, Zyllah
See Genesis 4:19-23.

Zina: Swahili, "beautiful"

Zinnia: Latin, the name of a
popular and colorful flower
Zeenia, Zina, Zinia, Zinnya,
Zinya

*Zipporah: Hebrew, "little bird"

Sippora, Sipporah, Zipora, Ziporah, Zippora

Zipporah was the wife of Moses (see Exodus 2:21).

> Train a child in the way he should go, and when he is old he will not turn from it.
>
> —PROVERBS 22:6

Zita: Greek, "seeker"—a diminutive of names such as Rosita

Zeeta, Zyta

Ziva: Hebrew, "to shine brightly"

Zeeva, Zeva, Ziv, Zivit

Zoe: Greek, "life"

Zoee, Zoeline, Zoelle, Zoey, Zoie

Zoila: Spanish, a feminine variation of Ziolo, which is derived from the Greek Zoe

Zola: Italian, "lump of earth"

Zona: Latin, "belt, girdle"—the name given to the belt in the constellation of Orion

Zonia

Zora: Slavic, "golden dawn"

Zarya, Zahrah, Zorah, Zorana, Zoreen, Zorene, Zorina, Zorine, Zorna, Zorra, Zorrah, Zorya, Zoya

Zuna: Bobangi (Nigeria), "abundance"

Zuri: Swahili, "beautiful"

Zuwena: Swahili, "good"

Boys' Names
A–Z

A

*Aaron: Hebrew, "enlightened one"

Aaran, Aaren, Aarin, Ahren, Aron, Arran, Arrand

Aaron was one of the most important men of the Old Testament. He was the brother of Moses and the first high priest of Israel. Read about him in the books of Exodus, Leviticus, Numbers, and Deuteronomy.

Abbott: Hebrew, "father"

Abbey, Abbot, Abott

*Abel: Hebrew, "breath of life"

Abe, Abell, Avel

Abel was the second son of Adam and Eve and was murdered by his older brother, Cain. Read Abel's story in Genesis 4:1-15 and Hebrews 11:4, 12:24

Abelard: Old German, "noble one"

Abelhard

*Abiah: Hebrew, "God is my father"

Abia, Abiel, Abija, Abijah

There were four men in the Bible named Abiah (1 Samuel 8:2, 1 Chronicles 3:10, 1 Chronicles 7:8, and Luke 1:5). Also one woman was named Abiah (1 Chronicles 2:24).

*Abner: Hebrew, "father of lights"

Ab, Abbie, Abby, Ebner

Abner served under his cousin Saul as captain of the Hebrew army. See 1 Samuel 14:50-51, 17:55-57.

*Abraham: Hebrew, "father of a multitude"

Abe, Abie, Abrahm, Abram, Ibrahim (Arabic)

---

* Names preceded by an asterisk are names that appear in the Bible.

Abraham was one of the most important patriarchs in the Old Testament. It was Abraham who was first justified by his faith. He was known as "the friend of God," and in his offering up of his son, Isaac, he became a model of God the Father, who offered up His Son for the atonement of our sins. Read about Abraham primarily in Genesis 11–25.

ABRAHAM LINCOLN
(1809–1865)

was the sixteenth president of the United States and one of the most beloved men in American history.

Ace: Latin, "one"—usually a nickname or an endearment
Acey

*Adaiah: Hebrew, "he who is pleasing to God"
Adia, Adiah
Adaiah was a popular Hebrew name, and there are several minor characters in the Old Testament with this pleasant name.

Adair: Scottish, "from the brook by the oak grove"

Adaire, Adare, Adaren, Aderrick

*Adam: Hebrew, "made from the earth"
Adamo (Italian), Adams
Adam was the first human created by God. See Genesis 1–3.

ADAM CLARKE
(1762–1832)

was an English Methodist pastor and a popular Bible commentator.

Addis: Old English, "child of Adam"
Ad, Addison, Addy

*Adlai: Hebrew, "God's justice"
See 1 Chronicles 27:29.

Adler: Old German, "he who is brave"

Adolph: Old German, "noble wolf"
Adolf, Adolfus, Adolphus, Dolf, Dolph, Dolphe, Dolphus

*Adoniram: Hebrew, "God is mighty!"
Ad
See 1 Kings 4:6, 5:14.

ADONIRAM JUDSON
(1788–1850)

was a great missionary to India and Burma.

ADONIRAM JUDSON (A.J.) GORDON
(1836–1895)

was given his first and middle name in honor of the missionary of the same name. A.J. Gordon was a popular Baptist pastor in Boston, founder of Gordon College and Divinity School, and author of several books on the Christian life.

Adrian: Latin, derived from the area of Adrian, Italy
Adrien, Adrion

*Adriel: Hebrew, "God, my majesty"
Adrial
See 1 Samuel 18:19; 2 Samuel 21:8.

*Aeneas: Greek, "he who is praiseworthy"
See Acts 9:33-34.

*Agabus: Hebrew, "locust"
See Acts 11:28, 21:10-11.

Aidan: Latin, "he who helps"
Aden, Adin, Aiden, Aydan

AIDEN WILSON (A.W.) TOZER
(1897–1963)

was a pastor with the Christian and Missionary Alliance denomination and author of several classic Christian books, most notably *The Knowledge of the Holy* and *The Pursuit of God*.

Aiken: English, "from the oak"

Ainsley: Scottish, "from my meadow"
Ainsleigh, Ansley

Akins: Yoruba (Nigeria), "he who is courageous"
Akens

Alain: a French variation of Alan

Alair: Latin, "he who is joyful"—a variation of Hillary
Alaire, Alare

Alan: Celtic, "attractive man" or "fair one"
Al, Alain (French), Alano (Spanish), Allan, Allen, Allyn

Alaric: German, "ruler"
Al, Alar, Larry

ALAN REDPATH
(1907–1989)
was a popular
British pastor, speaker,
and author.

Alastair: Irish variation of Alexander
Alastar, Alistair

Alban: Latin, "fair-complected one," or from the area of Alba, Italy
Albany, Alben, Albin

Albert: Old German, "he who is brilliant"
Al, Alberto (Spanish), Bert, Bertie, Berty, Elbert

ALBERT BENJAMIN (A.B.) SIMPSON
(1844–1919)
was the founder of the
Christian and Missionary
Alliance denomination
and author of many
excellent books on the
Christian faith.

Alden: Old English, "he who is friendly"
Aldan, Aldin

Aldo: Italian, "rich man"

Aldred: Old English, "he who is wise"
Eldred

Aldrich: Old English, "wise man"
Aldric, Aldrick, Aldridge, Eldric, Eldrick, Eldridge

Aldous: Old German, "wise man"
Al, Aldis

*Alexander: Greek, "he who defends"
Al, Alec, Alejandro (Spanish), Aleksander, Alessandro (Italian), Alex, Alexis, Lex, Sandy
There are at least three Alexanders named in the Bible. See Mark 15:21, Acts 4:6, and Acts 19:33 (some scholars say this is the same Alexander later referenced in 2 Timothy 4:14).

ALEXANDER CAMPBELL
(1788–1866)
was an evangelist and the
co-founder of the Disciples
of Christ denomination.

ALEXANDER CRUDEN
(1699–1770)
was an early compiler of the concordance to the Bible that bears his name and which is still in print.

Alfred: Old English, "wise counselor"
Al, Alf, Alfie, Alford, Alfredo, Alvord

Algernon: Old French, "noble warrior"
Alger, Elger, Elgernon

Allard: Old German, "he who is determined"
Alard

Allison: Old German, "he who is pious"
Al, Alison, Ally

Aloysius: Old German, "well-known warrior"

*Alpheus: Hebrew, "transient"
Alf, Alphaeus
See Matthew 10:3, Mark 2:14, 3:18, Luke 6:15, and Acts 1:13.

Alphonse: Old German, "he who is ready for battle"
Al, Alf, Alfie, Alfonso (Italian), Alphonsus, Alonzo (Spanish)

Alton: Old English, "from the old town"
Altan, Alten, Allton

*Alvah: Hebrew, "injustice"
Alva
See Genesis 36:40, 1 Chronicles 1:51.

*Alvan: Hebrew, "he who is sublime"
See Genesis 36:23, 1 Chronicles 1:40.

Alvin: Hebrew, "he who is beloved"
Al, Alwin, Alwyn, Vin, Vinny

Amadeus: Latin, "lover of God"
Amadeo (Italian), Amado, Amador

"For the mother is and must be, whether she knows it or not, the greatest, strongest, and most lasting teacher her children have. Other influences come and go, but hers is continual; and by the opinion men have of women we can generally judge of the sort of mother they had."

—HANNAH WHITALL SMITH
(1832–1911)

Ambrose: Greek, "immortal one"

Ambrosio

Ames: French, "he who is friendly"

Possibly from the Latin word for love, "amor," in which case Ames can be considered a male variation of the female Aimee/Amy.

*Ammiel: Hebrew, "kinsman of God"

Amiel

See Numbers 13:12, 2 Samuel 9:4-5, 1 Chronicles 3:5, 26:5.

Amory: Latin, "he who is loved"

Amery

*Amos: Hebrew, "he who bears a burden"

Amos was one of the minor prophets of the Old Testament. See the book bearing his name.

*Ananiah: Hebrew, "God has answered my plea"

See Nehemiah 8:4, 10:22.

Anastasias: Greek, "resurrection"

Anas, Anastasius, Stace, Stacey

Anatole: Greek, "from the east"

Anatolio

André: A French variation of Andrew (Greek, "strong, masculine")

Andrae, Andreas (Greek), Andres (Spanish)

ANDRAE CROUCH
(1942–)

is a popular Christian singer, songwriter, and pastor. His well-known songs include "My Tribute (To God Be the Glory)," "Through It All," and "The Blood Will Never Lose Its Power."

---

*Andrew: Greek, "strong, masculine"

Anders (Scandinavian), Andrae (French variation), André (French variation), Andreas (Greek), Andres (Spanish), Andry, Andy, Drew

Andrew was the first of the disciples chosen by Jesus and the brother of Peter. See Matthew 4:18, 10:2. Andrew died a martyr's death, crucified upon an X-shaped cross.

ANDREW MURRAY
(1828–1917)
was a South African pastor
and writer of many books
on the Christian life still
read by Christians today.

Angelo: An Italian variation of
angel, "messenger from God"
Angel, Angelos

Angus: Scottish, "he who is
strong"

*Annas: Hebrew, "the grace of
God"
Anas
See Luke 3:2, John 18:13,24,
and Acts 4:6.

Ansel: French, "he who is a
nobleman"
Ancel, Ancil, Ansell

Anselm: Old German, "he who
is protected by God"
Anselmo (Spanish)

Anson: Old German, "divine
one"

Anthony: Latin, "deserving of
high honor"
Anton (Slavic), Antoine
(French), Antonio (Italian),
Antony, Tony

*Ara: Hebrew, "he who is strong"
See 1 Chronicles 7:38.

*Aram: Hebrew, "exalted"
See Genesis 10:22-23, 22:21,
1 Chronicles 1:17, 7:34, and
Matthew 1:3-4.

Aran: Asian/Thai, "he who is
from the forest"

Archer: Latin, "bowman"
Arch, Archie

Archibald: Old German, "he
who is bold"
Arch, Archer, Archie

Arden: Latin, "he who is ablaze
with passion"
From the same root as the
word "ardent."
Ardan, Ardin, Ardy

Argus: Greek, "fully aware one"

Argyle: Irish, "from Ireland"

Aric: Old German, "one who
rules"
Arick, Arric, Arrick, Rick,
Ricky

*Ariel: Hebrew, "lion of God"
Ari, Arie, Arriel, Arye
See Ezra 8:16-17, 2 Samuel
23:20, and 1 Chronicles
11:22.

Arlan: Irish, "he who pledges or promises"

Arlen, Arlin, Arlyn

Arley: Old English, "he who hunts"—usually associated with hunting via archery, or a bowman

Arlie, Arleigh

Arlo: Spanish, "the barberry tree"

Armand: A Germanic variation of Herman

Arman, Armando (Spanish), Mandy, Manny

Armstrong: Old English, literally, as it sounds, "strong of arm"

*Arnan: Hebrew, "he who is strong"

See 1 Chronicles 3:21.

Arnold: Old German, "the glory of the eagle"

Arend, Arne, Arnie, Arnoldo

Arsenio: Greek, "manly"

Arsen, Arsene, Arsenius

*Artemus: Greek, "complete"

Art, Arte, Artemas, Artemis, Artie

See Titus 3:12. Some references denote the relationship of this name to the Greek goddess Artemis.

Arthur: English, "sturdy, like a rock; firm, unmovable"

Art, Artie, Artur, Arturo (Italian), Arty

Arvin: Old German, "he who is friendly"

Arv, Arvie, Arvind

*Asa: Hebrew, "healer"

Asa was the great-grandson of Solomon and a forebear of Jesus Christ (see Matthew 1:7-8). He was also the third king of Judah.

*Asaph: Hebrew: "he who gathers, collects"

There are three Asaphs in the Bible. The most notable was the Levite appointed by King David to be a director of choral music for the people of God. See 1 Chronicles 6:39, 15:17-19, 16:5-7, and 25:1-9.

Asaf

*Asaiah: Hebrew, "Jehovah is the cause"

There are several minor Old Testament references to men

with this name, the meaning of which gives glory to God.

Ash: Old English, from tree of the same name

Ashby, Ashton

*Asher: Hebrew, "blessed one"

Ash

Asher was the eighth son of Jacob. See Genesis 30:13, 35:26, 49:20, Deuteronomy 33:24-25.

Ashley: Greek, "starlike"

Ash, Aston (from the ash-tree village)

*Ashur: Hebrew, "free man"

See 2 Samuel 2:9.

Atherton: Old English, "village by the spring"

Athol: Possibly a Scottish place name

Atholl

Attica: Greek, a place name for a region of southern Greece

What's in a Name?

My son's name is Asaf. It comes from the Hebrew word meaning "to gather." Asaf, also written Asaph, was one of the writers of the Psalms and was on the praise and worship team for Israel. He was one of the people appointed to be a guardian of the ark of the covenant in his day. *Asaf* is also the root word for *asif*, which is the fall harvest, the spring harvest being *katzir* in the Bible. So in many ways my son's name represents worship, the last-days harvest, and the ark of the covenant. We thought about all these things when we named our son, who was born in Jerusalem in September of 2006. He is an Israeli citizen, and Asaf is also a popular name in Israel.

My daughter's name is Maayan. She is also Israeli and was born in Israel. Maayan is a popular name in Israel for both boys and girls. Since we wanted a modern name and one with lots of meaning and identity, we chose this one. It literally means "a living spring of water." This is what Yeshua describes as the Holy Spirit and what will flow out of our bellies (John 7:37). It also comes from the verse in Hebrew "Maayanei HaYeshua," or "wells of salvation" that we draw from.

SEAN FROM BEER SHEVA, ISRAEL

The variant name Atticus was made popular in recent decades as the protagonist (Atticus Finch) of the classic Harper Lee novel *To Kill a Mockingbird*.

Atticas, Atticus

Aubrey: Old German, "ruler"

Awbrey

August: Latin, "he who is respectable" or literally "august"

Agostino, Augie, Augustin, Augustine, *Augustus (see Luke 2:1, Acts 25:21, 27:1), Austin

---

AUGUSTINE
(354–430)

was the bishop of Hippo, a town on the North African coast. His writings endure 16 centuries after his death. Most notable are his *Confessions* and *The City of God*.

AUGUSTUS TOPLADY
(1740–1778)

was an English clergyman and hymn-writer, best remembered for "Rock of Ages."

Austen: Latin, "majestic"

Augey, Augie, Austin, Austino, Gus

Averill: Old English, "he who hunts the boar"

Ave, Averell

Avery: English, "ruler"

Ave

Avi: Hebrew, "God is my father"

Abi, Aviel

Axel: Hebrew, "father of peace"

Ax, Axe, Axell

Aylwin: German, "he who is beloved"—a variation of Alvin

*Azariah: Hebrew, "he who hears the Lord"

Az, Azaria, Azzy

There are at least 30 Azariahs in the Bible. It was a very common name, particularly in the Old Testament.

*Aziel: Hebrew, "God is mighty"

Az, Azzy

Aziel was a Levite who played the lyre in the tabernacle. See 1 Chronicles 15:20.

Azizi: Swahili, "he who is dear"

Azzizi, Azzy

Azriel: Hebrew, "God is my helper"

Baden: German, "bather"
Bay, Bayden

Bailey: Old French, "steward"—from the same root as the word "bailiff"
Bail, Baily, Bale, Bayley

Bain: Irish, possibly a diminutive for Bainbridge ("fine bridge")
Bane, Bayne

Baird: Irish, "poet" or "entertainer"
Bard, Bayard (can also mean "he who has red hair")

Baldwin: Old German, "treasured friend"

Ballard: Latin, "dancer"

Bancroft: Old English, "from the bean field"
Bank, Banky, Bink, Binky

Banner: English, "flag-bearer"
Ban, Banny

Bao: Asian/Vietnamese, "to place a bid"

*Barabbas: Hebrew, "a father's son"
Barabbas was the prisoner doomed to die on the cross, until the angry crowds demanded his freedom instead of Christ's. See Matthew 27:16-26.

*Barak: Hebrew, "sudden light" (as in a flash of lightning)
Barack, Barrak
Barak was a mighty warrior under the judge Deborah. Read about Barak in Judges 4:6 and Hebrews 11:32.

Baraka: Swahili, "he shall be blessed"

*Barnabas: Hebrew, "son of encouragement"
Barn, Barna (Italian), Barnaby, Barney
Barnabas was the apostle Paul's companion on many of his journeys. See Acts 4:36, 9:37.

Barrett: Old German, "bearlike"
Barret

Barnett: Old English, "he who is noble"
Barn, Barney

Baron: Latin, "warrior"

Barron

Barry: Irish, "valiant spearsman"

Baris, Barris, Bary, Berry

Barth: Usually a diminutive for Bartholomew.

It has also been used as a proper name honoring Karl Barth, an influential twentieth-century theologian.

***Bartholomew:** Hebrew, "son of the farmer"

Bart, Barth, Bartley

Bartholomew was one of Jesus's 12 disciples. He was also known by the name Nathanael. See Matthew 10:3; Mark 3:18; Luke 6:14; Acts 1:13.

***Bartimaeus:** Hebrew, "son of Timaeus"

Bart, Tim

Bartimaeus was the blind begger healed by Jesus. See Mark 10:36 and Luke 18:35.

Barton: Old English place name, possibly "the town where barley is grown"

Bart, Bartie, Barty

***Baruch:** Hebrew, "he who is blessed"

See Nehemiah 3:20, 10:6. See also Nehemiah 11:5 and Jeremiah 32:12-16.

Basil: Greek, "kingly"

Base, Basile, Bassel, Vaily (Russian)

BASIL THE GREAT
(330–379)
was born into a wealthy land-owning family known for their Christian faith. He became the bishop of Caesarea in 370.

Baxter: Old English, "baker"

Bax, Baxy

Beal: Old French variation of beau ("handsome man")

Beaman: Old English, "one who keeps bees"

Beeman, Beman, Bemon

Beauregard: Old French, "handsome man"

Beau, Bo

Beck: Old English, "stream" or "brook"

Bela: Slavic, "white"

Belah

Benedict: Latin, "blessed"

Ben, Benedictus, Benito (Italian), Bennet, Bennett

*Benjamin: Hebrew, "son of the right hand"

Ben, Benji, Benn, Benny, Benyamin

Benjamin was the youngest son of Jacob and Rachel and the first of the Israelite tribe bearing his name. Rachel died giving birth to him; she named him *Benomi* ("son of sorrows"). Later, Jacob changed his son's name to Benjamin. There are also several other Benjamins mentioned in the Old Testament.

BENJAMIN (BEN) CARSON
(1951–)

is a noted neurosurgeon and the author of *Gifted Hands* and *Think Big.*

Benson: English, "son of Ben"

Ben, Bensen

Bentley: Old English, "from the meadow with rough grass"

Ben, Bent

Benton: Old English, "from the town with rough grass"

Ben, Bent

*Beriah: Hebrew, "God has created"

See 1 Chronicles 8:13,21.

Berkeley: An Old English place name referring to "the forest of birch trees" or "the meadow where the birch trees grow"

Barclay, Berk, Berkley

Bernard: Old German, "true warrior"

Barnard, Barney, Barny, Bern, Bernardo (Spanish), Bernerd, Bernie

---

BERNARD OF CLAIRVAUX
(1090–1153)

was a medieval mystic and ardent proclaimer of the love of God.
His hymns include "Jesus, the Very Thought of Thee" and "O Sacred Head Now Wounded."

Bertram: Old German, "bright raven," or sometimes "glorious shield"

Bert, Bertie, Berton, Bertrand, Burt

Bevan: Welsh, "son of Evan"

Bev, Beven, Bevin, Bevon

Beverly: Old English, "from the beaver meadow"
Bev, Beverley

GEORGE BEVERLY SHEA
(1909–)
One of the most beloved gospel singers of the twentieth century. He frequently sang for the Billy Graham Crusades.

Bien: Asian/Vietnamese, "from the great sea"

Bijay: Asian/Bengali, "he who overcomes"

Bill: Old German, usually a diminutive for William
Bil, Billy, Will, Willy

WILLIAM "BILL" BRIGHT
(1921–2003)
was the author of the popular evangelistic tool "The Four Spiritual Laws" and founder of Campus Crusade for Christ, a successful ministry that began as an effort to reach college students with the gospel.

WILLIAM "BILLY" GRAHAM
(1918–)
is without doubt one of the most successful and widely known evangelists of all time. Through his crusades and his many books, literally hundreds of thousands—if not millions—have come to know Christ.

WILLIAM "BILLY" SUNDAY
(1862–1935)
was a baseball player before he was converted to Christ. He went on to become one of America's more famous and successful evangelists.

Binh: Asian/Vietnamese, "vase"

Bjorn: Scandinavian variation of Bernard

BIL KEANE
(1922–)
is the originator of the popular comic strip The Family Circus.

Blade: Old English, literally, as a knife blade, "sharp, sword-like"

Blaine: Irish, "thin one"
Blane, Blaney, Blayne

Blair: Irish, "from the field"

Blaise: French, "fiery, aflame"
Blase, Blaze (English)

BLAISE PASCAL
(1623–1662)
was a French mathematician and scientist who, upon converting to Christianity, became a noted apologist.

Blake: Old English, "white"
Blakely, Blakeley

Bo: Usually a diminutive for Beauregard

*Boaz: Hebrew, "strong, manly"
See Boaz's heroic story as a model of Christ the Redeemer in the book of Ruth, chapters 2–4.

Bob, Bobbie, and **Bobby:** Usually diminutives for Robert

Boniface: Latin, "doer of good deeds" or "of handsome appearance"

Booth: Old English, "small dwelling"
Boothe

Borden: Old English, "from the valley of the boar"
Bord, Bordy

Boris: Slavic, "fierce in battle, mighty warrior"
Borris

Boswell: French, "the town near the forest"
Bosworth, Boz

Bowen: Welsh, "son of Owen"
Bow, Bowe, Bowie

Boyce: Old French, "from the forest"
Boice, Boise, Boyse

Boyden: Scottish, "fair-haired one"
Boyd

Bradley: Old English, "large meadow or field"
Brad, Braden, Bradford, Bradwell, Brady

Brainard: Old English, "raven-like"
Brainerd

Brand: Middle English, "fiery one"—as in a firebrand
Brandt, Brant, Brantly

Brandon: Old English, "from the beacon hill"

Bran, Brand, Brandan, Brannon (Irish)

Breck: Irish, "freckled one"

Brede: Scandinavian, "glacial"

Brendan: Irish, "man of the sword"

Bren, Brenden, Brennan, Brennen

> Let the little children come to me, and do not hinder them, for the kingdom of heaven belongs to such as these.
>
> —MATTHEW 19:14

Brent: Old English, "from the hill"

Bret: Scottish, "from Brittany"

Brett, Brit, Britt, Britton

Brian: Irish, "honorable man"

Brien, Brion, Bryan, Bryant, Bryon

Brice: Welsh, "bright, alert one"

Bryce

Brick: English, "bridge"

Bridger

Brock: Old English, "badgerlike"

Brocke, Brocker

Broderick: Welsh, "son of renown"

Brodrick, Rick, Rickie, Ricky

Brody: German, "he with the unusual beard" or Gaelic, "ditch"

Brod, Brode, Brodie

Bronson: Old English, "son of Brown"

Bron, Bronnie, Bronny

Brook: Old English, "stream"— literally a brook

Brooks

Bruce: Old French, "from the woods"

Bruno: Old German, "darkly complected man"

Buck: American, "male deer"— usually a nickname or diminutive

Bucky

Bud: American, "friend"— usually a nickname or diminutive

Budd, Buddy

Burgess: Old English, "town dweller"

Burk: German, "castle"
Berk, Bourk, Burk, Burke

Burl: Old English, "knotty wood, tuft of wool"
Berl, Berle, Byrl

Burns: Scottish, "from the fountain"
Byrne, Byrnes

Burton: English, "he who is famous" or a place name
Berton, Burt

Buster: American, usually a nickname or diminutive

Butch: American, usually a nickname or diminutive

Buzz: American, usually a nickname or diminutive
Buzzy

Byrd: Old English, "birdlike"
Bird

Byrne: Old English, "by the brook"
Bern, Berne, Burne, Burns, Byrn

Byron: Old German, "cottage dweller"
Biron, Byran

C

Cable: Old French, "rope," literally, "cable"
Cabe, Cabel

Cade: Welsh, "warrior"
Caid, Caide

*Caesar: Latin, "long-haired one"
Cesar (Spanish), Cesare (Italian)

*Cain: Hebrew, "possessed"
Caine, Kane
Cain was Adam and Eve's firstborn son. His jealousy of his younger brother, Abel (due to Abel's sacrifice to God being accepted, and Cain's being rejected), resulted in the first murder noted in the Bible. See Genesis 4.

Calder: Irish, "from the stony stream"
Cal, Cald, Cale

*Caleb: Hebrew, "adventuresome" or "faithful"
Cal, Cale, Kaleb
Brave Caleb was one of the spies sent out by Moses to survey the Promised Land. See Numbers 13 and 14.

Calvin: Latin, "bald one"
　Cal, Calv, Kalvin, Vin, Vinnie,
　Vinny

CALVIN MILLER
(1936–)

is a popular pastor,
speaker, and author of
many books, including his
classic trilogy *The Singer.*

Cameron: Scottish, "one with
the crooked nose"
　Cam, Cammy, Kameron

Campbell: Scottish, "he who
has a crooked mouth," or perhaps "smile"
　Cam, Campy

Carey: Irish, "from the fortified
city"
　Cary, Kerry

Carl: Considered by many to be
a variation of Charles
　Carlson, Carlton, Karl

CARL F.H. HENRY
(1913–2003)

was an important leader
in twentieth-century
evangelical Christian circles. He served as editor
of *Christianity Today* from
1956 to 1958.

Carlin: Irish, "champion"
　Carl, Carlyn

Carlisle: Old English, "from the
tower of the castle"
　Carlyle

Carlo: A Spanish and Italian
variation of Charles
　Carlos

Carmichael: Scottish, "friend of
Michael"

Carmine: Latin, "song"
　Carm, Carmen

Carney: Irish, "warrior"
　Carn, Carny

Carroll: Irish, "champion"
　Caro, Carol, Karrell

Carson: Old English, "son of
Carr"
　Carse, Carsen

Carter: Old English, "one who
drives a cart"

Carver: Old English, "one who
carves wood"

Cary: Celtic, "he who is dark"
　Carey, Kerry

Case: Irish, "he who is full of courage"

Casey, Kase, Kasey

Cash: Latin, "he who is proud"

Caspar: German, "imperial one"

Cas, Casper, Cass, Cassie, Jaspar, Jasper, Kaspar, Kasper

Cassidy: Irish, "clever one"

Cass, Kassidy

Cassius: Latin, "he who is vain"

Though this is a negative connotation, it might be better construed as "he who is confident"

Cass, Cassio

Cato: Latin, "he who is wise"

Cecil: Latin, "blind one"

Cec

Cedric: Old English, "he who leads in battle"

Ced, Cedrick, Rick, Ricky

*Cephas: Greek, "small rock"

Cephas was the name given to Peter by Jesus. See John 1:42.

Chad: Irish, "valiant warrior"

Chadd, Chade, Chadwick

Chai: Asian (numerous languages), "tea"

Chaim: Hebrew, "life"

Chance: Middle English, "good fortune"

For a Christian, this might be construed as "he who is blessed."

Chan, Chanse

Chandler: Old English, "candle-maker"

Chan, Chaney

Chaney: French, "oak"

Chane, Cheney

Changa: African, "he who is strong"

Channing: Old English, "he who is wise"

Chan

Charles: Old German, "masculine, manly, virile"

Charles has many variations and diminutives, both male and female and in various foreign languages.

Carlo (Italian), Carlos (Spanish), Charlie, Charley, Chaz, Chazz, Chick, Chip, Chuck, Chucky

CHARLES GRANDISON FINNEY
(1792–1875)

was one of the most influential revivalists in American history. His autobiography has motivated many Christians to lead holy lives. Other works include his popular *Revival Lectures*.

CHARLES HADDON SPURGEON
(1834–1892)

was converted at age 15 and became one of the most successful evangelists of all time. His Metropolitan Tabernacle in London seated 6000 congregants.

CHUCK COLSON
(1931–)

was a key figure in the Watergate scandal involving former U.S. president Richard Nixon. Colson served seven months in prison for his crime. While incarcerated he became a Christian, and afterward, in 1976, he founded the hugely successful Prison Fellowship. His story is told in his bestselling book *Born Again*.

Charlton: A variation of Charles
Charl, Charleston

Chase: Old French, "he who seeks"

Chauncey: Latin, "official of the church"
Chaunce, Chauncy

Chester: Latin, "from the soldier's camp"
Ches, Cheston, Chet

Chilton: Old English, "farm by the brook"
Chilt, Chilty

Christian: Greek, "anointed one"—literally, a Christian
Chris, Chrystian, Cristian, Kris, Kristian

Christopher: Greek, "Christ-bearer"
Chris, Christos, Kris, Kristopher, Toph, Topher

Chuck: A diminutive of Charles

Chung: Asian/Chinese, "he who is wise"

Clair: Latin, "clear"
Clare (when spelled this way, usually a diminutive for Clarence)

Clancey: Irish, "red-headed man"
Clancy

Clarence: Latin, "clear, pure"
Clar, Clare, Clarry

Clark: Greek, from the word for "clerk," particularly a clerk in the Old English church
Clarke

***Claudius:** Latin, "he who is lame"
Claude, Claud, Claudel, Claudio (Spanish)
See Acts 11:28, 18:2, 23:26.

Clayton: Old English, "town near the clay beds," or "formed of clay"
Clay

Cleary: Irish, "he who is wise"

Cleavon: English, "from the cliff"

***Clement:** Latin, "he who shows mercy to others"—from the same root as the word *clemency*
Clem
Clement was a co-laborer with the apostle Paul. See Philippians 4:3.

CLEMENT OF ROME
(first century AD)

was an early Christian father and leader of the church in Rome. Some of his writings remain and are of use in learning how the church functioned in its earliest years.

CLEMENT OF ALEXANDRIA
(155–220)

was born in Athens to pagan parents, but converted to Christianity and wrote widely in his role as a teacher in Alexandria.

Cleon: Greek, "he who is well-known"

***Cleopas:** Greek, "glory"
Cleophas, Clopas
See the reference to Cleopas in Luke 24:18 and to Cleophas in John 19:25.

Cleveland: Old English, "from the cliff"
Cleve

Clifford: Old English, "from the cliff"
Cliff, Cliffy

Clifton: Old English, "from the town on the cliff"
Cliff, Clift

Clinton: Old English, "from the town on the hill"
Clint

Clive: Old English, often a diminutive for Clifford, Clifton, or Cleveland, but increasingly a proper name in its own right

---

CLIVE STAPLES (C.S.) LEWIS
(1898–1963)
was a British professor at the University of Cambridge and vibrant Christian author of such classics as *Mere Christianity* and The Chronicles of Narnia.

Clovis: Old German, "celebrated warrior"

Clyde: Welsh, "distant noise"

Cody: Old English, "pillow, cushion"
Code, Codey, Codie, Kody

Colby: Old English, a place name

Cole: Greek, originally a diminutive for Nicholas, or Old English, "he who is dark-skinned"
Kole, Koll

Coleman: Old English, "he who makes coal"
Cole, Colman

Colin: Irish, "young man"—also formerly a diminutive for Nicholas, but increasingly a proper name in its own right
Colan, Colen, Collin, Collins

Collier: Old English, "miner"
Collyer, Colyer

Colton: Old English, "from the dark town"

Conan: Irish, "worthy of praise"
Conant, Conley, Konan, Konant

Conn: Old English, often a diminutive for Connor, Conan, Conrad, Conroy, Conway, but increasingly a proper name in its own right

Connor: Scottish, "he who is wise"
Con, Conor, Konnor

Conrad: Old German, "wise counselor"
Con, Konrad

Conroy: Irish, "he who is wise"
Con, Roy

Constantine: Latin, "he who is reliable" or "constant"
Con, Conn, Constant, Costa, Konstantine, Stan

Conway: Celtic, "hound from the plains"
Con

CONSTANTINE
(285–337)
furthered the notion of a Christian empire through legalizing Christianity in the Roman Empire. This was in spite of the fact that his own spiritual beliefs were mixed at best. In 325 he organized the historic Council of Nicaea.

Cooper: Old English, "barrel-maker"
Coop

Corbett: Latin, "raven, warrior"
Corban, Corbin, Corby, Cory

Corcoran: Irish, "he with the ruddy complexion"
Corky

Cordell: Old French, "one who makes ropes"
Cord

Corey: Irish, "he who lives in the hollow"
Cory, Korey, Kory

Corin: Irish, "spearman"
Corrin, Korin, Korrin, Koryn

*Cornelius: Latin, "war crier"
Cornall, Cornel, Cornell, Corn
See the story of the conversion of the Roman soldier Cornelius and his family in Acts 10.

Cort: Old German, "he who is bold"
Corty, Kort

Cosmo: Greek, "of the universe," from the same root as the word *cosmos*
Cos, Cosimo (Spanish)

Courtney: English, "from the court"
Corey, Cort, Cory, Court, Courtenay

Craig: Irish, "rocky"—from the same root as the word *crag*, meaning "a rock formation"

Crandall: An Old English place name, "dale (valley) of the cranes"
Cran, Crandell

Crawford: Old English, "he who is from the ford of the crows"

Creighton: An Old English place name, "rocky area"
Cray, Crayton

Crispin: Latin, "curly-headed one"

*Crispus: Greek, "curly-headed one"
See Acts 18:8 and 1 Corinthians 1:14. Crispus, the leader of the synagogue at Corinth, was baptized by the apostle Paul upon his conversion to Christ.

Cruz: Spanish, "cross"

Cullen: Irish, "young animal"
Cullan, Culley, Cullin

Curran: Irish, "heroic one"
Curan, Currey, Curry

Curtis: Latin, "small one"
Curt, Curtiss, Kurt, Kurtis

Cuthbert: Old English, "he who is brilliant"
Bert

Cyprian: Greek, "he who is from Cyprus"

Cyrano: Greek, "from the Greek city of Cyrene"

Cyril: Greek, "lordly one"

CYRUS SCOFIELD
(1843–1921)
was a Congregational minister, author of several books, and editor of the still widely used Scofield Study Bible.

---

*Cyrus: Persian, "sun"
Cy
Cyrus was the founder of the Persian Empire and was responsible for helping to free the Jews from their captivity.

D

Dace: Irish, "from the south"
Dacey, Dacian, Dacias, Dacy

Dale: Old German, "one who lives in the valley (dale)"
Dallan, Dalle, Dayely, Dayle

Dallas: Celtic, "he who lives by the waterfall"

Daly: Gaelic, "he who offers wisdom"
Daley

Damian: Greek, "he who tames"
Daman, Damien, Damion, Damon

*Dan: Hebrew, "he who judges"
Dan was the fifth son of Jacob. The tribe of Dan is named for him. See Genesis 30:6 and Exodus 31:6. The name Dan in this Old Testament usage is complete in itself and does not serve as a diminutive for Daniel. Dan is also a diminutive for Daniel, as seen below.

Dana: Old English, "he who is from Denmark"
Dain, Dane, Dayn

*Daniel: Hebrew, "God is my judge"
Dan, Danal, Danby, Danforth, Dannel, Danno, Danny
Read the compelling story of the prophet Daniel in the book that bears his name.

Dante: Latin, "he who endures"
Donte

Darby: Irish, "he who is free"

Darcy: Irish, "dark one"
Darce, Darcey

"A mother is a chalice, the vessel without which no human being has ever been born. She is created to be a life-bearer, cooperating with her husband and with God in the making of a child. What a solemn responsibility. What an unspeakable privilege—a vessel divinely prepared for the Master's use."

—ELISABETH ELLIOT

Daren: Irish, "magnificent"
Darin, Darren

*Darius: Greek, "prosperous"
Darias, Dario, Darios
There are three men named Darius mentioned in the Bible. See Ezra 4:5,24. See also Nehemiah 12:22 and Daniel 5:31; 6:9; 9:1, and 11:1.

Darrell: French, "dear one"
Darryl, Daryl, Derrell, Deryl

*Dathan: Hebrew, "of the law"
Dathen, Dathon

See Numbers 16, 26:9, Deuteronomy 11:6, Psalm 106:17.

Daudi: Swahili, "he who is dearly loved"

*David: Hebrew, "beloved one"

Dave, Davey, Davian, Davion, Davis, Davon, Davy

David is one of the most beloved men in the Bible and is best described as a "man after God's heart." He can be read about in various books of the Old Testament, particularly 1 and 2 Samuel, 1 and 2 Kings, 1 and 2 Chronicles, and the Psalms, many of which he wrote.

DAVID BRAINERD
(1718–1747)

in his short life, worked among the American Indians and wrote an extensive diary, still in print, which has inspired Christians to this day.

DAVID LIVINGSTONE
(1813–1873)

was a Scottish missionary to Africa.

Davis: Scottish, "David's son"

Dawson: Old English, "son of David"

Daw, Dawes, Daws

DAWSON "DAWS" TROTMAN
(1906–1956)

was the founder of The Navigators, a successful evangelistic ministry, which has a global influence.

Dean: Old English, "valley"

Dino (Italian)

Dedric: Old German, "one who rules"

Dedrick, Rick, Ricky

Del: Old English, "valley"—sometimes a diminutive for Delbert and similar names, but often used as a proper name in its own right

Dell

Delany: Gaelic, "from he who challenges"

Del, Delain, Delane

Delbert: Old English, "brilliant as the sunshine"

Bert, Del, Dil, Dilbert

Delmar: Latin, "from the sea"
Del, Delmer, Delmore

*Demas: Greek, "he who rules"—also possibly a diminutive for Demosthenes
Demos, Dimas
Demas was an early companion of the apostle Paul (see Colossians 4:14; Philemon 24), but later forsook the apostle for "this present world" (2 Timothy 4:10).

*Demetrius: Greek, "he who follows [the false goddess] Demeter"
Demitri, Dmitri, Dmitrios
The two men named Demetrius found in the New Testament can be referenced in Acts 19:24, 38 and 3 John 12. The latter man was a brother in the Lord highly commended by the apostle John.

Dempsey: Irish, "he who is proud"

Denby: Scandinavian, "from Denmark"
Danby, Den, Denny

Dennis: Greek, "follower of [the false god] Dionysius"

Den, Denis, Dennison (son of Denny), Denny, Denys

Denton: Old English, "he who comes from the town in the valley"

Denver: Old English, "lush valley"

Denzel: English, "from Cornwall"
Denzil, Denzyl

Derek: Old German, "one who rules"
Darrick, Derric, Derrick, Dirk, Rick, Ricky

Deron: Hebrew, "he who is free"

Derry: Irish, "red-headed one"

Desi: Latin, "he who is desired"—often a diminutive for Desiderio
Des, Desiderio

Desmond: Latin, "created one"
Des, Desmund

Devin: Irish, "poet"
Devan, Devon

Devlin: Irish, "courageous"

Dewey: Irish, "dearly prized"

Dewitt: Welsh, "he who is blond"

DeWitt

Dexter: Latin, "easily movable" —from the same root as *ambidextrous* (adept with either the right or left hand)

Dex

Dick: Usually a diminutive for Richard

Dickson: English, "son of Dick"—Dick is usually a diminutive for Richard

Dick, Dickinson, Dicky, Dixon

Diego: A Spanish variation of James

Dietrich: German, "he who prospers"

Diederick, Dieter

Digby: Irish, "from the town by the dike or ditch"

What's in a Name?

When my husband and I named our older children, we blundered big time with the initials. My husband is from a large family, and our focus was on avoiding choosing names of other family members, both in our immediate and extended family. Assuming it was a safe choice, we named our oldest daughter Teri Lynn—making her TLP. That may sound okay...however, kids at school, such as they are, shortened her initials to "TP." That was embarrassing for her.

We didn't learn from that experience. I loved the name Pamela Sue, thus our second daughter had the shortened initials of "PP." This was doubly embarrassing for her. Yes, my face is now double-red.

Fortunately, both daughters married young men whose last names gave them an acceptable set of initials: TLC and PSF. You might say this was answered prayer!

We had finally learned our lesson when child #3 came along. My first pick for a boy's name was Phillip, but we knew that would never do! We named him Darren instead.

BARB FROM OREGON

Dillon: Irish, "man of faith"

Dill, Dillan, Dilly, Dylan

DIETRICH BONHOEFFER
(1906–1945)
was a German pastor who resisted the Nazis and was hung for his stance against Hitler's regime. His still-popular books include *The Cost of Discipleship* and *Life Together.*

Dino: Usually an Italian variation of Dean

Dion: Usually a diminutive for Dionysius (see below), but increasingly a proper name in its own right

Deion, Deon

*Dionysius: Greek name for their ancient god of wine

Deon, Deion, Dion

See the reference to this early Christian convert in Acts 17:34.

Dirk: Old German, "one who rules"—often a diminutive for Derrick, Theodoric, Roderick

Dolph: Old German, usually a diminutive for Adolph, Rudolph, or Randolph

Dolf, Dolfus, Dolphus

DOLPHUS WEARY
(1946–)
has been a tireless worker for racial reconciliation in the body of Christ. His story is told in his book *I Ain't Coming Back.*

Dominic: Latin, "he who belongs to the Lord"

Dom, Dominick, Domingo (Spanish), Nick, Nicky

Donald: Celtic, "powerful ruler"

Don, Donal, Donaldo (Spanish), Donel, Donner, Donnie, Donny, Donovan

Donato: Italian, "gift from God"

Don, Nat

Dooley: Irish, "dark warrior"

Doran: Greek, "gift from God"

Dore, Dorian, Dorien, Dorran, Dory

Dougal: Scottish, "dark stranger"

Douglas: Irish, "dweller by the brook"

Doug, Douglass

Dow: Irish, "one with dark hair"
Dowe, Dowell

Doyle: Irish, "dark stranger"—
usually an Irish variation of
Dougal

Drake: Middle English, "serpent"

Drew: Usually a diminutive for
Andrew
Dru

Driscoll: Celtic, "melancholy
one"

Drury: Old French, "he who
loves"

Duane: Irish, "dark one"
DeWayne, Dwayne, Dwain,
Dwaine

Dude: Usually a nickname, but
occasionally a proper name

Dudley: Old English, "from the
field"

Duff: Scottish, "dark one"
Duffy

Dugan: Irish, "dark one"
Doogan, Duggan

Duke: Latin, "one who leads"—
usually a nickname, but
occasionally a proper name

Duncan: Scottish, "warrior"

Dunstan: Old English, "strong
fortress"

Durant: Latin, "he who
endures"
Durand, Durante, Ran,
Randy

Durward: Old English, "he who
guards the gate"
Ward

Dustin: Old German, "courageous warrior"
Dustan, Dustyn, Dusty

Dutch: Literally "from the Netherlands"

Dwayne: See Duane

Dwight: German, "fair one"

DWIGHT L. MOODY
(1837–1899)
was one of America's most
successful evangelists. The
famed Moody
Bible Institute in Chicago
was founded by him in
1887 as the Chicago Evangelization Society.

Dylan: Welsh, "from the sea"
Dilan, Dillan, Dillon

Ɛ

Earl: Old English, "noble one"

Earle, Erle Errol, Erroll

Eban: Hebrew, "rock"

Eb, Eben

Ebenezer: Hebrew, "the Lord is my rock"

Eb, Eben

Eberhard: Old German, "strong like the boar"

Eb, Eberhardt, Evard, Everard

*Eden: Hebrew, "he who is a delight"

Edan

See 2 Chronicles 29:13 and 31:15.

Many names that begin with "Ed," as in the names below, have Anglo-Saxon roots. Ed in such names is indicative of "prosperity."

Edgar: Old English, "prosperous guardian"

Ed, Eddie, Medgar (German)

Edmund: Old English, "prosperous guardian"

Ed, Eddie, Edmond, Edmundo (Italian), Esmond (French)

Edric: Old English, "prosperous leader"

Ederic, Ederick, Edrick, Rick, Ricky

Edson: Old English, literally "Ed's son"

Ed, Eddie, Edison

Edward: Old English, "prosperous guardian"

Duarte (Portugese), Ed, Eddie, Eduardo (Spanish)

EDWARD V. (E.V.) HILL
(1933–2003)

was the pastor of Mt. Zion Missionary Baptist Church in the Watts section of Los Angeles, founder of the World Christian Training Center, and a popular Christian speaker.

Edwin: Old English, "treasured or prosperous friend"

Ed, Eddie, Eddy

Efrem: See Ephraim

Egan: Celtic, "ardent one"

Egbert: Old English, "he who wields the shining sword"

Bert, Bertie, Berty

Eldon: Old English, "from the hill of God"

Eldan, Elden, Eldin

Eldred: Old English, "wise counselor"

Eldrid

Eldridge: Usually a variation of Aldridge/Aldrich

Eldredge

*Elead: Hebrew, "God is witness"

See 1 Chronicles 7:21.

*Eleazar: Hebrew, "God has been my helper"

There are seven Eleazars in the Bible. In Matthew 1:15, we see an Eleazar in the ancestry of Christ.

*Eli: Hebrew, "Jehovah is my God"

Elias (the New Testament form of Elijah), Elihu, Elijah, Ely

See 1 Samuel 1–4 and 14:3.

*Eliah: Hebrew, "God is Jehovah"

See 1 Chronicles 8:27 and Ezra 10:26.

*Eliam: Hebrew, "the people of God"

Eliam was the father of Bathsheba, the consort of David. See 2 Samuel 11:3.

Elian: Spanish, of uncertain meaning

*Eliel: Hebrew, "God is God"

There were ten Eliels in the Old Testament, including a fellow warrior with King David (see 1 Chronicles 11:47).

*Eliezer: Hebrew, "God is my helper"

There are eleven Eliezers in the Bible, including an ancestor of Joseph, Mary's husband. See Luke 3:29.

*Elihu: Hebrew, "He is God"

There are five Elihus in the Bible, most notably the youngest of Job's friends. See Job 32:2-6, 34:1, 35:1, and 36:1.

*Elijah: Hebrew, "the Lord, my God"—a variation of Eli

Elijah was the greatest prophet in the Old Testament. His story can be found in 1 Kings 17–19 and 2 Kings 1–3, 9–10.

*Elisha: Hebrew, "the Lord is my salvation"

Elisha was a prophet and the successor to Elijah. See 1 Kings 19:16-19 and 2 Kings 2–13.

Eliot: French, "Jehovah is God"—a French variation of Eli

Elliot, Elliott

Ellis: An English variation of Eli

Ellison (son of Eli)

Elmer: Old English, "he who is noble"

Almer, Almo, Elmo

Elmo: Greek, "he who is easy to please"

Elroy: Latin, "royal one"

Roy

Elvin: Old English, "he who is elfish"

Elwin, Elwyn

Elvis: Scandinavian, "he who is wise"

Elvyn, Elwin, Elwyn

Elwood: English, "ancient forest"

Woody

Emery: Old German, "diligent worker"

Emerick, Emerson (son of Emery), Emory

Emil: German, "diligent worker"

Emile (French), Emilio (Spanish)

*Emmanuel: Hebrew, "God with us"

Emanuel, Immanuel, Manny, Manuel

Though this is not used as a proper name in the Bible, it is the prophesied appellation for the coming Savior who would indeed be "God with us." See Isaiah 7:14 and Matthew 1:23 in the New International Version.

Emmet: Hebrew, "he who speaks the truth"

Em, Emett, Emmett, Emmit, Emmitt

Emlyn: A Welsh place name

Em, Emlen, Emelyn, Emlyn

*Enan: Hebrew, "from the fountain"

See Numbers 1:15, 2:29, 7:78, 83, and 10:27.

*Eneas: Hebrew, "he who praises Jehovah"

Eneas was the man healed by the apostle Peter in Acts 9:33-34.

Engelbert: Old German, "bright angel"

Bert, Berty, Ingelbert

*Enoch: Hebrew, "he who is dedicated"

See Genesis 4:17-18 and 5:18-23.

*Enos: Hebrew, "man, mortal one"

Enosh

Enos was a son of Seth, and grandson of Adam and Eve. See Genesis 4.

Enrique: A Spanish variation of Henry

Rick, Ricky

*Epaphras: Greek, "he who is covered with foam"

See Colossians 1:7, 4:12, Philemon 23.

*Ephraim: Hebrew, "abundantly fruitful"

Efrem, Ephrem

See Genesis 41:52.

*Eran: Hebrew, "he who is watchful"

See Numbers 26:36.

Erasmus: Greek, "he who is friendly, lovable"

*Eri: Hebrew, "my watcher"

See Genesis 46:16 and Numbers 26:16.

Eric: Scandinavian, "he who is powerful"

Erich, Erick, Ericson ("son of Eric"), Erickson ("son of Erick"), Erik, Rick, Ricky

---

ERIC LIDDELL
(1902–1945)

was a gold-medal winner in the 400-meter run at the 1924 Olympics in Paris. His inspiring story was told in the popular movie *Chariots of Fire*. He later served as a missionary to China.

Ernest: Old German, "intent, purposeful"

Ern, Ernesto (Spanish), Ernie

Errol: See Earl

Erroll

Erskine: Old English, "from the cliff"

Erwin: Old English, "lover of the sea"

Ervin

*Esau: Hebrew, "he who is hairy"

Esau was the elder twin brother of Isaac, who later tricked him to gain Esau's birthright. See Genesis 25–28.

Esmond: Old English, "valued guardian"

Esteban: A Spanish variation of Steven/Stephen

Estevan, Steve

Estes: Italian, "from the east"

*Ethan: Hebrew, "he who is strong"

There are four Ethans in the Bible. The most notable was the wise Ezrahite mentioned in 1 Kings 4:31.

Eugene: Greek, "of noble birth"

Gene

EUGENE PETERSON
(1932–)

is a prolific Christian author and paraphraser of the popular *The Message* Bible.

Eusebius: Greek, "he who is godly"

Eustace: Greek, "fruitful"

*Eutychus: Greek, "he who is blessed"

See the interesting story of Eutychus, who fell asleep during one of the apostle Paul's lengthy sermons and fell out of his window seat to his death. Paul revived him (Acts 20:7-12).

Evan: Greek, "of noble birth"

Evans, Evin, Evyn

EVAN HOPKINS
(1837–1918)

was a popular Bible teacher at the Keswick conferences in late nineteenth-century England. His book *The Law of Liberty in the Spiritual Life* is considered by many to be a classic on the deeper life.

Everard: Old German, "he who is strong"

Everett: More common variation of Everard

Ev, Everet, Evert

*Ezekiel: Hebrew, "by the strength of the Lord"

Zeke

See the Bible book bearing this prophet's name.

*Ezra: Hebrew, "he who helps"
See 1 Chronicles 4:17, Nehemiah 10:2-8. See also the book bearing this prophet's name.

Fabian: Latin, "bean farmer"
Fabien (French), Fabio (Italian)

Fain: Old English, "he who is joyful"
Faine, Fane, Faniel, Fayne, Fein

Farley: Old English, "from the meadowlands"
Farleigh, Farly, Farr

Farran: English, "sojourner"
Farin, Faron, Farr, Farrin, Farron

Farris: English, "he who is strong"
Faris, Ferris

Farrell: Irish, "heroic one"
Farrel, Ferrell

Favian: Latin, "he who understands, perceives"

Felipe: A Spanish variation of Phillip

*Felix: Latin, "blessed one"
Feliciano, Felicio (Italian)
Felix was the Roman governor of Judea who was "almost persuaded" of the truth of the gospel through the preaching of the apostle Paul. See Acts 23:24-26, 24:2-27, and 25:14.

Fenton: Old English, "from the farm"
Fen, Fenny, Fent

Ferdinand: Old German, "adventurous one"
Ferd, Ferdy, Fernando (Spanish), Hernando (Spanish), Nando

Fergus: Irish, "masculine, virile"
Fergas, Ferguson (Fergus's son)

Ferris: Celtic, "rock"
Faris, Farris

Fernando: See Ferdinand.

*Festus: Latin, from the same root as our word "festive"

Festus was, like Felix above, a Roman governor of Judea. See Acts 24:27; 25; 26:24,32.

Fidel: Latin, "he who is faithful," from the same root as the word *fidelity*

Fidelio (Italian)

Filbert: Old English, "he who is brilliant"

Bert, Philbert

Fillmore: English, "well known"

Philmore

Findlay: Irish, "fair-complected one"

Fin, Finlay, Findley, Fyn, Fynn

Finian: Irish, "he who is fair-skinned"

Finnegan, Finnian

Firth: English, "from the forest"

Fitz: Old English, "son"

Whenever you see a name beginning with Fitz-, you can be assured that the meaning is "son of" the latter part of the name, as in the two entries below.

Fitzgerald: Old English, "son of Gerald"

Fitzpatrick: Old English, "son of Patrick"

Fleming: Old English, "he who is from the lowlands" or "from Flanders"

Flemming

Fletcher: Middle English, "arrowmaker"

Fletch

Children's children are a crown to the aged, and parents are the pride of their children.

—**PROVERBS 17:6**

Flint: Old English, "stone"

Flynt

Flip: English, usually a nickname. Sometimes a diminutive for Philip.

Floyd: Celtic, "gray"

Flynn: Irish, "son of the red-haired man"

Flin, Flyn

Foluke: Yoruba (Nigeria), "he who is protected by God"—can be either male or female

Forbes: English, "he who is prosperous"

Forrest: Old English, "forest" Forest, Forrester, Forster

Foster: Old English, a variation of the occupational name Forrest, "he who works in the forest"

Fowler: Old English, "one who hunts fowl"

Francis: German, "free man" Frances (usually the female variation of this name), Francisco (Spanish), Francois, Franchot (both French variations), Franco (Italian), Frank, Franky

---

FRANCIS OF ASSISI
(1182–1226)

was one of the most influential Christians of all times. His life was marked by service to the poor and a deep devotion to Christ.

FRANCIS ASBURY
(1745–1816)

is considered the father of American Methodism.

FRANCIS SCHAEFFER
(1912–1984)

was the founder, with his wife Edith, of the L'Abri Fellowship in Switzerland. His many important books include *True Spirituality, He Is There and He Is Not Silent,* and *How Should We Then Live?*

FRANÇOIS FENELON
(1651–1715)

was a popular French clergyman and author.

Frank: English, sometimes a diminutive for Franklin or Francis, but often a proper name in its own right Frankie, Franky

---

FRANK LAUBACH
(1884–1970)

was a pioneer in the field of literacy and author of the classic book *Prayer, the Mightiest Force in the World.*

Franklin: Middle English, "he who is a free landholder" Frank, Franklyn, Franky

Franz: A German variation of Francis

Frantz

Frazer: Old English, "he who has curly hair"

Fraizer, Fraser, Frasier

Frederick: Old German, "peaceful ruler"

Fred, Freddie, Freddy, Frederic, Fredric, Fredrick, Rick, Ricky

Freeman: Old English, "free man"

Fremont: Old German, "free man"—usually a German variation of Freeman

Fritz: German, sometimes a German diminutive for Frederick, but occasionally a proper name in its own right, or simply a nickname

Fuller: Old English, an occupational name. A fuller was "one who shrinks cloth"

Fulton: Old English, "from the town near the open field"

Gable: Possibly a diminutive of Gabriel

*Gabriel: Hebrew, "God is my strength"

Gabby, Gabe, Gaby, Gavriel

Gabriel was the angel who interpreted Daniel's vision (see Daniel 8:16-26, 9:20-27) and proclaimed the births of John the Baptist (Luke 1:11-20) and Jesus (Luke 1:26-38).

Gage: Old French, "he who promises"

Gaige, Gaije

*Gaius: Latin, "he who rejoices"

There are four references to men named Gaius in the New Testament. It's uncertain if there are actually four distinct men named Gaius; however, it's possible that the following references pointed to the same man. See Acts 19:29, 20:4, Romans 16:23, 1 Corinthians 1:14, and 3 John 1 and 3:5-8.

Gale: Old French, "gentlemanly"—from the same root as the word *gallant*

Gael, Gail, Gayle

Galen: Greek, "peaceful one"

Galin, Gaylan, Gaylen, Gaylin, Gaylon

Gallagher: Irish, "devoted helper"

Galvin: Irish, "small bird" (sparrowlike)
Galvan, Galven

*Gamaliel: Hebrew, "God is my rewarder"
See Numbers 1:10, 2:20, 7:54, 10:23. See also Acts 5:34 and 22:3.

Gannon: Irish, "fair-complected one"

García: Spanish, "strong spearman"

Gardner: Latin, "one who works with the land"—from the same origin as the word *gardener*
Gard, Gardiner, Gardnar

Gareth: Welsh, "he who is gentle"
Garath, Garith, Garreth, Gary, Garry

Garfield: Old English, "from the battlefield"

Garland: French, "decorative wreath"
Gar, Garlan, Garlin, Garlind, Garr

Garner: Old German, "warrior who protects the weak"

Garrett: Old German, "mighty spearman"
Garet, Garett, Garret

Garrick: Old German, "one who rules with the spear"

Garson: French, "he who protects"

Garth: a Scandinavian variation of Gardner

Gary: Old German, "brave spearman"
Garey, Garry

Gavin: Welsh, "he who is like a hawk"
Gavan, Gaven, Gawain, Gawayne

Gaylord: Old French, "he who is joyous, happy, jolly"

Gaynor: Irish, "son of the fair-complected one"
Gaine, Gayner

Geary: Middle English, "he who is adaptable"

Gene: Usually a diminutive for Eugene
Geno, Gino

Geoffrey: Old German, "the peace of God"—a variation of Jeffrey

Geof, Geoff, Jeff, Jeffery, Jeffrey

George: Greek, "worker of the land" (farmer, husbandman)

Georges (French), Georgio (Italian), Jorge (Spanish), Jorgen (Danish)

GEORGE WASHINGTON CARVER
(1861–1943)

was born into slavery the same year the American Civil War began. He became a leading agriculturist and his work with the "lowly peanut" led him to greatness.

GEORGE MÜLLER
(1805–1898)

was a British Christian, active among the Plymouth Brethren. He's largely remembered for his faith in God to provide for the daily needs of the several orphanages he founded. His autobiography is still popular among Christians everywhere.

GEORGE VERWER
(1938–)

was converted to Christ at age 17 and was led by God to start Operation Mobilization (OM), an outreach to foreign lands, enhanced by the ministry's ship, the *Logos*, and later, the *Logos II*.

GEORGE WHITEFIELD
(1714–1770)

was a contemporary of John Wesley and a great preacher and teacher of the Bible. It was Whitefield who popularized the large outdoor meetings that characterized the Great Awakening.

Gerald: Old German, "mighty spearman"

Geraldo (Spanish), Gerrald, Gerrold, Gerry, Jerry

GEORGE FOX
(1624–1691)

was the founder of the Quakers (the Society of Friends).

Gerard: Old German, "courageous spearman"
Gerrard, Gerry, Jerry

GERARD MANLEY HOPKINS
(1844–1889)
was an English poet and
priest. Among his most
notable poems is the classic "God's Grandeur."

Germain: French, "he who
comes from Germany"
Germaine

Gian: Italian—Gian is the Italian variation of John. It can
be combined with other Italian variations to produce an
attractive name. An example
is Giancarlo (John Charles).

*Gideon: Hebrew, "mighty warrior"
The story of Gideon, God's
"mighty man of valor," is
recounted in Judges 6–8.

Gifford: Old German, "generous
giver"
Giff, Giffard

Gilbert: Old German, "bright
pledge or promise"
Bert, Gil, Gilberto (Italian),
Gilburt

GILBERT KEITH
(G.K.) CHESTERTON
(1874–1936)
was the popular writer of
the Father Brown mystery
stories and several books
on the Christian faith still
popular today (*Orthodoxy*
and *The Everlasting Man*).

---

*Gilead: Hebrew, "he who is
strong"
There are three men named
Gilead in the Bible. Gilead is
also a region of the nation
Jordan.

Giles: Greek, "protected by a
shield"
Gil, Gilles

Gilman: Irish, "servant of Gil,
Gil's man"
Gil, Gill

Gilmer: Old English, "notable
hostage"
Gil, Gill

Gilroy: Irish, "he who serves
royalty"
Gil, Gill, Gillroy

Gino: Italian variation of Gene
(from Eugene)

Giovanni: An Italian variation of John, as is Gian
Gian, Gianni, Van, Vanny

Giuseppe: An Italian variation of Joseph

Glade: Old English, "he who brings happiness"
Glades

Glen: Irish, "a glen or valley"
Glenn, Glyn, Glynn

Glendon: Scottish, "he who lives in the glen"
Glen, Glenden, Glenn

Goddard: Old German, "the firmness of God"
Gothart

Godfrey: Old German, "the peace of God"

***Goliath:** Hebrew, "he who is sent away"
See the story of the giant man whom David killed in 1 Samuel 17.

***Gomer:** Hebrew, "to make complete"
See Genesis 10:2-3, 1 Chronicles 1:5, and Ezekiel 38:6.

Gonzales: Spanish, "wolf"
Gonsalve, Gonzalo, Gonzo

Goodwin: Old German, "godly friend"
Godwin, Goodwyn

Gordon: Old English, "he who comes from the hill"
Gord, Gordan, Gorden, Gordie, Gordy

Gower: Welsh, "he who is pure"

Grady: Latin, from the same root as our word *grade*, meaning a step or level

Graham: Old English, "lavish home"
Graeham, Grahame

Granger: Middle French, "he who farms"
Grange, Gray

Grant: French, "he who bestows, or grants"
Grantley

Granville: Old French, "from the big town"
Grenville, Greville

Gregory: Greek, "watchman"
Greg, Gregg, Gregor

GREG LAURIE
(1952–)
is a popular pastor, speaker, and author.

GREGORY OF NYSSA
(330–395)
was the bishop of Nyssa and an important figure in the fourth-century church.

Gresham: Old English, "from the village by the grazing land"

Griffin: Latin, "hook–nosed one"
Griff, Griffen

Griffith: Welsh, "powerful leader"
Griff, Griffyth

Grover: Old English, "one who comes from the grove"
Grove

Guido: Italian, "he who guides"

Guillaume: A French variation of William

Guillermo: A Spanish variation of William

Gunnar: Norse, "warrior"

Gunther: Scandinavian, "warrior"
Gunnar, Gunter (German), Gunthar

Gustav: German, "God's staff"
Guss, Gussie, Gustaf (Swedish), Gustave, Gustavo (Spanish), Gustavus

Guy: Irish, "he who guides"
Guido (Italian), Guyon (French)

H

Haddon: Scottish, "from the heather"
Haddan, Hadden, Hadyn

Hale: Old English, "whole, complete"
Hayle

Haley: Irish, "he who has a superior mind; bright man"
Hailey, Haily, Hale

Hallan: English, "he who dwells at the hall"
Halen, Hallin, Halyn

Hamilton: Old English, "from the privileged estate"
Hamel, Hamil

Hamlin: Old German, "he who cherishes his home"
Hamblyn, Hamlyn

*Hamuel: Hebrew, "God is my warmth"
See 1 Chronicles 4:26.

*Hanan: Hebrew, "he who has grace"
There are several Hanans in the Bible, including a descendant of Saul and his son Jonathan. See 1 Chronicles 8:38, 9:44.

*Hananiah: Hebrew, "Jehovah is full of grace"
There are 14 Hananiahs in the Bible, all of them minor characters.

*Haniel: Hebrew, "he who has the grace of God"
Hanniel
See Numbers 34:23 and 1 Chronicles 7:39.

Hank: English, usually a diminutive for Henry

Hansel: German, usually a diminutive of Johannes, the German variation of John
Hans, Hannes

*Haran: Hebrew, "he who is strong"
There are three Harans in the Bible, all minor characters.

Harbin: German, "small and strong warrior"

Harden: Old English, "from the valley of the Hares"
Hardin, Hardyn

Hardy: Old English, "he who is enduring"

Harlan: German, "from the warriors"
Harland, Harlen, Harlin, Harlon

Harley: Old English, "from the long pasture"
Harleigh, Harly

Harold: German, "noted warrior"
Hal, Haroldo (Spanish), Harry

Harper: Old English, "he who plays the harp"

Harrison: Old English, "son of Harry"
Harris, Harry

Harry: Usually a diminutive for Harold, Harrison, or Henry, but used occasionally as a proper name in its own right

The Names of God and What They Tell Us

In the Bible, names usually reveal certain facts or qualities about a person. This is especially true about the names of God. The many names given to Him in Scripture help reveal who He is and what He does. Here are some of His Old Testament Hebrew names and their meanings:

Elohim	The Creator	Genesis 1:1
El Shaddai	The All-Sufficient One	Psalm 91:1
El Elyon	The God Most High	Genesis 14:17-20
El Roi	The God Who Sees	Genesis 16:13-14
Adonai	The Lord	Malachi 1:6
Jehovah	The Self-Existent One	Exodus 3:13-15
Jehovah-jireh	The Lord Will Provide	Genesis 22:13-14
Jehovah-raah	The Lord My Shepherd	Psalm 23:1
Jehovah-rapha	The Lord Our Healer	Exodus 15:26
Jehovah-shalom	The Lord Is Peace	Judges 6:22-24
Jehovah-shammah	The Lord Who Is Present	Ezekiel 48:35
Jehovah-tsidkenu	The Lord Our Righteousness	Jeremiah 23:5-6

Hart: Old German, "a male deer, a stag"
Harte, Hartley

Harvey: Old German, "ready warrior"
Harve, Herve (French), Hervey

Hasani: Swahili, "he who is handsome"
Hasain, Hasan, Hason

Haven: Old English, "place of safety, refuge"

Heath: Middle English, "he who comes from the heath"
Heathe, Heith

Heathcliff: Middle English, "he who comes from the cliff near the heath"

Hector: Greek, "he who is firm, resolute"

Hein: Asian/Vietnamese, "he who is gentle"—can be male or female

Henry: Old German, "he who rules the home"
Hank, Hendrick (Dutch), Henri (French)

Herbert: Old German, "illustrious warrior"
Bert, Hebert, Herb, Herbie

Herman: Old German, "warrior"
Harmon, Hermon

Herschel: Hebrew, "deer"
Herschell, Hershel

HENRY DRUMMOND
(1851–1897)

was a Scottish evangelist and author whose classic book on love, *The Greatest Thing in the World,* is still in print after more than 125 years.

---

*Hezekiah: Hebrew, "God is my strength"
Hezekiah was a king of Israel whose prayer for additional years of life was granted by God. See 2 Kings 20:1-11.

Hiatt: Old English, "from the high gate"
Hi, Hyatt

Hillary: Latin, "he who is cheerful"
Hil, Hilarian, Hilario (Spanish), Hilary, Hill, Hilaire (French), Hillery

*Hillel: Hebrew, "he who is highly esteemed"
See Judges 12:13-15.

*Hiram: Hebrew, "he who is exalted"

Hi, Hyram

There are two minor characters in the Bible named Hiram.

*Hodiah: Hebrew, "he who honors God"

Hod

See 1 Chronicles 3:24.

Hogan: Irish, "youthful one"

"In Scripture, God gives us a blueprint for how the family is to function. The father is head of the family. Together with his wife, he raises his children in a home where Jesus Christ is the focus. The Bible is the most important book in the home. It is the responsibility of the parents, and ultimately that of the father, to make sure the children grow up in an environment that will enable them to one day become competent, responsible parents in their own right. This ensures the continuity of the biblical family for the next generation."

—STEVE FARRAR

Holden: Old German, "he who is kind"

Hollis: Old English, "he who lives by the holly groves"

Holmes: Norwegian, "from the land by the waters"

Holm, Hume

Holt: Old English, "from the forested hill"

Homer: Greek, "he who is held hostage"

Horace: Latin, "he who keeps the time"

Horatio, Horatius

*Hosea: Hebrew, "he who has God's salvation"

See the Bible book that bears the name of this prophet.

Houston: Scottish, "from Hugh's town"

Huston

Howard: Old German, "he who guards"

Howe, Howie

Hoyt: Norse, "of the soul"

Hubert: Old German, "he who is mentally sharp, bright"

Bert, Hobart, Huber, Hugh

Hugh: Old German, "wise one, mentally sharp"

Huey, Hughes, Hugo

Humbert: Old German, "notable Hun"

Humberto, Umberto (Italian)

Humphrey: Old German, "peacemaker"

Humphry

Hunter: Old English, "he who hunts"

Hunt, Huntley

Hyde: English—a land measurement of approximately 120 acres

Hyman: Hebrew, "life"—a variation of Chaim

Haim, Hy, Hymie

Ian: A Scottish variation of John

Ean, Iain

*Ichabod: Hebrew—a sad name, signifying "the spirit of the Lord has departed"

Ignatius: Latin, "full of enthusiasm, eager"

Ignace, Ignacio

IGNATIUS
(d. c. AD 110)
was a first-century Christian who served as the bishop of Antioch. His writings provide much insight into the function and beliefs of the early church.

Igor: Norse, "he who is heroic"

Ike: Usually a diminiatuve for Isaac

(MAJOR) IAN THOMAS
(1913–)
founded the ministry of Torchbearers International and has had a worldwide teaching ministry for many decades. His several books include *The Saving Life of Christ.*

Ilias: A Greek variation of Elijah

Immanuel: See Emmanuel

Ingmar: Scandinavian, "noted son"

Ing, Inge, Inger

Ingram: Old English, "angel, messenger of God"

Innis: Irish, "he who is from the island"

Innes

Ira: Hebrew, "he who watches, guards"

IRA SANKEY
(1840–1908)

was a noted gospel singer who traveled with evangelist Dwight L. Moody.

---

*Iri: Hebrew, "he who is watched by God"

See 1 Chronicles 7:7.

Irving: Irish, "he who is handsome"

Irv, Irvin, Irvine, Irwin

ISAAC WATTS
(1674–1748)

was an English writer of more than 500 hymns, many of which are still beloved today. Best known are the popular Christmas carol "Joy to the World" and the year-round favorite "When I Survey the Wondrous Cross."

---

*Isaac: Hebrew, "he who laughs"

Ike, Itzaak, Itzak, Izaak, Izak, Izzy, Zak

Isaac was the son of Abraham, born through his wife Sarah, in fulfillment of God's promise to Abraham. Isaac's story begins in Genesis 17 and is one of the most dramatic in the Bible.

*Isaiah: Hebrew, "God is my salvation"

Isa, Isiah, Issiah

Isaiah was one of Israel's most important prophets. Many prophecies of the coming Messiah are recorded in the book of Isaiah.

*Ishmael: Hebrew, "God has heard"

Ishmael was the son born to Abraham through Hagar, Sarah's handmaiden. Ishmael eventually became the founder of the tribal people called the Midianites. See Genesis 16 and 17.

*Israel: Hebrew, "he who has prevailed with God" or "a prince of God"

Israel was the new name given to Jacob at Jabbok after he prevailed against the angel of God. See Genesis 32:28.

*Issachar: Hebrew, "He who is rewarded"

There are two Issachars in the Bible, one of whom was the ninth son of Jacob and the head of one of the 12 tribes of Israel. See Genesis 30:18.

Ivan: A Russian variation of John

Ivano, Ivo, Vanya

Ives: Old English, "hunter with a bow and arrow"—literally, an archer

Yves (French)

*Izziah: Hebrew, "God exalts"

See Ezra 10:25.

J

*Jaanai: Hebrew, "God answers my prayer"

Janai

See 1 Chronicles 5:12.

*Jabez: Hebrew, "he is born of pain"

Jabe, Jay

Jabez was born into affliction, but his life was blessed because he prayed and trusted in God to enlarge his circumstances. See 1 Chronicles 4:9-10.

*Jabin: Hebrew, "God, the creator"

See Joshua 11:1-14, Judges 4, and Psalm 83:9.

*Jachin: Hebrew, "God establishes"

There are three Jachins in the Bible, all minor characters.

What's in a Name?

Your adopted child may wish to choose a new name to celebrate joining your family. When Jesse and Carole were fostering a six-year-old in hopes of adopting him, they and their son decided to change his first name. Eager to participate in choosing his new moniker, their son suggested his favorite names: Pikachu, Squirtle, and Charizard. Not wishing to saddle their boy with the name of a Pokemon character, Jesse and Carole quickly redirected him, steering him toward three more appropriate names. Their son eventually decided Isaiah was a good fit.

LAURA CHRISTIANSON
AUTHOR OF *THE ADOPTION DECISION*

Jack: Usually a diminutive for John, Jacob, or Jackson, but also often used as a proper name in its own right

Jackie, Jacko, Jackson (son of Jack), Jock

JACK HAYFORD
(1934–)
is a leading pastor in the Foursquare denomination and a prolific author. His works include *Prayer Is Invading the Impossible* and the popular worship chorus "Majesty."

---

*Jacob: Hebrew, "he who supplants another"

Jack, Jacobus, Jake, Jakob

Jacob was born the second of a pair of twins to Isaac and Rebekah. He later traded a bowl of food to his hungry twin, Esau, in exchange for Esau's birthright. See the story in Genesis 25.

JACOBUS ARMINIUS
(1559–1609)
was a Dutch theologian and pastor whose teachings have long been held in contrast to those of John Calvin.

Jacques: A French variation of Jacob

*Jadon: Hebrew, "God has heard"

Jaden, Jay, Jaydon

See Nehemiah 3:7.

Jael: Hebrew, "mountain goat"

Yael

*Jahleel: Hebrew, "God is patient"

Jaleel

See Genesis 46:14 and Numbers 26:26.

Jaime: A Spanish varation of James

*Jairus: Hebrew, "God gives light"

See Mark 5:22 and Luke 8:41.

Jake: Usually a diminutive for Jacob

*Jakeh: Hebrew, "he who is devout"

See Proverbs 30:1.

Jamal: Arabic, "he who is handsome"

Jamaal, Jahmal, Jahmil, Jamar

*James: An English variation of Jacob, "he who supplants another"

Jamie, Jaymes, Jim, Jimmie, Jimmy

There are four men named James in the New Testament. One was one of Jesus' 12 disciples and the brother of John. Jesus referred to the two brothers as "sons of thunder." A second James was the son of Alphaeus, who is mentioned in Matthew 10:3, Mark 3:18, and Luke 6:15. A third James was the half-brother of the Lord Jesus—see Matthew 13:55, Mark 6:3, Acts 12:17, 15:13, 21:18, 1 Corinthians 15:7, Galatians 1:19, 2:9,12, and James 1:1. The fourth James was the father of Judas, the apostle—see Luke 6:16.

JAMES HUDSON TAYLOR
(1832–1905)

was a pioneering missionary to China. His book, *Hudson Taylor's Spiritual Secret*, is considered a classic on living the victorious Christian life.

Jameson: English, "son of James"

Jamison, Jim, Jimmie, Jimmy

Jamie: English, usually a diminutive for James, but also often a proper name in its own right

JAMES (JIM) ELLIOT
(1927–1956)

was one of the five missionaries to Ecuador who were martyred by the Huaorani (Auca) people, whom they wished to reach. Their story has been told in books written by Jim's widow, Elisabeth Elliot. He penned the widely known Christian motto, "He is no fool who gives what he cannot keep to gain what he cannot lose."

Jamil: Arabic, "he who is handsome"

Jamal, Jameel, Jamel

*Jamin: Hebrew, "he who is highly favored"

Jamian, Jamien, Jamon, Jaymin

There are three Jamins in the Old Testament, all minor characters.

*Jamlech: Hebrew, "Jehovah is king"
See 1 Chronicles 4:34.

Jan: Usually a Dutch variation of John, but also a proper name in its own right

Janson: English, "son of Jan"
Jan, Jans, Janse, Janzen

*Japheth: Hebrew, "he who is beautiful"
Japeth, Japh, Japhet, Jay
Japheth was the second son of Noah. See Genesis 5:3, 6:10, 7:13, 9:18-27, and 10:1-32.

*Jarah: Hebrew, "honey"
Jara, Jera, Jerah
See 1 Chronicles 9:42.

*Jared: Hebrew, "he who descends"—from the same root as Jordan
Jerad, Jered, Jareth, Jarrod
See Genesis 5:15-20; 1 Chronicles 1:2; and Luke 3:37.

Jarman: Old German, "he who comes from Germany"

Jaron: Hebrew, "he who sings"
Jaran, Jaren, Jarin

Jarrett: Old English, "brave spearman"
Jaret, Jerrett, Jerry

Jarvis: Old German, "spearlike, sharp"

*Jashen: Hebrew, "he who sleeps"
See 2 Samuel 23:32.

*Jason: Greek, "he who heals"
Jase, Jasen, Jasin, Jay, Jayce, Jayson
See Romans 16:21 and Acts 17:5-9.

Jasper: Jasper was a stone in the breastplate of the Old Testament high priest
Jaspar, Jazz

*Jathniel: Hebrew, "God gives gifts"
See 1 Chronicles 9:14 and 26:2.

*Javan: Hebrew, "made of clay"
Javan was a grandson of Noah—see Genesis 10:2; 1 Chronicles 1:5-7; Isaiah 66:19.

Jay: Often a diminutive for many "J" names, such as Jeremiah, Jason, and Jacob, or a proper name in its own right

Jean: A French variation of John

*Jeconiah: Hebrew, "established by God"
Jeconia, Jeconias
See Matthew 1:11-12.

*Jediah: Hebrew, "God knows"
Jed, Jedaiah, Jedia
There are several Jediahs in the Bible, all minor characters.

*Jedidiah: Hebrew, "God is my friend"
Jed, Jedediah, Jedi
See 2 Samuel 12:25.

Jeffrey: Old English, "kept by the peace of God"
Geoffrey, Jeff, Jeffery, Jefferson (son of Jeff), Jeffy

*Jehiah: Hebrew, "God lives"
See 1 Chronicles 15:24.

*Jemuel: Hebrew, "God is light"
See Genesis 46:10, Exodus 6:15.

Jens: A Scandinavian variation of John
Jenson ("son of Jens")

*Jeremiah: Hebrew, "God is exalted"
Jeremia, Jeremias, Jerry
There are several Jeremiahs in the Bible. The most notable is the prophet whose book in the Bible bears his name.

> Blessed is the man who fears the LORD, who finds great delight in his commands. His children will be mighty in the land; the generation of the upright will be blessed.
>
> **—PSALM 112:1-2**

Jeremy: An English variation of the Hebrew Jeremiah/Jeremias, "God is exalted"
Jaramy, Jeremey, Jerry

Jeriah: Hebrew, "God has seen"

*Jeriel: Hebrew, "founded of God"
See 1 Chronicles 7:2.

Jermaine: French, "to sprout," from the same root as the word "germinate"—or "from Germany"
Germaine, Jermain, Jermane

Jerome: Greek, "sacred name"
Jerom, Jeron, Jerrome, Jerry

Jerry: Usually a diminutive for Gerald or Gerard

JERRY JENKINS
(1949-)

is a hugely popular Christian author with more than 160 books to his credit, including the megaselling Left Behind series.

---

*Jesher: Hebrew, "he who is righteous"

Jesh, Jeshar

See 1 Chronicles 2:18.

*Jesiah: Hebrew, "God exists"

See 1 Chronicles 12:6 and 23:20.

*Jesse: Hebrew, "he who is graced by God"

Jess, Jessie, Jessy

Jesse was the father of King David and thus an ancestor of the Lord Jesus Christ. He was also the grandson of Ruth and Boaz. See 1 Samuel 17:12-14.

JESSE OWENS
(1913–1980)

won four Gold Medals at the 1936 Olympic games in Berlin, Germany. His story is told in his autobiography, *Jesse*.

---

*Jesus: Hebrew, "God is my salvation"

Jesus Christ, the Savior of mankind, is, of course, the primary individual in the Bible. Accordingly, Jesus means "Jehovah is salvation," which was literally true, as God Himself came in the form of man to bear our sins. The name Jesus can also be translated Jeshua, Jehoshua, and Joshua. The name Jesus (pronounced "hay-sus") in modern times has been extremely popular in Latin American cultures, far less so elsewhere. This name has been referred to in the Bible as the one name that "is above every name" (Philippians 2:9).

*Jethro: Hebrew, "he who is prosperous"

Jethro was the father-in-law of Moses. See Exodus 3:1, 4:18, 18:1-12.

*Jibsam: Hebrew, "he who is sweet"

See 1 Chronicles 7:2.

Jim: Almost always a diminutive for James

Jimmie, Jimmy

*Joab: Hebrew, "God is my good father"

There are several Joabs in the Old Testament, mostly minor characters.

*Joachim: Hebrew, "the Lord is my judge"

*Joah: Hebrew, "God is my brother"

There are several Joahs in the Bible, who are mostly minor characters.

Joaquín: A Spanish variation of Joachim

*Job: Hebrew, "he who is afflicted"

Jobe, Joby

See Job's miraculous story of tragedy and restoration in the book bearing his name.

*Joda: Hebrew, "he who is hasty"

See Ezra 3:9 and Luke 3:26.

Jody: English, usually a diminutive for Joseph, but often a proper name in its own right

*Joed: Hebrew, "Jehovah is my witness"

See Nehemiah 11:7.

*Joel: Hebrew: "the Lord Jehovah is God"

There are several Joels in the Bible, including the prophet Joel, whose book in the Bible bears his name.

*Joha: Hebrew, "Jehovah lives"

See 1 Chronicles 8:16 and 11:45.

*Johanan: Hebrew, "God is gracious"

There are 11 Johanans in the Bible, all minor characters.

Johan: A German variation of John. See next entry.

Johann, Johannes

JOHANN GUTENBERG
(1398–1468)

was a German metalworker who developed a press with movable type, which revolutioned the printing process.

*John: Hebrew, "God is gracious"

Giovanni (Italian), Hannes (Finnish), Hans (Scandinavian), Ian (Scottish), Ivan (Russian), Jack, Jackie, Jean (French), Jens (Danish), Johann (German), Johnny, Juan (Spanish), Sean (Irish), Yanni (Greek)—see also Jonathan

The two most notable Johns in the Bible are John the Baptist and the apostle John. The great apostle was the author of several books in the Bible, including the gospel, the three epistles bearing his name, and the book of Revelation.

JOHN BUNYAN
(1628–1688)

was a preacher in seventeenth-century England who dissented from the practices of the Anglican church. His book *Pilgrim's Progress* is arguably the bestselling fictional work of all time.

JOHN CALVIN
(1509–1564)

was a key figure in the Protestant Reformation.

JOHN NEWTON
(1725–1807)

was a debauched slave trader until his conversion at age 23. He's best remembered today for his hymn "Amazing Grace."

JOHN PERKINS
(1930–)

was born into poverty in Mississippi. Converted to Christ at age 27, he began helping and serving poor communities in his home state. His courageous story is told in his book *With Justice for All*.

JOHN SUNG
(1901-1944)

was a native-born Chinese evangelist.

JOHN WESLEY
(1707-1788)

was one of the most influential theologians and preachers of all time. For generations, male sons have been blessed with the first and middle names John and Wesley.

*Joiakim: Hebrew, "Jehovah establishes"
See Nehemiah 12:10,26.

*Jonah: Hebrew, "dove"
Jonah was, in a sense, the first missionary. The prophet was sent to Nineveh to call

the people of the city to repentance. See the book bearing Jonah's name for the story of his mission.

*Jonan: Hebrew, "God has been gracious"
See Luke 3:30.

*Jonas: A variation of John

*Jonathan: Hebrew, "he who is a gift from the Lord"
Jon, Jonathon, Jonny
There are 14 Jonathans in the Bible, the most notable being the great warrior and beloved friend of King David. Read about their friendship in 1 Samuel 18.

JONATHAN EDWARDS
(1703–1758)

was one of the most influential clergymen in American history. Many of his writings are still read today, including his well-known sermon "Sinners in the Hands of an Angry God."

---

*Jorah: Hebrew, "he who teaches"
See 1 Chronicles 5:13 and Ezra 2:18.

*Joram: Hebrew, "God is on high"
There are five Jorams in the Bible, all minor characters.

Jordan: Hebrew, "descending" (apparently a reference to the descending waters of the Jordan River)
Jordy, Jordyn

JONATHAN GOFORTH
(1859–1936)

along with his wife, Rosalind (1864–1942), gave his life to Christ in service as a missionary to China. The couple suffered great hardship, but their efforts bore much fruit in advancing the gospel in Asia.

Jorge: A Spanish variation of George

*Jorim: Hebrew, "he who exalts the Lord"
See Luke 3:29.

José: A Spanish variation of Joseph

*Joses: Hebrew, "he who pardons"
There are three men with the name Joses in the Bible.

*Joseph: Hebrew, "God shall add"

Giuseppe (Italian), Joe, Joey, José (Spanish), Josef (German), Yusseff (Hebrew)

There are several Josephs in the Bible. Two of them are key characters. In the Old Testament, Joseph, the beloved son of Jacob, was betrayed by his brothers, and yet that betrayal would ultimately result in the saving of his family. In the New Testament, Joseph was the husband of Mary, the mother of the Lord Jesus.

JOSH MCDOWELL
(1939–)

is a Christian evangelist and apologist who has influenced many through his books and ministry. His *Evidence that Demands a Verdict* (1972) has served as a documentation of the historical facts of the Gospel accounts for nearly a generation.

---

*Joshua: Hebrew, "my salvation is of God"

Josh, Joshuah

Joshua was the successor of Moses in leading the Hebrews into the Promised Land. See his story in several books in the Old Testament, including Exodus, Numbers, Deuteronomy, Joshua, and Judges.

*Josiah: Hebrew, "may God protect"

Josiah was one of the good kings of Judah. His reign began when he was eight years old—see 1 Kings 13:2 and 2 Chronicles 34:3.

*Jotham: Hebrew, "God is perfect"

There are three Jothams in the Bible—see Judges 9:5, 1 Chronicles 2:47. and 2 Kings 15:32.

Jovan: A Slavic variation of John

Jovani, Jovann, Jovin

Juan: A Spanish variation of John

*Jubal: Hebrew, "the horn's ram"

See Genesis 4:21.

*Judah: Hebrew, "he who is praised"

Judas (Latin), Judd, Jude

There are several men in the Bible with variations of this

popular name. Judah was the fourth son of Jacob and Leah, and he became the leader of the tribe of Judah. See Genesis 29:35; Numbers 26:19-21; and 1 Chronicles 2:3-6.

Julian: Greek, "he who is youthful"

Julien, Julius, Jule, Jules, Julio (Spanish)

Julio: A Spanish variation of Julian

Junius: Latin, "he who is young"—the Latin variation of Julian

Justin: Latin, "he who is upright, just"

Juss, Justis, Justiss, Justus, Justyn

K

*Kadmiel: Hebrew, "God is from of old"

Cadmiel

There are three Kadmiels in the Bible, all minor characters.

Kai: Welsh, "he who protects, secures" as with a lock and key

Kala: African, "he who is tall"

Cala, Kalla

Kalil: Arabic, "he who is a friend"

Kahlil

*Kallai: Hebrew, "God is fast"

See Nehemiah 12:20.

Kalle: Scandinavian, "virile, masculine"

Cale, Kael, Kail, Kale, Kayle

Kane: Celtic, "he who is fair-complected"

Kain, Kaine, Kayne

Karl: A German variation of Charles

Carl, Karel (Slavic), Karlis, Karol (Slavic)

KARL BARTH
(1886–1968)
was a very influential theologian and writer of the twentieth century.

Karsten: A Slavic variation of Christian

Kashka: Yoruba (Nigeria), "he who is friendly to others"

Kavan: Irish, "he who is attractive"

Caven, Kaven, Kavin, Kavyn

Kean: Old English, "sharp, keen"

Keane, Keenan, Keene

Keefe: Irish, "he who is attractive"

Keef, Kief, Kiefe

Keegan: Irish, "little determined one"

Keeley: Irish, "he who is attractive"

Keely

Keenan: Irish, "little ancient one"

Keen, Kienan

*Keilah: Hebrew, "he who is enclosed"

See 1 Chronicles 4:19.

Keir: Celtic, "he who is dark-skinned"

Kerwin, Kerwyn

Keith: Welsh, "he who is from the wooded area"

Kellen: Irish, "victorious warrior"

Kell, Kellan, Kelly

Keller: Irish, "faithful friend"

Kelly: Irish, "courageous warrior"

Kelley

Kelsey: Old German, "he who lives by the water"

Kelcey, Kelsy

KEITH GREEN
(1953–1982)

was a popular singer, evangelist, and exhorter during the days of the Jesus Movement. His inspiring story is told in his biography *No Compromise.*

Kelvin: Scottish, "from the narrow brook"

Celvin, Kelvan, Kelwin

Kempton: Middle English, "from the warriors"

Kemp, Kemper

*Kemuel: Hebrew, "our God stands"

There are three Kemuels in the Bible, all minor characters.

*Kenan: Hebrew, "he who is begotten"

A grandson of Adam—see Genesis 5:9.

Kendall: Celtic, "he who comes from the valley"

Ken, Kendal, Kendell, Kenny

Kendrick: English, "strong ruler"

Ken, Kendric, Kenny, Kenrick, Rick, Ricky

Kennedy: Gaelic, "he who wears the helmet"

Kenner: Irish, "he who is of great courage"

Ken, Kennar, Kennard

Kenneth: Celtic, "he who is attractive"

Ken, Kenn, Kenny

Kent: Celtic, "fair-complected one"

Kenton

Kenyon: Irish, "he who is fair-haired, towheaded"

Ken, Kenny

Kenzie: Scottish, "worthy master"

Kermit: Dutch, "he who is from the church"

Kerry: Irish, "he who is dark"

Cary, Carey, Keary

Kerwin: Celtic, "he who is dark-skinned"

Keir, Kerwyn

Kevin: Celtic, "he who is gentle"

Kevan, Kevyn

KENNETH TAYLOR
(1917–2005)

was a giant in the Christian publishing industry of the twentieth century. His paraphrase of the Bible *(The Living Bible)* brought easier access to the Word of God for millions of readers. He was the founder of Tyndale House Publishers, one of the largest Christian publishing companies in America today.

Kiefer: A German variation of Cooper

Keefer

Kieran: Irish, "he who is dark"

Kier, Kiernan

Killian: Gaelic, "small warrior"

Kilian, Killy, Killyan, Kilyan

Kimball: Old English, "brave warrior"
Kim, Kimble

Kimberly: An English place name, referring to a meadow
Kim

Kincaid: Scottish, "he who leads in battle"
Kinkade

King: Old English, "he who rules"

Kingsley: Old English, "he who is from the king's meadow"

Kingston: Old English, "he who is from the king's manor"

Kipp: Old English, "he who is from the steep hill"
Kip, Kipper, Kippy

Kirby: Old English, "he who is from the church village"
Kerby

Kirk: Scottish, "he who is from the church"—sometimes a diminutive for Kirkland or Kirkham

What's in a Name?

At eight-and-a-half months pregnant, I was sitting in a salon chair having my hair cut. Noting that I was obviously expecting, the stylist asked if my husband and I had names picked out. I explained that this was our third child and we couldn't think of a boy's name we both liked. For our first two kids we had lists five to seven names long for both sexes. But this time we were blank for boys' names.

"If I had been a boy, my name would have been Keeve," she said while clipping away.

I asked her how to spell the name, and from the moment I heard it, I loved it. When my husband arrived home from work I asked, "What do you think of the name Keeve?"

He repeated it twice and proclaimed, "It's cool. That's it!"

Our daughter had been named after my side of the family. Our first son was named after my husband's side. So we compromised and gave Keeve the middle name Kennedy. We made everyone happy because Keeve's grandpas are Ken-n-Eddy.

LINDA ANN FROM ARIZONA

Kit: Usually a diminutive for Christopher
Kitt

Kivi: Hebrew, "he who is protected"
Akiva, Kiva

Klaus: A German diminutive of Nicholas
Klaas, Klas

Knox: English, "he who is from the hill"

Knute: Danish, "he who is kind"
Canute, Knut

Konrad: A German variation of Conrad

Kristopher: An alternate spelling of Christopher
Kris, Topher

Kurtis: Alternate spelling of Curtis
Kurt

Kyle: Irish, "a narrow strip of land"
Kiel, Kile, Kiley, Ky, Kylie, Kyler

Kynan: Welsh, "he who rules"
Ky

Kyne: English, "he who has royal blood"

*Laban: Hebrew, "he who is white"
Laban was the brother of Rebekah, the father of Rachel and Leah, and the brother-in-law of Jacob. See Genesis 24, 27, and 28.

*Lael: Hebrew, "he who is committed to God"
See Numbers 3:24.

Laird: Scottish, "lord"

Lamar: Old French, "from the sea"
Lamarr, Lemarr

Lambert: Old German, "beautiful land"
Bert, Bertie, Berty, Lamberto

*Lamech: Hebrew, "he who overthrows"
There are two Lamechs in the Bible, including the father of Noah. See Genesis 5:26-31 and Luke 3:36.

Lamont: French, "the mountain"

Lamond

Lance: Originally a diminutive for Lancelot, but more often a proper name on its own

Launce

Lancelot: Latin, "he who serves"

Lan, Lanny, Lance, Launce, Launcelot

Landers: French, "he who is from the grassy plains"

Lan, Land, Lander, Landis, Landess

Landon: Old English, "he who comes from the meadowlands"

Lan, Landan, Lanny

Lane: Middle English, "he who is from the lane, the simple road"

Laine, Layne

Lang: Scandinavian, "he who is tall"

Lange

Langston: Old English, "long town"

Lanh: Asian/Vietnamese, "he who is peaceful"

Larken: Irish, "he who is determined"

Lark, Larkin, Larkyn

Larnelle: An apparently American name with unknown roots

Larnel, Larnell

BROTHER LAWRENCE
(1611–1691)

was originally named Nicholas Herman. He served many years in the French Army, and then in midlife, joined a religious order where he served as a simple layman—a cook in the order's kitchen for the next 30 years. And yet, his small but powerful book, *The Practice of the Presence of God*, continues to encourage and refresh Christians more than 300 years after his death.

Larry: Usually a diminutive for Lawrence, Laurence, or Lars

Lars: Swedish, originally a diminutive for Lawrence, but also a proper name on its own

Laris, Larris, Larson (son of Lars)

Latham: Scandinavian, "from the barn"

Laurence: Latin, "he who wears the laurel wreath"

Lan, Lanny, Larren, Larry, Lars, Laurie, Lawrence

Lavan: Hebrew, "white"

Lavi: Hebrew, "lion"

> These commandments that I give you today are to be upon your hearts. Impress them on your children. Talk about them when you sit at home and when you walk along the road, when you lie down and when you get up.
>
> —**DEUTERONOMY 6:6-7**

*Lazarus: Hebrew, "grace"

Lazar, Lazaro (Italian)

There are two men named Lazarus in the Bible. The first one is the man in Jesus' story about the poor man (Lazarus), who died and was taken to Abraham's bosom... and the rich man who was separated from Lazarus by a wide unspannable gulf (see Luke 16:19-31). The other Lazarus was the brother of Mary and Martha. Jesus raised him from the dead and restored him to his sisters. See the story in John 11; 12:1-7.

Leaf: English, literally a tree leaf

Leal: Latin, "he who is faithful"

Leander: Greek, "he who is as fierce as a lion"

Ander, Anders, Lee

Leben: Yiddish, "life"

Lee: Old English, "from the meadow"

Leigh

Leif: Scandinavian, "he who is dearly loved"

Leighton: Old English, "from the farm meadowlands"

Lee

Leith: Celtic, "wide"

Leland: Old English, "from the land of shelter"

*Lemuel: Hebrew, "he who is dedicated to God"

Lem, Lemmy

See Proverbs 31:1,4.

Leon: Usually a diminutive for Leonard

Leonard: Old German, "he who is like unto the lion"
Leo, Leon, Len, Lenny, Leonardo, Leonid, Leonidas

LEONARD RAVENHILL
(1907–1995)
was a British evangelist and exhorter to prayer and holiness among Christians during the latter half of the twentieth century.

Leopold: Old German, "he who is bold as a lion"
Leo

Leroy: Old French, "he who is royal"

Leslie: Scottish, "from the meadow in the valley"
Les, Lesley

Lester: Old English, a place name—"coming from Leicester"
Les

Lev: Hebrew, "heart"

*Levi: Hebrew, "united one"
There are four Levis in the Bible, including the third son of Jacob through Leah. His descendants formed the Levitical priesthood.
Levy

Lewis: English, "noted warrior"
Lew, Lewie, Louis

LEWIS SPERRY CHAFER
(1871–1952)
was the founder of the influential Dallas Theological Seminary. His several books include *Grace, He That Is Spiritual,* and *True Evangelism.*

Lex: Greek, "the word"—also a diminutive for Alexander
Lexy, Lexxy

Liam: An Irish variation of William

Lincoln: Old English, "he who comes from the town by the waters"
Linc

Lindsay: Old English, "from the island of linden trees"
Lin, Lind, Lindsey, Lindy, Lyn

*Linus: Greek, "he with flax-colored hair"
See 2 Timothy 4:21.

Lionel: Latin, "he who is like unto the lion"

Llewellyn: Welsh, "he who is like unto the lion"

Lloyd: Celtic, "gray, dark-complected one"
Loyd

Locke: Norse, "he who is last"
Loch, Lock

Logan: Scottish, "from the small hollow"

Lombard: German, "he who is bearded"
Bard, Lombardo

Lon: English, usually a diminutive for Alonzo, Lawrence, or Leonard
Lonnie, Lonny

London: A British place name, from the city of the same name
Lon, Lonnie

Loren: Latin, a variation of Laurence
Lorin, Lorren

Lorenzo: An Italian variation of Laurence
Lorenso, Lorentz, Lorry, Ren, Rennie

LORENZO DOW
(1777–1834)

was a hugely popular revivalist of the Second Great Awakening—so popular that by the mid-nineteenth century, Lorenzo was one of the most favored names for male babies in the United States.

Lorne: Latin, a variation of Laurence.

*Lot: Hebrew, "he who is hidden"
Lot was Abraham's brother. See Genesis 13, 14, 19.

Louis: Old German, "noted warrior"
Lewis, Lou, Louie

Lowell: Old English, "he who is praiseworthy"
Lovell, Lowe, Lowel

Lucas: A variation of Luke that has become popular as a proper name in its own right
Lukas, Luke

Lucian: Latin, "he who brings light"
From the same root as Lucifer, the angel of light, who

fell into condemnation due to pride. However, in the original intention, the variations of this name should represent any child of God who will bring the true light of Christ to those who know him.

Luciano (Italian), Lucien, *Lucius (see Acts 13:1, also Romans 16:21)

Ludwig: A German variation of Louis

Luigi: An Italian variation of Louis

Luís: A Spanish variation of Louis

LUIS PALAU
(1934–)

is an Argentine-born evangelist who has led hundreds of thousands to Christ in his extensive international ministry.

---

*Luke: Latin, "he who brings light"

Lucas, Lukas, Luken

Luke was a physician, a man of great learning, and a committed follower of Jesus Christ. In addition to the Gospel bearing his name, Luke also wrote the book of Acts.

Luther: Old German, "he who is a renowned warrior"

Lyle: Old French, "from the island"

Lyman: Old English, "he who comes from the meadow"

LYMAN BEECHER
(1775–1863)

was the father of Henry Ward Beecher and Harriet Beecher Stowe, two of the most influential religious figures of the nineteenth century. Beecher was an ardent revivalist and helped to found the American Bible Society.

Lyndon: Old English, "linden tree"

Linden, Lindin, Lyn

Lynn: Old English, "beside the flowing water"

Lin, Lyn

Lysander: Greek, "he who sets free"

Lysan, Sandy

*Lysias: Greek, "he who sets free"
See Acts 23:26, 24:7, 22.

*Maacah: Hebrew, "compression"
Maachah
There are five Maacahs in the Old Testament, with perhaps the two more notable ones being Abraham's brother (Genesis 22:24) and one of King David's mighty men (1 Chronicles 11:43).

Mabry: Old English, meaning is uncertain

Mac: English, Irish, and Scottish prefix that means "son of"—also used as a standalone name
Mack, Mackey, Mackie

Macabee: Hebrew, "hammer"
Maccabee

Macadam: Scottish Gaelic, "son of Adam"
MacAdam, McAdam

Macallister: Scottish Gaelic, "son of Alistair"
MacAlister, McAlister, McAllister

Macdonald: Scottish Gaelic, "son of Donald"
MacDonald, McDonald

Mack: A diminutive of Mackenzie

Mackenzie: Irish Gaelic, "son of the wise ruler"—a name for both boys and girls
MacKensie, McKenzie, McKensie

Mackinley: Irish Gaelic, "learned ruler"
MacKinlay, McKinlay, McKinley

Macon: Old English, "to make, create"
Makon

Macy: Old French, "Matthew's estate"
Mace, Macey, Maceo

Maddock: Old Welsh, "he who is benevolent"
Madoc, Madoch, Madock

Maddox: Old Welsh, "benefactor's son"
Madocks, Maddocks, Madox

Madison: Old English, "valiant warrior"

Maddie, Maddison, Maddy, Madisson

*Magdiel: Hebrew, "honor of God"

See Genesis 36:43.

Magee: Irish Gaelic, "son of Hugh"

MacGee, MacGhee, McGee

Magen: Hebrew, "protector"

Magnus: Latin, "he who is great"

Magnes, Magnusson, Manus

Maguire: Irish Gaelic, "son of the beige one"

MacGuire, McGuire, McGwire

*Mahlah: Hebrew, "mildness"

Mahalah

See 1 Chronicles 7:18.

Makaio: Hawaiianized variation of Matthew

Makani: Hawaiian, "breeze"

Makimo: Hawaiianized variation of Maximus

*Malachi: Hebrew, "messenger of God"

Malachai, Malachie, Malachy, Malaki, Maleki

Malachi was an Old Testament prophet, the author of the last book of the Old Testament. You can read about him in the Bible book that bears his name.

Malakai: Hawaiianized variation of Malachi

*Malchiah: Hebrew, "God is my king"

Malchijah

See 1 Chronicles 6:40.

*Malchiel: Hebrew, "God is my king"

See 1 Chronicles 7:31.

Malcolm: Scottish Gaelic, "servant of St. Columba"

Mal, Malkolm

Maleko: Hawaiianized variation of Mark

Malin: Old English, "strong warrior"

Mallen, Mallin, Mallon

Mallory: Old German, "army counselor"

Mallery, Mallorie, Malory

Maloney: Irish Gaelic, "pious"
Malone, Malonee, Malonie, Malony

Malvin: variation of Melvin
Malvyn

*Manasseh: Hebrew, "causing forgetfulness"
Manasseh and his brother, Ephraim, were sons of Joseph, the son of Jacob. Manasseh's descendants became one of the tribes of Israel (Genesis 41:51). Also the name of a wicked king of Israel (2 Kings 21:1-2).

Mandel: German, "almond"
Mandy, Mannie, Manny

Manfred: Old English, "man of peace"
Fred, Freddie, Freddy, Manifred, Mannie, Manny—additional variations are possible to create with this name

Manley: Middle English, "meadow, guardian of a pasture"
Manleigh, Manly, Mansfield, Manton

Manning: Old English, "to station, guard"
Mannyng

*Manoah: Hebrew, "rest, quiet"
Manoah was a godly man and the father of Samson. See Judges 13.

Mansfield: Old English, "field by the little river"

Manton: Old English, "man's town"
Manten, Mannton

Manuel: Spanish, a variation of Emmanuel
Mano, Manolo, Manny

Manville: Old French, "great town"
Mandeville, Manvel, Manville, Manvill

Marc: French variation of Mark

Marcel: Latin, "he who is a hard worker"
Marceau, Marcelin, Marcello (Italian), Marcellus, Marcelo (Spanish)

Marcos: Spanish variation of the Latin Marcus

Marcus: Latin, "brilliant warrior, warlike"
Marc, Marco, Marko, Markus

MARCUS WHITMAN
(1802–1847)
was a physician who helped pioneer missionary work in the 1830s and 1840s in the Oregon Territory.

Marden: Old English, "sheltered place near the sea"
Marsden

Mario: Italian variation of Mark
Marianus, Marius, Meirion

Marion: Hebrew, "bitter, rebellious"—a name for both boys and girls
Mariano

*Mark: Latin, "warlike"
Marc (French), Marceau, Marcel, Marco, Marcos, Marcus, Mario, Marius, Marko, Markos (Greek), Markus, Marq—additional variations are possible to create with this name
John Mark was a helper to Paul and Barnabas and a close companion of Peter. See Acts 12:25.

Marland: Old English, "land near the lake"
Marlin, Marion, Marlond, Marlondo

Marley: Old English, "meadow near the lake"
Marleigh, Marly

Marlin: Old English, "sea"
Mar, Mario, Marle, Marlis

Marlon: Old French, "wild hawk"
Marlen, Marlin, Marlinn, Marlonn

Marlow: Old English, "hill near the lake"
Marlo, Marloe, Marlowe

Marsden: Old English, "field near water"
Marsdon, Marston, Marden

Marsh: Old English, "swamp, marsh"

Marshall: Old French, "horse groomer"
Marchall, Marschal, Marsh, Marshal, Marshell

MARSHALL BROOMHALL
(1866–1937)
oversaw the literature ministry of China Inland Mission and wrote the classic biography of J. Hudson Taylor.

Marston: Old English, "town by the marsh"

Martin: Latin, "warlike one"
Mart, Marten, Marti (Spanish), Martie, Martine, Martino (Italian), Martinus, Marty, Martyn (Russian)

MARTIN LUTHER
(1483–1546)
was a successful Catholic priest who became a Protestant Reformer. His mastery of the biblical languages enabled him to write an excellent German translation of the Bible.

MARTYN LLOYD-JONES
(1899–1981)
was initially a medical doctor, but then became a Protestant minister noted for his exceptional, verse-by-verse style of preaching through the Bible. He taught at Westminster Chapel in London.

Marvel: Latin, "a miracle"
Marvell, Marvelle

Marvin: Old English, "good or famous friend"

Marv, Marven, Mervin, Mervyn, Merwin, Merwyn, Murvin

Masato: Japanese, "justice"

Mason: Old French, "stonecutter"
Maison, Masen, Sonnie, Sonny

Mataio: Hawaiianized variation of Matthew

Mateo: Spanish variation of Matthew

Mather: Old English, "conqueror, powerful army"
Maither, Matther

*****Mathusala:** see Methuselah

*****Mattaniah:** Hebrew, "gift of Jehovah"
There are nine Mattaniahs in the Old Testament, all of them minor characters.

*****Matthan:** Hebrew, "a gift"
There are two Matthans in the New Testament—see Matthew 1:15 and Luke 3:29.

*****Matthew:** Hebrew, "gift of the Lord"
Mat, Mateo (Spanish),

Matheu (German), Mathew, Mathias, Matias, Matt, Mattaus, Matteo (Italian), Matthaus, Mattheus, Matthias, Mattias, Mattie, Matty—additional variations are possible to create with this name

Matthew was also known as Levi. He was a tax collector who gave up everything to become a disciple of Jesus. See Luke 5:27,29.

MATTHEW HENRY
(1662–1714)
An English non-Conformist minister and popular Bible commentator.

---

*Matthias: Hebrew, "gift of God"

Mathias, Mattias

Matthias was the disciple chosen to replace Judas. You can read the account about him in Acts 1:23-26.

Maurice: Latin, "dark-skinned"

Maurey, Maurie, Maurise, Maury, Morey, Morice, Moris, Morrice, Morrie, Morris

Mawuli: Ewe (Ghana), "there is a God"

Max: A diminutive of Maxwell or Maximilian

Maks, Maxence, Maxson

Maximilian: Latin, "greatest, distinguished one"

Mac, Mack, Maks, Max, Maxey, Maxemillan, Maxie, Maxim, Maximillian, Maximo (Spanish), Maximos (Greek), Maxy—additional variations are possible to create with this name

Maxwell: Old English, "Mack's stream"

Maxwelle

Mayer: Latin, "he who is greater"

Maier, Meir, Meyer

Mayfield: Old English, "strong one's field"

Mayhew: Hebrew "gift of the Lord"—an Old French variation of Matthew

Mayhue

Maynard: Old German, "powerful"

May, Mayne, Maynhard, Menard

Mead: Old English, "from the meadow"

Meade, Meed, Meid

Medwin: Old German, "strong friend"
Medvin, Medwyn

*Mehida: Hebrew, "famous"
See Ezra 2:52.

*Mehir: Hebrew, "price of dexterity"
See 1 Chronicles 4:11.

Meir: Hebrew "radiant"
Mayer, Meier, Meiri, Meyer, Myer

Mel: A diminutive of Melvin

*Melatiah: Hebrew, "Jehovah has set free"
See Nehemiah 3:7.

Melbourne: Old English, "mill stream"
Mel, Melborn, Melburn, Milbourn, Milbourne, Milburn, Millburn

*Melchi: Hebrew, "Jehovah is my king"
There are two Melchis in the New Testament, both of whom are ancestors of Christ (see Luke 3:24 and 3:28).

*Melchizedek: Hebrew, "king of righteousness"
Melchizedek was the king

and priest of Salem; Abraham received a blessing from him. You can read the account of this event in Genesis 14:17-24.

> Love...always protects, always trusts, always hopes, always perseveres. Love never fails.
>
> —1 CORINTHIANS 13:7-8

Meldon: Old English, "mill hill"
Melden

Melville: Old English, "town with a mill"
Mel, Melburn, Meldon, Melford, Melton, Melwood

Melvin: Irish Gaelic, "chief"
Malvin, Malvyn, Mel, Mell, Melvyn, Melwin, Melwyn, Vin, Vinnie, Vinny

*Menahem: Hebrew, "comforter"
Menachem, Nachum, Nahum
See 2 Kings 15:14-23.

Mendel: Hebrew, "wisdom"
Mandel

Mercer: Middle English, "store-keeper"

Merce

Meredith: Welsh, "protector of the sea"

Meredyth, Merideth, Meridith, Merri, Merry

Merle: Latin, "thrush" (a bird)

Merlin: Middle English, "falcon, hawk"

Marion, Marlon, Merlyn

Merrick: Old English, "ruler of the sea"

Merrik, Meyrick

Merrill: Latin, "he who is a famous one"

Meril, Merill, Merrel, Merrell, Merril, Meryl

Merton: Old English, "town by the sea"

Merwyn, Murton

Mervin: Old Welsh, "famous friend"

Merv, Merven, Mervyn, Merwin, Merwyn

*Mesha: Hebrew, "freedom"

There are three Meshas in the Old Testament, all of whom are minor characters.

*Meshach: Hebrew, "that draws with force"

Meshach was one of the friends of Daniel who refused to worship an idol and was protected while in a fiery furnace. You can read about this miraculous event in Daniel 3.

*Meshech: Hebrew, "drawing out"

Mesech

See 1 Chronicles 1:5,17.

*Methuselah: Hebrew, "it shall be sent"

Mathusala

Methuselah lived longer than anyone else in history—969 years (Genesis 5:21-27). God sent the flood upon the earth after Methuselah died.

Meyer: German, "farmer"

Mayer, Mayor, Meier, Meir, Myer

Mhina: Swahili, "he who is delightful"

*Micah: Hebrew, "Who is like God?"—a variation of Michael

Micaiah, Mike, Mikey, Mikal, Mycah

There are seven Micahs in

the Old Testament, with the most significant one being the prophet who wrote the Bible book that bears his name.

*Michael: Hebrew, "Who is like God?"

Maguel, Micael, Mical, Michal, Michail, Micheal, Michel, Michele (Italian),

The Names of the Twelve Disciples

At the beginning of His ministry, Jesus chose 12 helpers who would follow Him for three years. Because we are able to learn so much about the disciples from the New Testament, it's easy to feel endeared toward them and feel as though we know them. And it's common for Christian parents to name their sons after one of the men (except for Judas Iscariot, who betrayed Jesus). Here are the 12 names and their meanings:

Peter	"rock"
Andrew	"strong, masculine"
James, son of Zebedee	"heel catcher, supplanter"
John, son of Zebedee	"God is gracious"
Philip	"lover of horses"
Bartholomew/Nathaneal	"given by God"
Thomas	"twin"
Matthew	"gift of the Lord"
James, son of Alphaeus	"heel catcher, supplanter"
Judas (not Iscariot)	"praised"
Simon the Zealot	"one who hears"
Judas (who betrayed Jesus)	"praised"

Mick, Mickey, Mickie, Micky, Miguel (Spanish), Mikael, Mike, Mikel, Mikey, Mikhail (Russian), Mikkel, Miky, Mitch, Mitchell, Mychal—additional variations are possible to create with this name

There are ten Michaels in Scripture, and there is also the archangel Michael—see Daniel 10:13,21; Jude 9; Revelation 12:7.

MICHAEL W. SMITH
(1957–)

is a Christian singer and songwriter who has had numerous #1 hit songs and has won both Dove awards and Grammy awards.

---

*Midian: Hebrew, "contention"

Midian was a son of Abraham and his wife Keturah (Genesis 25:2).

Miguel: Spanish, variation of Michael

Mikala: Hawaiianized variation of Michael

Miles: Old German, "beloved, gentle"

Milan, Mills, Milo, Myles

MILES COVERDALE
(1488–1569)

was an English Bible translator who produced the first complete English Bible.

Millard: Old English, "caretaker of the mill"

Millerd, Millward, Milward

Miller: Old English, "one who works in a mill"

Millar, Myller

Mills: Old English, "near the mills"

Milo: German variation of Miles

Mylo

*Mishael: Hebrew, "who is what God is"

There are three Mishaels in the Old Testament, the most significant being a friend of Daniel's. See Daniel 1:6-7.

Milton: Old English, "village mill"

Milt, Milten, Miltin, Milty, Mylton

Minkah: Akan (Ghana), "justice"

Mitchell: A variation of Michael

Mitch, Mitchel, Mitchill, Mytch

Moises: Spanish variation of Moses

Monroe: Irish Gaelic, "mouth of the Roe River"
Monro, Munro, Munroe

Montague: French, "steep mountain"
Montagew, Montagu, Monte, Monty

Montgomery: Old English, "wealthy one, mountain hunter"
Monte, Montie, Montgomerie, Monty

Monty: A diminutive of Mont-names such as Montgomery

Moore: Old English, "the moors"
More

*Mordecai: Hebrew, possibly "a little man" or "worshiper of Marduk"
Mordechai, Mordy, Mort, Mortie, Morty
Mordecai raised up Esther, adopting her after her parents died. Esther later became the queen of Persia and, with Mordecai's encouragement, helped save the Jewish people from annihilation. This story is told in the Bible book of Esther.

Morgan: Welsh, "dweller by the sea"
Morgen, Morgun

Morley: Old English, "meadow by the moor"
Moorley, Moorly, Morlee, Morleigh, Morly

Morris: Old English, "uncultivated marshland"
Mo, Morey, Morice, Moris, Morrey, Morrie, Morrison, Morry

Morse: Old English, "son of Maurice"
Morrison

Mortimer: Latin, "quiet water"
Mort, Morty, Mortymer

Morton: Old English, "town on the moor"
Morten

*Moses: Hebrew, possibly "saved" or "the one drawn out" (from the water)
Mioshe, Mioshye, Mo, Moe, Moise (French/Italian), Moises (Spanish), Mose, Moshe, Mozes
Moses was chosen by God to lead the people of Israel out of slavery from Egypt and into the Promised Land.

The account of his life spans the Bible books of Exodus through Deuteronomy.

Muir: Scottish Gaelic, "moor"

Murdock: Irish Gaelic, "sailor"
Murdo, Murdoch, Murtagh, Murtaugh

Murphy: Irish Gaelic, "from the sea"
Murfee, Murfey, Murfie, Murphee, Murphey, Murphie

Murray: Scottish Gaelic, possibly "seaman, sailor"
Murrey, Murry

Myles: A variation of Miles

Myron: Greek, "fragrant oil"
Marion, Marino, Marwin, Merwin

N

*Naaman: Hebrew, "pleasant"
There are four Naamans in Scripture, the most notable being the Syrian army captain who was cured of leprosy by the prophet Elisha—see 2 Kings 5.

Nachman: Hebrew, "comforter"
Menachem, Menahem, Nacham, Nachmann, Nahum

*Naham: Hebrew, "consolation"
See 1 Chronicles 4:19.

*Nahum: Hebrew, "full of comfort"
Nehemiah, Nemiah
Nahum was a prophet who warned of God's judgment upon the city of Nineveh. You can read about what happened in the Bible book that bears his name.

Naoko: Japanese, "honest"

Napana: Hawaiianized variation of Nathan

Napoleon: Italian, "from Naples"
Leon, Leone, Nap, Napoleone

Nassor: Swahili, "he who is victorious"

Nat: A diminutive of Nathan Nathaniel

*Nathan: Hebrew, "giver, gift of God"
Nat, Natan, Nataniel (Spanish), Nate, Nathen

There are ten Nathans in the Bible, with two of the key ones being the third child of David (2 Samuel 5:14) and the prophet who confronted King David about his sin with Bathsheba (2 Samuel 7:2-17).

*Nathaniel: Hebrew, "given by God"

Nat, Natanael, Nataniel, Nate, Nathan, Nathaneal, Nathanial, Natty, Neal, Nethanel, Nethaniel, Niel, Thaniel

Jesus said Nathaniel was "an Israelite...in whom is no deceit!" (John 1:47).

NATHANIEL WILLIAM TAYLOR
(1786–1858)

was a graduate of Yale who, in 1822, was appointed the first professor of theology at the school.

Neal: Irish variation of Neil

Neale, Neall, Nealle, Niles

*Nebai: Hebrew, "fruit of the Lord"

See Nehemiah 10:19.

Ned: A diminutive of names such as Edward and Edmund

NED BERNARD STONEHOUSE
(1902–1962)

was a New Testament scholar at Westminster Theological Seminary who was influenced by the great theologian J. Gresham Machen.

---

*Nehemiah: Hebrew, "God's compassion"

Nechemia, Nechemiah, Nechemya

Nehemiah helped a large group of Israelites to return to Jerusalem at the end of their Babylonian captivity and rebuild the walls of Jerusalem—a story that is told in the Bible book of Nehemiah.

*Nehum: Hebrew, "consolation"

See Nehemiah 7:7.

Neil: Gaelic, "champion"

Neal, Neale, Neall, Nealle, Neel, Neile, Neill, Neille, Niel—additional variations are possible to create with this name

Nelson: English, "son of Neil, champion"

Nealson, Neils, Neilson, Nels, Nelsen, Nilson

L. NELSON BELL
(1894–1973)

was a longtime missionary in China and the father of Ruth Bell Graham, the wife of evangelist Billy Graham.

Nemesio: Spanish, "justice"

*Nemuel: Hebrew, "God is spreading"
See Numbers 26:9,12.

*Neriah: Hebrew, "lamp of Jehovah"
Neriah was the scribe and messenger of the prophet Jeremiah (Jeremiah 32:12).

Nestor: Greek, "traveler, aged wisdom"
Nester, Nesterio, Nestore, Nestorio

Neville: Latin, "new estate"
Nev, Nevil, Nevile, Nevyle

Nevin: Old English, "middle"
Nev, Nevan, Neven, Nevins

Newell: Old English, "new hall"
Newall, Newel, Newhall

Newman: Old English, "newcomer"
Neuman, Neumann, Newmann

Newton: Middle English, "new town"

Ngoli: Ibo (Nigeria), "happiness"

Ngozi: Ibo (Nigeria), "blessing"

Niall: Irish Gaelic, "champion"
Neil, Nial

Niamke: Yoruba (Nigeria), "he who is God's gift"

NICHOLAS OF HEREFORD
(d. 1420)

had a role in helping to produce John Wycliffe's early version of the Bible by translating text from the Latin Vulgate into English.

*Nicolas: Greek, "victorious people"
Claus, Cole, Klaas, Klaus, Niccolo (Italian), Nicole (French), Nichol, Nicholas, Nichole, Nicholl, Nichols, Nick, Nickey, Nickie, Nicklas, Nickolas, Nicky, Nicol, Nicola, Nicolas, Nicolaus, Niki, Nikki, Nikkolas, Nikky, Niklas, Nikolai (Russian), Nikolas, Nikolaus—additional variations are possible to create with this name; some of the spelling

variations above are used for both boys and girls

See Acts 6:5.

NICKY CRUZ
(1938–)

is a former gang member turned evangelist who reaches out to troubled teens through Teen Challenge and Nicky Cruz Outreach. His story is told in his bestselling autobiography, *Run, Baby, Run* (1968).

***Nicodemus:** Greek, "the people's conqueror"

Nicodemus was a Pharisee, a Jewish religious leader during the time of Jesus. You can read about a conversation between him and Jesus in John 3:1-9.

Nigel: Latin, "dark one"
Nig, Nye

Nikolao: Hawaiianized variation of Nicolas

***Noah:** Hebrew, "peace, comforter, rest"
Noa, Noach, Noak, Noë
Noah built the ark and warned people of God's coming judgment upon the earth. The account of the great flood is given in Genesis 6–8.

Noel: French, "Christmas"—a name for both boys and girls
Natal, Natale, Nowel, Nowell

Noelani: Hawaiian, "heavenly mist"

Nolan: Irish Gaelic, "famous, noble"
Noland, Nolen, Nolin, Nollan

Norbert: Old German, "brilliant hero"
Bert, Bertie, Berty, Norb, Norberto

Norman: Old English, "man from the north"
Norm, Normand, Normando (Spanish), Normen, Normie

NORMAN GEISLER
(1932–)
A theologian, philosopher, and prolific author who has written extensively on defending the Christian faith.

Norris: Latin, "northerner"

Northrop: Old English, "from the north farm"

Northrup

Norton: Old English, "from the northern town"

Norval: Old German, "he who is of the north"

Norville: Old French, "northern town"

Norval, Norvel, Norvell, Norvil, Norvill

Norvin: Old English, "northern friend"

Norvyn, Norwin, Norwyn

Norwell: Old English, "woods in the north"

Norwood: Old English, "north forest"

Nuncio: Italian, "messenger"

Nunzio

Nyamekye: Akan (Ghana), "God's gift"

Nye: Middle English, "islander, island dweller"

Nyle

O

*Obadiah: Hebrew, "servant of God"

Obadias, Obadya, Obe, Obed, Obediah

There are several Obadiahs in the Bible, the most prominent being the prophet of Judah who wrote the Bible book Obadiah.

*Obed: Hebrew, "servant"

There are five Obeds in the Bible, with the most notable one being the son of Boaz and Ruth, which makes him an ancestor of Jesus Christ (Ruth 4:17-22).

Octavius: Latin, "eighth child"

Octave, Octavian, Octavio, Octavo, Octavus

Ogden: Old English, "oak valley"

Ogdan, Ogdon

Okechuku: Ibo (Nigeria), "gift of God"

Olaf: Scandinavian, "ancestor"

Olaff, Olav, Olave, Ole, Olen, Olin, Olie, Olif

Oliver: Latin, "olive tree," or Old Norse, "kind one"

Oliverio (Spanish), Olivero, Olivier (French), Oliviero (Italian), Olivio, Olley, Ollie, Olliver

OLIVER HOLDEN
(1765–1844)

an American minister and hymn-writer who also served in the Massachusetts House of Representatives.

OLE KRISTIAN HALLESBY
(1879–1961)

was a Norwegian theologian and writer who also supported foreign missions. He resisted the Nazi movement in World War II and spent time in a concentration camp. His best-known book is titled *Prayer*.

Olubayo: Yoruba (Nigeria), "highest joy"

Olujimi: Yoruba (Nigeria), "God gave this to me"

Olushola: Yoruba (Nigeria), "God has blessed"

Oluyemi: Yoruba (Nigeria), "fulfillment from God"

*Onesimus: Greek, "profitable"

Onesimus was a slave who ran away from his master, Philemon. After he became a Christian, the apostle Paul urged him to return. Onesimus's story is told in the Bible book of Philemon.

Oran: A variation of Oren

Oren, Orin, Orran, Orren, Orrin

Orel: Latin, "golden"

Oral, Oriel, Orrel

OREL HERSHISER
(1958–)

was a pitcher for the Los Angeles Dodgers baseball team and won the Cy Young Award and World Series MVP award in 1988. Orel shares about his faith in his book *Out of the Blue*.

Oren: Hebrew, "pine tree," or Irish Gaelic, "pale-skinned"

Oran, Orin, Orren, Orrin

Orlando: Spanish variation of Roland

Arlando, Lanny, Orlan, Orland, Roland, Rolando

Orman: Old German, "he who is a mariner"

Ormand

Ormond: Old English, "from the bear mountain"
Ormand, Ormonde

Orson: Latin, "bear"
Orsen, Orsin, Orsis, Orsonio, Urson

Orville: Latin, "from the golden village"
Orv, Orval, Orvell, Orvil

Orvin: Old English, "spear friend"
Arvin, Arvyn, Ervin, Ervyn, Irvin, Irvyn, Orwin, Orwyn

Osahar: Fon (Benin), "God hears"

Osakwe: Fon (Benin), "God agrees"

Osayaba: Fon (Benin), "God forgives"

Osaze: Fon (Benin), "whom God likes"

Osborn: Old English, "divine warrior"
Osborne, Osbourn, Osbourne, Osburn, Osburne, Ozzie

Oscar: Old Norse, "divine spear, spear of God"
Oskar, Osker, Ossie, Ozzy

Osten: Variation of Austin
Austen, Austin, Ostin, Ostyn

Oswald: Old English, "god of the forest"
Ossie, Osvald, Oswall, Oswell, Ozzie, Ozzy, Waldo (German)

OSWALD CHAMBERS
(1874–1917)
became a Christian under the ministry of Charles Spurgeon and became a lecturer, preacher, and writer. He is best known for the classic devotional book *My Utmost for His Highest.*

J. OSWALD SANDERS
(1902–1992)
was an active missions spokesman and statesman as well as a Bible teacher in New Zealand and Southeast Asia. He also wrote 32 books, including the classics *Spiritual Leadership* and *Spiritual Maturity.*

---

*Othni: Hebrew, "lion of God"
See 1 Chronicles 26:7.

*Othniel: Hebrew, "lion of God"
Othniel was the younger brother of Caleb and the first of Israel's judges—see Joshua 15:17 and Judges 3:7-11.

Otis: Greek, "acute hearing"
Oates, Otes

Otto: Old German, "he who is prosperous"
Odo, Othello, Otho, Ottmar

Owen: Welsh, "young warrior"
Ewan, Ewen, Owain, Ovin, Owin

OWEN THOMAS
(1812–1891)
a Welsh preacher, was also a theologian and a writer who translated some key Christian works into Welsh.

Oz: Hebrew, "strength"
Ozzie, Ozzy

Pablo: Spanish variation of Paul
Pablos

Page: French, "young attendant"
Padget, Padgett, Paget, Pagett, Paige

Pakelika: Hawaiianized variation of Patrick

Pakiana: Hawaiianized variation of Sebastian

Palani: Hawaiianized variation of Frank

Palmer: Old English, "peaceful pilgrim"
Pallmer, Palmar

Parker: Old English, "guardian of the park"
Parke, Parkes, Parkman, Parks

Parkin: Old English, "little Peter"
Parken

Parnell: Old French, "little Peter"
Parrnell, Pernell

Parrish: Middle English, "from the churchyard"
Parrie, Parrisch, Parry

Pascal: Italian, "pertaining to Easter or Passover"
Pascale, Pasquale

Patrick: Latin, "member of nobility"

Pat, Patric, Patrice, Patricio, Patryk

PATRICK HAMILTON
(1503–1528)

was influenced by the writings of Martin Luther and was the first martyr of the Scottish Reformation.

Patton: Old English, "from the warrior's estate"

Pat, Paten, Paton, Patten

*Paul: Latin, "small"

Pablo (Spanish), Paolo (Italian), Paulin, Paulinus, Paulos, Paulus, Pavel (Russian)—additional variations are possible to create with this name

Paul (first known as Saul) was a zealous Jewish religious leader who persecuted the early Christians. His miraculous conversion story is told in Acts 9. He wrote many of the New Testament epistles.

Paulo: Spanish and Hawaiianized variations of Paul

Paxton: Latin, "town of peace"

Paxon, Payton

Payne: Latin, "countryman"

Paine

Payton: Old English, "warrior's estate"

Paton, Patton, Paxton, Peyton

*Pedaiah: Hebrew, "redemption of the Lord"

There are six Pedaiahs in the Bible, all of whom are minor characters.

Pedro: Spanish variation of Peter

Pedrio, Pepe, Petrolino, Piero (Italian)

Pekelo: Hawaiianized variation of Peter

Peleke: Hawaiianized variation of Fred

Peleki: Hawaiianized variation of Percy

Pell: Middle English, "parchment"

Pembroke: Celtic, "from the headland"

Pembrook

Penley: Old English, "enclosed meadow"

Penleigh, Penly, Pennleigh, Pennley

Penn: Old English, "enclosure"

Pen

Percival: Old French, "pierce the veil"

Perce, Perceval, Percey, Percivall, Perci, Percy, Purcell

Percy: French, "the perceptive"

Pearcy, Percey, Perci, Percie

"Each child bears the personal imprint of the Master—His brush strokes, His color scheme, His loving attention to detail. And each treasure is given to us freely by God, delivered into our hands with great pride and joy."

—STEVE MILLER

*Perez: Hebrew, "bursting through"

Phares, Pharez

See Genesis 38:29.

Perkin: Old English, "little Peter"

Perkins, Perkyn, Perrin

Perry: Middle English, "pear tree"

Parry, Perrie

*Peter: Greek, "rock"

Peder, Pedro (Spanish), Pete, Petey, Petr, Pierce, Piero (Italian), Pierre (French), Peirson (Peter's son), Pieter, Pietr—additional variations are possible to create with this name

Peter was one of the 12 disciples (Matthew 10:2), and wrote the New Testament books of 1 and 2 Peter.

PETER MARSHALL
(1902–1949)

was born in Scotland and became a popular preacher and served as chaplain to the U.S. Senate from 1947 to 1949. His story is told in the best-selling book (and popular movie) *A Man Called Peter* (1951).

PEDER PALLADIUS
(1503–1560)

was a key leader in the Danish church who was a Reformer and Bible translator.

*Pethuel: Hebrew, "God delivers"

Pethuel was the father of the prophet Joel (Joel 1:1).

Peyton: Old English, "fighting man's estate"

Payton

*Phanuel: Hebrew, "face of God"

Phanuel was the father of Anna the prophetess, who gave thanks to God when she saw the baby Jesus. The account of this event is told in Luke 2:36-38.

Phelan: Gaelic, "little wolf"

Phelps: Old English, "son of Philip"

*Philemon: Greek, "loving"

Philemon was a well-to-do Christian whom the apostle Paul remembered for his love and kindness. Paul encouraged Philemon to be forgiving when his runaway slave, Onesimus, returned. Paul's words to Philemon are found in the Bible book of Philemon.

Philip: Greek, "lover of horses"

Felip, Felipe (Spanish), Felippo (Italian), Filip, Filippo, Fillip, Phil, Philippe, Phillip, Phillipe, Phillips

Philip was one of the 12 apostles and an evangelist.

One of his amazing witnessing encounters is recorded in Acts 8:26-40.

PHILIP PAUL (POPO) BLISS
(1838–1876)

was an American hymnwriter and gospel singer. He wrote "Hallelujah! What a Savior!" and "It Is Well with My Soul."

PHILLIPS BROOKS
(1835–1893)

was an American minister in the Episcopalian church. He wrote the words to "O Little Town of Bethlehem."

Philmore: A variation of Fillmore

Pickford: Old English, "from the ford at the peak"

Pierce: A variation of Peter

Pearce, Pearson, Peerce, Peirce, Pierson

Pierre: French variation of Peter

Pila: Hawaiianized variation of Bill

Pilipo: Hawaiianized variation of Phillip

Pitney: Old English, "island of the stubborn one"
Pittney

> **PIERRE ROBERT OLIVETAN**
> *(c. 1506–1540)*
> was a cousin of John Calvin. His translation of the Bible into French was used by the French Reformers.

Pitt: Old English, "pit"

Placido: Spanish, "he who is serene"
Placedo, Placidus, Placijo

Plato: Greek, "broad-shouldered"
Platon

Pollard: Middle English, "cropped hair"
Poll, Pollerd

Pomeroy: Old French, "apple orchard"
Pommeray, Pommeroy

Ponce: Spanish, "fifth"

Porter: Latin, "gatekeeper"
Port

Powell: Old English, a surname related to Paul
Powel

Prentice: Middle English, "apprentice, a learner"
Prentis, Prentiss

Prescott: Old English, "priest's dwelling"
Prescot, Scott, Scottie, Scotty

Presley: Old English, "priest's meadow"
Presly, Pressley, Prestley, Priestley, Priestly

Preston: Old English, "priest's estate"

Preye: Ibo (Nigeria), "God's gift, God's blessing"

Proctor: Latin, "official"
Prockter, Procter

Puluke: Hawaiianized variation of Bruce

Quentin: Latin, "the fifth"
Quent, Quenten, Quenton, Quint, Quintin, Quinton, Quintus

Quigley: Irish Gaelic, possibly "messy hair"

Quillan: Irish Gaelic, "cub, endearing"
Quill, Quillen

Quimby: Old Norse, "dweller at the woman's estate"

Quincy: Latin, "estate of the fifth son"
Quin, Quincey, Quinsy

Quinlan: Irish Gaelic, "he who is strong"
Quin

What's in a Name?

My daughter, Emily, and her husband, Ryan, have dedicated their lives to missions in Africa. When Emily gave birth to twins—a boy and a girl—the unusual names they chose reflects their passion for the ministry God has called them to, which is, in effect, to explain the Word to those who do not otherwise understand.

In Acts, we read,

> On his way he met an Ethiopian eunuch, an important official in charge of all the treasury of Candace, queen of the Ethiopians. This man had gone to Jerusalem to worship, and on his way home was sitting in his chariot reading the book of Isaiah the prophet. The Spirit told Philip, "Go to that chariot and stay near it." Then **Philip ran** up to the chariot and heard the man reading Isaiah the prophet. "Do you understand what you are reading?" Philip asked. "How can I," he said, "unless someone explains it to me?" So he invited Philip to come up and sit with him (Acts 8:27-30).

This Scripture says Philip was so excited to obey the Spirit that he *ran* to the eunuch.

And, yes.... my grandson's name is Philip Ran.

Philip Ran's twin sister is named Esther Malaika. Esther was chosen because (in my daughter's words) "Esther was used by God to save the entire Jewish nation. She changed history, and yet never seems to get the credit she really deserves."

Malaika means "angel" in the Swahili language, which is native to the area Emily and Ryan's ministry serves in Eastern Africa.

BECKY FROM GEORGIA

Quinn: Irish Gaelic, "he who is wise"

Quinto: Spanish variation of Latin Quintus

Quinton: Variation of Quinten

Quon: Chinese, "bright"
Kwan

Radbert: Old English, "bright counselor"
Rad, Bert

Radburn: Old English, "red stream"
Rad, Radborn, Radborne, Radbourn, Radbourne, Radburne

Radcliff: Old English, "red cliff"
Radcliffe, Radclyffe, Raddy

Radford: Old English, "red ford"

Radley: Old English, "red meadow"
Radlee, Radleigh, Radly

Radnor: Old English, "red shore"

Rafael: Spanish variation of Raphael

Rafferty: Irish Gaelic, "prosperous"
Rafe, Raff, Raferty, Rafferty

*Raguel: Hebrew, "shepherd, friend of God"
Raguel (also known as Jethro and Reuel) was the father-in-law of Moses (Numbers 10:29).

*Raham: Hebrew, "friend, affection"
See 1 Chronicles 2:44.

Rainart: German, "mighty judgment"
Rainhard, Rainhardt, Reinart, Reinhard, Reinhardt, Reinhart

Rainier: Old German, "deciding warrior"
Rainer, Rayner, Raynier

Raleigh: Old English, "dweller of the roe-deer meadow"
Ralegh, Rawleigh, Rawley, Rawly

Ralph: Old English, "advisor, counselor"
Rafe, Raff, Ralf, Ralston, Raul, Rawley, Rolf, Rolph

Ralston: Old English, "Ralph's settlement"

Ramiro: Portuguese, "he who is a great judge"

Ramón: Spanish variation of Raymond

Ramsay: Old English, "strong island"
Ram, Ramsey

Rand: A diminutive of Randolph

Randall: Old English, "strong shield"
Rand, Randal, Randel, Randell, Randey, Randi, Randie, Randl, Randle, Randy

Randolph: Old English, "shield-wolf"
Rand, Randal, Randall, Randell, Randolf, Randy

Randy: A diminutive of Randall, Randolph
Randey, Randi, Randie

Ranger: Old French, "guardian of the forest"
Rainger, Range

Ransom: Latin, "redemption"—or Old English, "Ronald's son"
Ransome

Raoul: French variation of Ralph
Raúl (Spanish), Roul, Rowl

*Rapha: Hebrew, "he has healed"
Raphah
See 1 Chronicles 8:2,37.

Raphael: Hebrew, "God has healed"
Rafal, Rafael (Spanish), Rafaele (Italian), Rafaelo, Rafe, Rafel, Raffael, Rafi, Ravel
Jewish tradition teaches that Raphael is one of the four angels that stand next to God's throne (the others are Gabriel, Michael, and Uriel).

Raúl: Spanish variation of Ralph

Ravi: Hindi, "sun"
Ravid, Raviv

RAVI ZACHARIAS
(1946–)
a descendant of a line of Hindu priests, is a Christian apologist who speaks internationally and has written several books, among them *Can Man Live Without God?*

Rawlin: Old French, a diminutive of Roland
Rawlinson, Rawson

Ray: A diminutive of Raymond
Rae, Rai, Raye, Reigh, Rey

Rayburn: Old English, "a stream where deer go"

Raeborn, Raeborne, Raeburn, Ray, Rayborn, Raybourne, Rayburne

Rayford: A variation of Ray

Raymond: Old English, "wise guardian"

Raemond, Raimond, Raimundo, Ramón, Ramond, Ramonde, Ramone, Ray, Raymon, Raynold, Raymundo (Portuguese/Spanish)

Raynor: Scandinavian, "mighty army"

Ragnar, Rainer, Rainier, Rainor, Raynar, Rayner

Read: Old English, "red-haired"

Reade, Red, Redd, Reed, Reid, Reide

Redford: Old English, "river crossing with red stones"

Ford, Red, Redd

Redley: Old English, "red meadow"

Radley, Redleigh, Redly

Redmond: Irish variation of Raymond

Radmond, Radmund, Redmund

Reece: Welsh, "fiery, enthusiastic"

Rees, Reese, Rhys, Ries

Reed: Old English, "red-haired"

Read, Reade, Reid

Reese: A variation of Reece

Regan: Irish Gaelic, "little king"

Reagan, Reagen, Regen

Reginald: Old English, "powerful"

Naldo, Rainault, Rainhold, Raynald, Reg, Reggie, Regin, Reginaldo (Spanish), Reginalt, Reginauld (French), Reginault (French), Reinald, Reinhold, Renaud, Renault, Rene, Reynold, Reynolds

---

REGINALD HEBER
(1783–1826)

was a missionary and songwriter who served in India and wrote more than 50 hymns, including "Holy, Holy, Holy."

Reinhart: Old German, "brave counsel"

Remington: Old English, "raven-family settlement"

Renatus: Latin, "to be born again"
Rene

René: French, "reborn"—also a name for girls

Renfred: Old English, "powerful peace"

Renny: Irish Gaelic, "small and mighty"

Renshaw: Old English, "raven woods"
Renishaw

Renzo: A diminutive of Lorenzo

REUBEN ARCHER TORREY
(1856–1928)

was an evangelist invited by D.L. Moody to become the first superintendent of what is now Moody Bible Institute. He also served as dean of what is now Biola University and wrote more than 40 books.

---

*Reuben: Hebrew, "behold, a son"
Reubin, Reuven, Rube, Rubén (Spanish), Rubens, Rubin, Ruby
Reuben was the firstborn

son of Jacob and Leah and the ancestor of one of the 12 tribes of Israel (Genesis 49:1-3).

*Reuel: Hebrew, "God is a friend"
There are four Reuels in the Old Testament—see Genesis 36:4-17; Exodus 2:18; Numbers 2:14; and 1 Chronicles 9:8.

Rex: Latin, "king"
Rei, Rexer, Rexford

Rexford: Old English, "king's ford"

Rey: Spanish, "king"
Reyes

Reynard: Old German, "mighty, brave"
Rainard, Ray, Raynard, Reinhard, Reinhardt, Renard, Renardo (Spanish), Renaud, Renauld, Rey, Reynaud, Reynauld

Reynold: A variation of Reginald
Reinaldo, Reinold (Dutch), Renaldo, Renauld, Renault (French), Reynaldo (Spanish), Reynolds, Rinaldo

Rhett: Welsh variation of Reece

Rhodes: Greek, "roses"
Rhoads, Rhodas, Rodas

Rhys: Welsh, "he who is fiery, zealous"
Rase, Ray, Reece, Reese, Rey, Royce

Richard: Old German, "strong ruler"
Dick, Dickie, Dicky, Ric, Ricardo (Spanish), Riccardo (Italian), Rich, Richardo, Richart (Dutch), Richie, Rick, Rickard (Swedish), Rickey, Ricki, Rickie, Ricky, Rikard, Riki, Rikki, Ritchard, Ritchie—additional variations are possible to create with this name

---

RICHARD BAXTER
(1615–1691)
was an English Puritan minister and prolific author known for his book *The Saints' Everlasting Rest*. He was also a noted hymnwriter.

Richmond: Old German, "powerful, protector"

Rick: A diminutive of Richard
Frederick, Ric, Rickey, Rickie, Ricky, Rik, Rikki, Rikky

Rico: Italian diminutive of names such as Enrico and Ricardo

Rider: Old English, "horseman"
Red, Ridder, Ridley, Ryder, Ryerson

Ridge: A modern name, "a narrow range of hills or mountains"

Ridley: Old English, "red meadow"
Riddley, Ridly

Riley: Irish Gaelic, "valiant"
Reilly, Ryley

Ripley: Old English, "from the shouter's meadow"
Rip, Ripleigh, Riply

Roald: Old German, "famous ruler"

Roarke: Irish Gaelic, "famous ruler"
Rorke, Rourke

Rob: A diminutive of Robert

Robert: Old English, "bright, famous"
Bert, Bertie, Bob, Bobbie, Bobby, Rob, Robb, Robby, Robers (French), Roberto

(Spanish), Robertson, Robi, Robson, Robyn, Robynson, Rubert, Ruberto (Italian), Rupert, Ruperto—additional variations are possible to create with this name

ROBERT CHARLES (R.C.) SPROUL
(1939–)

is an American pastor and theologian and the founder of Ligonier Ministries. He is a prolific author whose many works include *Faith Alone* and *Scripture Alone*.

ROBERT MORRISON
(1782–1834)

was a London Missionary Society worker in China from 1807 to 1834. He helped translate the Bible into Chinese.

Robin: A diminutive of Robert—also a name for both boys and girls
Roban, Robben, Robbyn, Robyn

Robinson: Old English, "son of Robert, shining with fame"
Robeson, Robynson, Robyn

Rocco: German/Italian "rock, rest"
Roch, Roche, Rochus, Rock, Rocko, Rocky

ROBERT MURRAY M'CHEYNE
(1813–1843)

a minister in the Church of Scotland, was a much-loved preacher, pastor, poet, and prayer warrior who died of typhus at the young age of 29.
His story is told in Andrew Bonar's classic *Memoir and Remains of the Rev. Robert Murray M'Cheyne*.

Rochester: Old English, "stone fortress"
Chester, Chet, Rock, Rocky

Rock: A variation of Rocco
Rocky

Rockley: Old English, "rock meadow"
Rocklee, Rockleigh, Rockly

Rockwell: Old English, "rocky spring, a well in the rocks"
Rock, Rockne, Rocky

Rocky: A variation of Rocco

Rod: A diminutive of Roderick
Rodd, Roddie, Roddy

Roderick: Old German, "famous ruler"

Broderick, Brodrick, Rhoderick, Rod, Rodd, Roddie, Roddrick, Roddy, Roderic, Rodrick, Rodrik, Rodrigo (Spanish), Rodrigue (French), Rodrigues, Rodriguez, Rodrique (French), Rodriquez—additional variations are possible to create with this name

Rodney: Old English, "island clearing"

Rod, Rodd, Roddy, Rodnee, Rodnie

Rodrigo: Spanish variation of Roderick

Roe: Middle English, "roe deer"

Row, Rowe

Rogan: Irish Gaelic, "red-head"

Roan

Roger: Old German, "famous spearman"

Rodge, Rodger, Rodgers, Rog, Rogers, Rogiero (Italian), Roj, Ruggiero (Italian)

Roland: Old German, "fame of the land"

Orlando (Italian), Roeland, Rolan, Rolando (Portuguese, Spanish), Roley, Rollan, Rolland, Rollie, Rollin, Rollins, Rollo, Rolly, Rowe, Rowland

Rolf: A variation of Rudolph

Rolfe, Rolle, Rollo, Rolph, Rowland

Ronald: Old Norse, "mighty power"

Ranald, Renaldo, Ron, Ronaldo (Portuguese), Ronel, Roneld, Ronell, Roni, Ronnie, Ronny

Ronson: Old English, "son of Ronald"

Roper: Old English, "he who is a rope-maker"

Rory: Irish Gaelic, "red king"

Roric, Rurik

Rosario: Italian, "rosary, crown"

Roscoe: Old Norse, "from the deer forest"

Rosco, Ross, Rossie, Rossy

Ross: Scottish Gaelic, "from the peninsula"

Roscoe, Rossie, Rossy, Roswald, Royce

Rowan: Irish Gaelic, "red-haired," Old English, "rugged"

Roan, Rohan, Rowe, Rowen, Rowney

> May your father and mother be glad; may she who gave you birth rejoice!
>
> —**PROVERBS 23:25**

Rowe: A variation of Roland

Rowland: A variation of Roland

ROWLAND HILL
(1744–1833)
was a prominent evangelical minister and the first chairman of the Religious Tract Society in the United Kingdom.

Roy: Gaelic, "red," Old French, "king"

Roi, Roye, Royle, Royston

Royce: Old English, "royalty, son of the king"

Roice, Roy

Royden: Old English, "rye hill"

Roy, Roydan, Roydon

Royston: Old English, "Royce's town"

Rudolph: Old German, "famous for courage, famous wolf"—use with care, in light of the well-known children's story character Rudolph the red-nosed reindeer

Raoul (French), Raúl (Spanish), Rolf, Rolfe, Rolph, Rolphe, Roul, Rudey, Rudi, Rudie, Rudolf, Rudolfo (Spanish and Italian), Rudy

Rudy: A diminutive of names beginning with Rud-.

Rudee, Rudey, Rudi, Rudie

Rudyard: Old English, "red paddock"

Rudd, Ruddie, Ruddy, Rudel, Rudy

Ruford: Old English, "red ford, rough ford"

Rufford

*Rufus: Latin, "red-haired, fair countenance"

Rufe, Ruffus, Rufous, Ruskin, Russ, Rusty

Rufus was the son of Simon the Cyrenian, who was told

to carry Jesus' cross (Mark 15:21). Some believe the Rufus mentioned in Mark is the same one mentioned in Romans 16:13 by the apostle Paul.

Rupert: Italian and Spanish variations of Robert
Ruprecht (German)

Rushford: Old English, "ford with rushes"

Ruskin: Old French, "red-haired"
Rush, Russ

Russell: French, "red-haired, red-skinned"
Russ, Russel

RUSSELL HERMAN CONWELL
(1843–1925)
was an atheist who, after being seriously wounded during the Civil War, became a Christian and an author and biographer. He is best known for his classic *Acres of Diamonds*.

Rusty: French, "red-haired"
Rustin

Rutherford: Old English, "from the cattle crossing"

Ryan: Irish Gaelic, "king"
Rhyan, Rian, Rien, Ry, Ryane, Rye, Ryen, Ryuan, Ryun

Ryder: English, "one who rides"

Ryland: Old English, "land where rye is grown"
Ryeland, Rylan

Ryle: Old English, "rye hill"
Ryal, Ryel

Sadiki: Swahili, "a man of truth"

Salehe: Swahili, "he who is righteous"

Salem: Hebrew, "peace"
Salim, Shalom, Shelomi, Shlomi, Sholom

Salim: Swahili, "peaceful"

*Salmon: Hebrew, "peace"
Salma, Salmah, Zalman
See Ruth 4:20.

Salvador: Latin, "preserved, savior"

Sal, Salvadore, Salvator, Salvatore, Salvidor, Xavier, Xaviero, Zavier, Zaviero

Sam: A diminutive of Samuel or Samson

*Samson: Hebrew, "strong, child of the sun"

Sam, Sammie, Sammy, Sampson, Sams, Sansom, Sanson, Sansone

Samson was one of Israel's most famous judges. He led Israel for 20 years, and was of legendary strength. Yet he repeatedly disobeyed God, which led to his downfall. For this reason, the name is rarely used by parents. His life story is told in Judges 13–16.

SAMSON OCCOM
(1723–1792)

was a Native American (Mohican) who became a Christian during the Great Awakening. He became one of the best-known missionary preachers to the American Indians.

*Samuel: Hebrew, "heard by God, appointed by God"

Sam, Sammey, Sammie, Sammy, Samuele (Italian), Samuelle, Samwell, Samy

Samuel was a prophet, a priest, and one of Israel's last judges. He was Israel's spiritual leader in the transition from God as King to the human kings Saul and David. He is among the key characters in the Bible books of 1 and 2 Samuel.

SAMUEL MARSDEN
(1764–1838)

an Englishman who worked and served in a convict settlement in New South Wales, he also pioneered missionary work in New Zealand.

SAMUEL POLLARD
(1864–1915)

was an evangelist and philanthropist in China for nearly 20 years. Many became Christians under his ministry.

Sanborn: Old English, "from the sandy brook"

Sandy

Sancho: Latin and Spanish, "sacred"

Sanche, Sanchez, Sancos

Sanders: Middle English, "son of Alexander"

Sanderson, Sander, Saunders, Saunderson, Zanders

SAMUEL RUTHERFORD
(1600–1661)
was a Scottish minister who was persecuted and sent into exile. During that exile, he wrote much of his classic *Letters*.

Sandy: A diminutive of Alexander—also a name for both boys and girls

Sandey, Sandie

Sanford: Old English, "sandy river crossing"

Sandford, Sandy

Santiago: Spanish, "St. James"

Sandiago, Sandiego, Santeago, Santigo

Santo: Italian and Spanish, "holy"

Santos

Sargent: Old French, "officer"

Sarge, Sargeant, Sergent

*Saul: Hebrew, "the one who asks"

Saulo, Shaul, Sol, Sollie, Solly

Saul was the first king of Israel. However, he misused God's blessings and was disobedient, so God took the kingdom away from him and appointed David as king. Many details of his life story are told in 1 Samuel. In the New Testament, Saul was the original name of the apostle Paul, whose conversion to Christianity is described in Acts 9.

Sawyer: Middle English, "he who saws"

Saw, Sawyere

Sayer: Old German, "victorious people"

Saer, Say, Sayers, Sayre, Sayres

Schuyler: Dutch, "shield, scholar"

Schuylar, Skuyler, Skylar, Skyler, Skylor

Scott: Old English, "from Scotland"

Scot, Scoti, Scotti, Scottie, Scotty

Sean: Irish variation of John—a name for both boys and girls

Shane, Shannon, Shanon, Shaughn, Shaun, Shawn

Sebastian: Greek, "honorable, respected"

Bastian, Bastien, Seb, Sebastiano (Italian), Sebastien, Sebastian, Sebo

---

SEBASTIAN
(d. c. 303)

was a martyr who was killed during the persecution under the Roman emperor Diocletian.

SEBASTIAN CASTELLIO
(1515–1563)

was a Protestant theologian who wrote translations of the Bible in classical Latin and colloquial French.

Sedgwick: Old English, "sword place"

Sedgewick, Sedgewyck, Sedgwyck

Seeley: Old French, "he who is blessed"

Sealey, Seely, Seelye

Segel: Hebrew, "treasure"

Segev: Hebrew, "majestic"

Sekou: West Africa, "great warrior, leader"

Seldon: Old English, "willow valley"

Selden, Shelden, Sheldon

Selwyn: Old English, "friend of the family"

Selwin, Win, Winnie, Winny, Wyn, Wynn

Sergio: Latin, "he who is a servant"

Sergei, Sergey, Sergi, Sergio, Sergios

*Seth: Hebrew, "the appointed of God"

Seth was the third son born to Adam and Eve (Genesis 4:25-26).

Seton: Old English, "seaside town"

Seward: Old English, "sea guardian"

Sewerd, Siward

Sewell: Old English, "victory and strength"

Sewald, Sewall

Seymour: Old French, "from St. Maur"

Seamore, Seamor, Seamour, Seymore

Shad: A diminutive of Shadrach

*Shadrach: Babylonian, "command of Aku" (the Babylonian moon god)

The name given to Hananiah, one of Daniel's three friends (Daniel 1:7). Together with Abednego and Meshach, he was protected from harm in the fiery furnace (Daniel 3:12-20).

Shalom: Hebrew, "peace," a common greeting in Hebrew

Sholom, Solomon

*Shamgar: Hebrew, "sword"

Shamgar was the third judge of Israel. He helped to deliver the people from the Philistines. See Judges 3:31.

*Shammua: Hebrew, "famous"

Shammuah

There are four Shammuas in Scripture, the two most notable being a man sent by Moses to spy out the Promised Land (Numbers 13:4), and a son of King David and Bathsheba (2 Samuel 5:14).

Shanahan: Irish Gaelic, "clever"

Shanan, Shannan

Shane: A variation of Sean

Shaine, Shayne

What's in a Name?

When I was pregnant for the third time, having already given birth to two sons, I really wanted to have a girl. But one day my husband told me he'd had a dream and was certain we were having a boy and his name was to be Samuel. I didn't like the name Samuel. I had a girlfriend whose boy was called Sam. I just knew I didn't want to use that name. It wasn't too long, though, before I too had a dream in which I was calling our soon-to-come baby Samuel. From then on we called him Samuel, which ended up being a perfect fit. I learned that it is the child that makes the name, not the other way around.

VIRGINIA FROM OREGON

Shannon: Hebrew, "peaceful," Irish Gaelic, "wise one"

Shanan, Shanen, Shannan, Shannen, Shanon

*Shaul: Hebrew, "asked"

There are three Shauls in the Old Testament, all of whom are minor characters.

Shaun: variation of Sean

SHAUN ALEXANDER
(1977–)

is a running back for the Seattle Seahawks football team and won the league MVP award in 2005. The story of God's work in his life is told in his book *Touchdown Alexander*.

Shaw: Old English, "from the grove"

Shawn: A variation of Sean
Shawne, Shawnel, Shawnell, Shawon

Shay: A variation of Shea

Shea: Gaelic, "admirable"—also a name for both boys and girls
Shae, Shay, Shaye, Shaylon, Shays

Sheffield: Old English, "crooked meadow"
Sheff, Sheffie, Sheffy

Shelby: Old English, "from the ledge estate," or "place where willows grow"
Selbey, Shelbey, Shelbi, Shelbie

Sheldon: Old English, "from the ledge hill"—also a variation of Seldon
Shelden, Sheldin

SHELDON JACKSON
(1834–1909)

was a Presbyterian minister who served for many years as a missionary in the western frontier and Alaska. He helped begin many schools for Eskimos.

Shelton: Old English, "lives on the edge of town"

*Shem: Hebrew, "renown"
Sem
Shem was one of Noah's sons, and also an ancestor of Jesus Christ (Genesis 5:32).

*Shemaiah: Hebrew, "God is fame, Jehovah has heard"
Shemaiah is one of the more common names in the Bible. Among those given this name were a number of priests and Levites (1 Chronicles 9:14,16, 2 Chronicles 17:8, 2 Chronicles 31:15, 2 Chronicles 35:9; Ezra 10:21).

*Shemuel: Hebrew, "heard of God"

There are three Shemuels in Scripture, all of whom are minor characters.

Shepherd: Old English, "shepherd"

Shep, Shepard, Shephard, Shepp, Sheppard, Shepperd

Shepley: Old English, "sheep meadow"

Shapley, Shepleigh, Shepply, Ship, Shipley

Sherborn: Old English, "bright stream"

Sherborne, Sherbourn, Sherburn, Sherburne

Sheridan: Irish Gaelic, "seeker, wild one"

Sheredan, Sheridon, Sherridan

Sherlock: Old English, "he who has bright hair"

Sherlocke, Shurlock, Shurlocke

Sherman: Old English, "woodcutter, cloth cutter"

Scherman, Schermann, Shearman, Shermann

Sherwin: Middle English, "swift runner"

Sherwind, Sherwinn, Sherwyn, Sherwynne

Sherwood: Old English, "from the forest"

Sherwin, Sherwoode, Shurwood, Wood, Woodie, Woody

*Shiloh: Hebrew, possibly "God's gift"

A place name in the Bible— see Joshua 18:1 and 1 Samuel 1:3, 3:21.

*Shimei: Hebrew, "Jehovah is famous"

Shimi, Shimhi

Shimei appears numerous times in Scripture and evidently was popular. Among its appearances are in 1 Kings 4:18, 1 Chronicles 3:19, 8:21, 25:3, 2 Chronicles 31:12-13, Zechariah 12:13.

Shimron: Hebrew, "a guard"

See Genesis 46:13.

Shing: Chinese, "victory"

Shlomo: A variation of Solomon

Shelomi, Shelomo, Shlomi

Sidney: Old French, "from St. Denis"—also a contraction of St. Denis

Sid, Syd, Sydney

Siegfried: Old German, "victorious peace"

Sig, Sigfrid, Sigvard

*Silas: A variation of Silvanus

Silas was one of the apostle Paul's key companions in ministry—see Acts 15:40, 16:19,25,29.

Silvanus: Latin, "of the forest"

Silvain (French), Silvana, Silvano (Italian), Silvio, Sylas, Sylvan, Sylvanus, Sylvio

Silvester: Latin, "from the forest"

Silvestre, Silvestro, Sylvester

*Simeon: See Simon

*Simon: Greek variation of the Hebrew name Shimeon, "one who hears"

Shimon, Shimone, Si, Sim, Simeon, Simion (Slavic), Simmonds, Simmons, Simms, Simone, Sims, Sy, Symms, Symon

The variation Simeon appears several times in the Bible, with the two more notable ones being a son of Jacob and Leah (Genesis 29:33), and a devout man awaiting the Christ's coming (Luke 2:25-34).

Sinclair: Old French, "from St. Clair"

Sinclare, Synclair

Siyolo: Zulu (South Africa), "this is joy"

Skerry: Old Norse, "stony isle"

Skip: Middle Dutch, "ship's boss"

Skipp, Skipper, Skippie, Skippy

Skyler: Dutch, "scholar"

Schuyler, Schyler, Skylar, Skylor

Slade: Old English, "child of the valley"

Slaide, Slayde

Slater: Old English, "hewer of slates"

Sloan: Irish Gaelic, "he who is a warrior"

Sloane

Smith: Old English, "blacksmith"

Smithson, Smitty, Smyth, Smythe, Smythson

Snowden: Old English, "snow, sheltered place"

Snowdon

Sol: Latin/Spanish, "sun, sunshine"

*Solomon: Hebrew, "peaceful, man of peace"

Salamón (Spanish), Salman, Salmon, Salmone, Salomon, Salomone, Shalmon, Sheloma (Yiddish), Solaman, Solmon, Solomon, Zalman (Yiddish)

Solomon was the son of King David and Bathsheba. After David's death, Solomon ascended the throne and ruled for 40 years. His life story is recorded in 1 Kings 1–11.

SOLOMON STODDARD
(1643–1729)
was a key leader in the Protestant church in America, who had a strong interest in revival. He was the grandfather of Jonathan Edwards.

Somerset: Old English, "summer settlement"

Soren: Scandinavian variation of Severus, an old Latin name

Spark: Middle English, "happy"
Sparke, Sparkie, Sparky

Spencer: Middle English, "dispenser of provisions"
Spence, Spens, Spense, Spenser

Spike: Latin, "point, spike"

Ssanyu: Uganda, "he brings happiness"

Stacy: Old English, "stable, prosperous"
Stace, Stacee, Stacey

Stafford: Old English, "shallow river crossing"
Staffard, Staford

Stancliff: Old English, "stony cliff"

Standish: Old English, "stony parkland"

Stanfield: Old English, "stony field"
Stansfield

Stanford: Old English, "stony ford"
Stan, Stamford, Standford

Stanislaus: Latin, "stand of glory"
Stanislas (French), Stanislus, Stanislao (Spanish)

Stanley: Old English, "rocky meadow"
Stan, Stanfield, Stanlee, Stanleigh, Stanly

Stanton: Old English, "stone settlement"

Stan, Stanten, Staunton

Stanwood: Old English, "stone woods"

Steadman: Old English, "farmstead occupant"

Steadmann, Stedman

Stein: German, "stone"

Steen, Sten, Steno, Stensen, Stenssen

STEPHEN CHARNOCK
(1628–1680)

was an English Puritan theologian and writer. His classic *Discourses Upon the Existence and Attributes of God* is considered one of the best studies on God.

---

*Stephen: Greek, "crowned one"

Esteban (Spanish), Estefan, Estevan, Stafan, Staffan, Steban, Steben, Stefan (German), Stefano (Italian), Steffen, Stephan, Stephens, Stephenson, Stevan, Steve, Steven, Stevie, Stevy—additional variations are possible to create with this name

Stephen was the first Christian martyr in the New

Testament. The accounts of his selection for ministry service and his martyrdom are found in Acts 6–7.

Sterling: Old English, "high quality, genuine"

Stirling

Steve: A diminutive of Stephen

Stewart: Old English, "steward"

Steward, Stuart

Stoddard: Old English, "he who is a horse herder"

Stoddart

Storm: Old English, "storm, turbulent"

Stratford: Old English, "shallow river crossing"

Strafford

Struthers: Irish Gaelic, "near the brook"

Struther

Stuart: Old English, "a steward"

Steward, Stewart, Stu

Suhuba: Swahili, "a good friend"

Sullivan: Irish Gaelic, "dark eyes"

Sullavan, Sullevan, Sully

Sumner: Old French, "summoner"

Sutcliff: Old English, "south cliff"
Sutcliffe

Sutton: Old English, "from the southern town"

Suubi: Uganda, "he who brings hope"

Sven: Scandinavian, "youthful"
Svein, Sveinn, Svend, Swain, Swen, Swensen, Swenson

Sydney: A variation of Sidney

Sylvester: Latin, "of the forest"
Silvester, Sly

T

Tabor: English, "drum beater"
Tab, Tabb, Tabby, Taber

Tad: A diminutive of Thaddeus
Tadd, Thad

Taggart: Irish Gaelic, "son of the priest"
Taggert

Talbot: Old French, "valley-bright, reward"
Talbert, Talbott

Tanner: Old English, "leather worker"
Tan, Tanier, Tann, Tannen, Tanney, Tannis, Tannon, Tanny

Tate: Middle English, "cheerful, happy"
Tait, Taitt, Tayte

Taylor: Middle English, "a tailor"
Tailer, Tailor, Tayler

Teague: Irish Gaelic, "poet"
Taig, Teagan, Tegan, Teger, Teigan, Teige, Teigen, Teigue

Ted: A diminutive of Theodore
Tedd, Teddey, Teddie, Teddy

Telford: Old French, "iron-piercer"
Telfer, Telfor, Telfour, Tellfer, Tellfour

Tennant: Old English, "tenant, one who rents"
Tenant, Tennent

Tennessee: Cherokee (Native American)—the name of a state in the United States
Tenn, Tenny

Teodoro: Spanish variation of Theodore

*Terah: Hebrew, "turning, duration"
See Genesis 11:26, 20:12.

Tennyson: Middle English, "son of Dennis"
Tenny

Terrance: Latin, "smooth, polished one"
Tarrance, Terence, Terrence, Terrey, Terri, Terris, Terry, Torrance, Torrence, Torrey

Terrell: Old German, "belonging to Thor" (god of thunder in Norse mythology)
Tarrall, Terrall, Terrel, Terrill, Terryl, Terryll, Tirrell, Tyrrell

Terry: A diminutive of Terence—also a name for both boys and girls
Terrey, Terri, Terrie

Tex: A modern name, an abbreviation of the state Texas

*Thaddeus: Greek, "courageous, tender"
Tad, Tadd, Thad, Thaddaos, Tadeo (Spanish), Taddeo (Italian), Thaddaeus, Thaddaus, Thadeus
Thaddeus was one of the 12 disciples. He is also called

Judas, son of James. He is mentioned in Matthew 10:3, Luke 1:16, Acts 1:13.

Thane: Old English, "warrior, landowner"
Thain, Thaine, Thayne

Thatcher: Old English, "he who is a roof thatcher"
Thacher, Thatch, Thaxter

Thayer: Old English, meaning uncertain

Theo: A diminutive of Theodore

Theodore: Greek, "gift of God"
Fedor, Feodor (Russian), Fyodor (Russian), Tadd, Taddeus, Ted, Tedd, Teddie, Teddy, Teodoro (Spanish), Thaddeus, Theo, Theodor, Tod, Todd—additional variations are possible to create with this name

---

THEODORE JACOBUS FRELINGHUYSEN
(1691–1748)
a Dutch Reformed minister who moved to America, was among the early forerunners of the religious revival known as the Great Awakening.

Theophilus: Greek, "loved by God"

Theophilus was the recipient of the books of Luke and Acts (Luke 1:3, Acts 1:1).

*Thomas: Aramaic, "twin"

Thom, Thoma, Thomason, Thomson, Thompson, Tom, Tomas (German), Tommey, Tommie, Tommy—additional variations are possible to create with this name

Thomas was one of the 12 disciples. See Matthew 10:3, Mark 3:16-19, Luke 6:13, Acts 1:13.

THOMAS AQUINAS
(1225–1274)

was a prominent and influential philosopher and theologian of his day, and the writer of the classic *Summa Theologiae.*

THOMAS CHALMERS
(1780–1847)

was a key organizer of the Free Church of Scotland. He was active in evangelizing, teaching, and meeting the needs of the poor in Scottish cities.

THOMAS WALKER
(1859–1912)

was an extremely devoted missionary to India and the subject of Amy Wilson-Carmichael's biographical work *Walker of Tinnevelly.*

Thor: Old Norse, "thunder"

Tor, Tore, Torre, Tyrell, Tyrus

Thornton: Old English, "town near thornbushes"

Thorn, Thorndike

Thorpe: Old English, "village"

Thorp

Thurman: Old English, "servant of Thor"

Thurmon

We will tell the next generation the praiseworthy deeds of the LORD, his power, and the wonders he has done.

—PSALM 78:4

Thurston: Scandinavian, "Thor's stone"

Thorstan, Thorsten, Thorston, Thurstain, Thurstan, Thursten

Till: German, "people's ruler"
Thilo, Tillman, Tilmann

Timoteo: Spanish varation of the Greek name Timotheos

*Timothy: Greek, "honored of God"
Tim, Timmie, Timmy, Timoteo (Spanish), Timothe, Timotheus (German), Timothey, Tymothy

Timothy grew up in a Christian home and was the apostle Paul's "son in the faith." He was an evangelist and church leader. Paul's exhortations to him are found in the Bible books of 1 and 2 Timothy.

TIMOTHY RICHARD
(1845–1919)

was considered one of the great missionaries to China. He was involved in both ministry and education and had a key role in establishing the first modern university in Shansi province.

Tino: Spanish diminutive of Agostino and other -tino names
Teeno, Teino, Tyno

Tito: Spanish variation of Greek Titos

TIM LaHaye
(1926–)

formerly a pastor and the writer of over 50 books, is also the coauthor (with Jerry Jenkins) of the megaselling Left Behind series and cofounder of the Pre-Trib Research Center, a Bible-prophecy study group.

*Titus: Greek, "honor"
Tito, Titos, Tytus

Titus was a Greek who became a Christian under the apostle Paul's ministry. He proved to be a faithful servant (2 Corinthians 7:6,13). Paul's words to him are found in the Bible book of Titus.

TITUS COAN
(1801–1882)

was a very active pastor and Bible teacher in Hawaii for nearly 50 years. He helped establish several churches, most of which were led by native Hawaiian pastors.

*Tobiah: Hebrew, "God is good"

Tobe, Tobee, Tobey, Tobi, Tobias, Tobie, Tobijah, Tobin, Toby, Tobye, Tobyn

See 2 Chronicles 17:8 and Zechariah 6:10,14.

Toby: A diminutive of Tobiah

Tavi, Tobe, Tobee, Tobey, Tobi, Tobie, Tobin

TOBYMAC (TOBY MCKEEHAN)
(1964–)

is the lead singer for the Christian music group dcTalk. The group released the books *Jesus Freaks* and *Jesus Freaks, Volume 2,* books for teens about the persecution and martyrdom of Christians through the ages.

Todd: Middle English, "fox"

Tod, Toddie, Toddy

Tom: A diminutive of Thomas

Thom, Tomm, Tommy

Tomás: Spanish variation of Thomas

Tommy: A diminutive of Thomas

Tommey, Tommie

Tony: A diminutive of Anthony

Toney, Toni, Tonie, Tonio (Portuguese)

TONY (ANTHONY) EVANS
(1949–)

is the first African American to receive a PhD from Dallas Theological Seminary. He is the senior pastor of a multicultural church and is the founder of Urban Alternative, an organization committed to bringing both spiritual and community growth to urban areas.

Tor: Hebrew, "turtledove," Norwegian, "thunder"

Thor

Torrance: Irish Gaelic, "from the hills"

Tore, Torey, Torin, Torr, Torrence, Torrens, Torrey, Torry

Townsend: Old English, "from the end of town"

Town, Towney, Towny

Tracy: Latin, "bold, courageous"—also a name for both boys and girls

Trace, Tracey, Treacy

Travis: Old French, "at the crossroads"
Traver, Travers, Travus, Travys

Trent: Latin, "rapid stream"
Trenten, Trentin, Trenton

Trevor: Welsh, "large homestead"
Trefor, Trev, Trevar, Trever

Trey: Middle English, "three"
Trai, Traye, Tre

Tristan: Welsh, "sorrowful"
Tris, Tristam

Troy: Irish Gaelic, "foot soldier"
Troi, Troye

Truman: Old English, "faithful one"
Trueman, Truett, Trumaine, Trumann

Tucker: Middle English, "a tucker of cloth"
Tuck, Tuckerman

Tudor: Welsh variation of Theodore

Tumaini: Nwera (Kenya), "hope"

Tumwebaze: Uganda, "Let us remember God"

Turner: Middle English, "lathe worker, woodworker"

Tusabomu: Uganda, "We pray thanks to God"

Ty: Short form of names that begin with Ty-

***Tychicus:** Greek, "he who is fortunate"
Tychicus was a helper to the apostle Paul and sometimes accompanied Paul on his journeys (Acts 20:4). Paul speaks highly of him (Colossians 4:7).

Tyler: Middle English, "maker of tiles"—also a name for both boys and girls
Tilar, Ty, Tylar, Tyller, Tylor

Tyrone: Greek, "sovereign"
Tirone, Tirown, Ty, Tye, Tyron

Tyson: Old French, "high-spirited, firebrand"
Thyssen, Ty, Tye, Tyssen

U

Udell: Old English, "yew-tree valley"
Del, Dell, Udale, Udall

Udolf: Old English, "wolf wealth"
Udolfo, Udolph

Ugo: Italian variation of Hugh

Uleki: Hawaiianized variation of Ulysses

Ulf: Old German, "wolf"

Ulmer: Old English, "fame of the wolf"
Ullmar, Ulmar

Ulrich: Old German, "power of the wolf"
Uli, Ullric, Ulrick, Ulrik

ULRICH VON HUTTEN
(1488–1523)
was a German Reformer who came under the influence of Martin Luther.

ULRICH ZWINGLI
(1484–1531)
was a key leader of the Swiss Reformation and founder of the Swiss Reformed Churches. He had a major influence on bringing about positive changes in civil and state matters in Zurich, Switzerland.

Ulysses: Latin/Greek, "one who dislikes injustice, wrathful"
Ulises, Ulisses, Ulysse

Umberto: Italian, "umber" (earth-colored)

Umi: Yao (Malawi), "life"

Upton: Old English, "upper settlement"

*Uriah: Hebrew, "Jehovah is my light"
Uri, Yuri, Yuria, Yuriah
The name Uriah appears several times in the Bible, the most notable being the husband of Bathsheba. See 2 Samuel 11.

*Uriel: Hebrew, "flame of God"
Uri, Yuri
See 1 Chronicles 6:24 and 2 Chronicles 13:2.

*Uzziel: Hebrew, "God is strong, power"
Uziel, Uzziah
Six different men bear the name Uzziel in Scripture, including a man who, during King Hezekiah's reign, carried out a successful military campaign against the Amalekites (1 Chronicles 4:42-43).

V

Vail: Old English, "valley"
Vaile, Vaill, Val, Vale

Val: A diminutive of Valentine

Valdemar: Old German, "famous ruler"
Waldemar

Valentine: Latin, "strong, brave"
Val, Valentin (French/Spanish), Valentino (Italian), Valentinus, Valentyn

Valerian: Latin, "strong"
Valerio, Valerius, Valery, Valeryan, Valory

Van: Dutch, "of noble descent"—also a short form of some Dutch surnames
Vann, Von, Vonn

Vance: Old English, "marshland"

Varick: Old German, "leader who defends"
Varrick, Warick, Warrick

Vaughn: Welsh, "small"
Vaughan, Von

Venturo: Spanish variation of Latin Valerius

Vern: A diminutive of the names Verne and Vernon

Verne: Latin, "springlike"
Vern

Vernon: Latin, "belonging to spring"
Lavern, Laverne, Vern, Vernal, Verne, Vernen, Verney

J. VERNON MCGEE
(1904–1988)

was a longtime pastor and popular radio teacher on the Thru the Bible Radio Network, a broadcast in which he took his listeners through studies of each book of the Bible.

Verrill: Old French, "he who is loyal"
Verill, Verrall, Verrell, Veryl

Veston: Latin, "town of churches"

Victor: Latin, "conqueror"
Vic, Vick, Victer, Victoir, Victoriano, Victorio (Spanish), Viktor, Vittorio (Italian)

Vincent: Latin, "conqueror"
Vicente (Spanish), Vin,

Vince, Vincene, Vincento, Vincenzo (Italian), Vinnie, Vinny

Vincento: Spanish variation of Vincent

Virgil: Latin, "staff bearer"
Verge, Vergil, Virge

Vladimir: Slavic, "world prince"
Ladimir, Vladmir

W

Wade: Old English, "river crossing"
Waddell, Wadell, Wayde

Wagner: Old German, "wagon builder, wagon driver"
Waggoner, Wagoner

Waite: Middle English, "guard, watchman"
Waite, Wayte

Walaka: Hawaiianized variation of Walter

Walcott: Old English, "cottage by the wall"
Wallcot, Wallcott, Wolcott

Walden: Old English, "from the forest valley"
Waldon

Waldemar: Old German, "famous ruler"
Valdemar

Waldo: A diminutive of Waldemar
Wald, Wallie, Wally

Walena: Hawaiianized variation of Warren

Walford: Old English, "brook ford"

Walfred: Old German, "ruler of peace"
Walfried

Walker: Old English, "thickener of cloth"

Wallace: Gaelic, "from Wales"
Wal, Wall, Wallach, Wallas, Wallie, Wallis, Wally, Walsh, Welch, Welsh

Wally: A diminutive of names such as Walter and Wallace
Wallie

Walter: Old German, "powerful warrior"
Wally, Walt, Walterio (Spanish), Walther

WALLIE AMOS (W.A.) CRISWELL
(1909–2002)
was an outstanding Baptist preacher and prolific author and the senior pastor of First Baptist Church of Dallas, Texas, for nearly 50 years.

Walton: Old English, "fortified town"
Walt

Walwyn: Old English, "Welsh friend"
Walwin, Walwinn, Walwynn, Welwyn

Ward: Old English, "defender, guard"
Warde, Warden, Worden

Wardell: Old English, "watchman's hill"

Wardley: Old English, "watchman's meadow"
Wardleigh

Warner: Old German, "army guard"
Werner, Wernher

Warren: Old English, "he who is a protector, watchman"
Varner, Ware, Warrin, Warriner

WARREN WIERSBE
(1929–)
is a Bible teacher who taught on the popular *Back to the Bible* radio broadcast and has written more than 80 books.

Washington: Old English, possibly a village name
Wash, Washburn

Watson: Old English, "son of Walter"

Wayland: Old English, "land by the path"
Walen, Way, Waylan, Waylen, Waylin, Waylon, Weyland, Weylin

Wayne: Old English, "wagon maker"
Duane, Dwaine, Dwayne, Wain, Waine, Wayne

Webb: A diminutive of Webster

Webster: Old English, "a weaver"
Web, Webb

Welby: Old German, "well-farm"
Welbey, Welbie, Wellbey, Wellby

Weldon: Old English, "well-hill"
Welden

Wells: Old English, "from the springs"

Wendell: Old German, "wanderer"

Wendall, Wendel, Wyndell, Wynn

Werner: Old German, "protecting warrior"

Warner, Wernhar, Wernher

Wes: Short form of names that begin with Wes-

Wesley: Old English, "from the west meadow"

Lee, Leigh, Wes, Wesly, Wessley, West, Westley

Westby: Old English, "western farmstead"

Westbey, Westbie

Westcott: Old English, "western cottage"

Wescot, Wescott, Westcot

Weston: Old English, "west farm"

Westen, Westin

Wheatley: Old English, "wheat field"

Wheatly

Whitby: Old English, "white farm"

Whitbey, Whitbie

"The best way to think about fatherhood is this: God has chosen you for a special assignment. Out of the three billion other men on earth right now, He's chosen *you* to be the father of this particular child who is about to erupt into the world. Whether this unique individual is born to you and your wife or has come to you through adoption doesn't really matter—*God chose you.*"

—NICK HARRISON

Whitcomb: Old English, "white valley"

Whitcombe

Whitfield: Old English, "white field"

Whitley: Old English, "white meadow"

Whitney: Old English, "from the white island"

Whit

Wikoli: Hawaiianized variation of Victor

Wilbert: Old German, "he who is bright"

Wilburt

Wilbur: Old German, "brilliant"
Wilber, Wilbert, Wilburt,
Willbur

Wiley: Old English, "crafty"
Willey, Wylie

Wilford: Old English, "willow-ford"

Wilfred: Old English, "resolute and peaceful"
Wilfrid, Wilfried, Wilfryd,
Will, Willfred, Willfrid, Will-fried, Willfryd

WILFRED THOMASON GRENFELL
(1865–1940)

a British medical mission-ary, served for more than
40 years with fishermen
and native Eskimos
and Indians in Labrador
and Newfoundland.

Will: The short form of names
beginning with Will-, and a
diminutive of William

Willard: Old German, "he who
is brave"
Will, Willerd, Willie, Willy

William: Old German, "resolute
protector"

Bill, Billie, Billy, Vilhelm, Vil-liam, Wil, Wilem, Wilhelm,
Will, Willem, Wilhelm, Willi,
Willie, Willis, Wills, Willson,
Willy—additional variations
are possible to create with
this name

WILLIAM FOXWELL ALBRIGHT
(1891–1971)

was a prominent American
archaeologist and scholar
of the Bible lands.

WILLIAM BOOTH
(1829–1912)

was an evangelist and
the founder of the
Salvation Army.

WILLIAM CAREY
(1761–1834)

is often called the "father
of modern missions." He
was a pioneer missionary
to India and started the
Baptist Missionary Society.

WILLIAM TYNDALE
(1494–1536)

an English Reformer and
martyr, translated the
Bible from its original lan-guages into English.

Wilson: Old English, "son of William"

Willson

WILSON CARLILE
(1847–1942)

was an Anglican minister in England who founded the Church Army, which reached out to those who lived in urban slums.

Winfred: English, "peaceful friend"

Winslow: Old English, "friend's hill"

Winston: Old English, "friendly town"

Win, Winnie, Winny, Winsten, Winstonn, Winton, Wynston, Wystan

Winthrop: English, "friend's village"

Wolcott: English, "wolf's cottage"

WOLFGANG FABRICIUS CAPITO
(1478–1541)

was a Protestant Reformer and theologian who had contact with Martin Luther and Huldrych (Ulrich) Zwingli.

Wolfgang: Old German, "traveling wolf"

Woodrow: Old English, "row by the woods"

Wood, Woodie, Woody

Woodward: Old English, "forest warden"

Woodard

Woody: A diminutive of Woodrow

Wyatt: Old French, "small fighter"

Wiatt, Wyatte, Wye, Wyeth

Wycliff: Old English, "white cliff"

Wycliffe

Wylie: Old English, "he who is clever"

Wiley, Wye

Wyndham: Old English, "village near a winding way"

Windham, Wynndham

Wynn: Welsh, "fair one"

Win, Winn, Winnie, Winny, Wynne

Xan: A diminutive of Alexander

Xanthus: Latin, "golden-haired"

Xavier: Basque, "new house"
Javier, Saviero, Xaver
(German), Xever, Zavier

Xenos: Greek, "hospitality"
Zeno, Zenos

Xerxes: Persian, "monarch"

Ximenes: Spanish variation of
Simon
Ximenez

*Note: Some names beginning with
Y can also be altered to begin with
I or J.*

Yagil: Hebrew, "rejoice"
Yagel

Yahya: Swahili, "God's gift"

Yankov: Hebrew variation of
Jacob
Yancob, Yachov, Yacov,
Yakob, Yakov

Yale: Old English, "heights,
upland"
Yael

Yancy: possibly a Native American word that means
"Englishman"
Yance, Yancey, Yantsey

Yannis: Greek variation of John
Yanni, Yannakis

Yardley: Old English, "fenced
meadow"
Yardlee, Yardleigh, Yardly,
Yarley

Yasuo: Japanese, "calm"

Yavin: Hebrew, "God will understand"
Jabin, Jehoram, Joram,
Yadin, Yadon, Yavniel, Yediel,
Yehoram

Yehudi: Hebrew, "praise"—
related to the masculine
Jude and feminine Judith
Judah, Yechaudi, Yehuda,
Yehudah

Yigal: Hebrew, "God will
redeem"
Yagel, Yigael, Yigdal

Yitzhak: Hebrew, "laughter"
Itzak, Izaak, Yitzchak

Yochanan: Hebrew, "the Lord is
gracious"
Johanan, Yohannan

Yohance: Hausa (Nigeria), "God's gift"

Yora: Hebrew, "to teach"
Jorah, Yorah

York: Celtic, "boar settlement, yew-tree settlement"

Yves: French, a variation of the German name Ivo
Ives

Z

*Zacchaeus: Hebrew, "God remembers"

Zacchaeus was a Jew whom fellow Jews despised because he worked as a tax collector for the Roman government. His encounter with Jesus and subsequent conversion is described in Luke 19:1-10.

*Zachariah: Hebrew, "the Lord has remembered"

Zacarias (Spanish), Zacary, Zach, Zachari (German), Zacharias, Zachary, Zack, Zackariah, Zackerias, Zackery, Zak, Zakarias, Zecheriah, Zekariah, Zeke—additional variations are possible to create with this name

Zacharias was the father of John the Baptist. The fascinating account of an angelic visitor who announces John the Baptist's birth and Zacharias being unable to speak until the baby is born is given in Luke 1.

Zachariah was the son of Jeroboam II, a king of Israel (2 Kings 14:29) and the grandfather of King Hezekiah (2 Chronicles 29:1).

ZACHARIAS URSINUS
(1534–1583)

was a German Reformer who helped to craft the Heidelberg Catechism, a key document expressing the beliefs of Christians.

*Zacharias: See Zachariah

Zachary: Hebrew, "the Lord has remembered"—a popular form of Zachariah

Zaccary, Zaccery, Zachery, Zackarey, Zackary, Zackery

ZACHARY MACAULAY
(1768–1838)

was a longtime advocate in the fight to end the slave trade.

Zack: A diminutive of Zachary

*Zadok: Hebrew, "fair, righteous"

Zadoc, Zaydok

Zadok appears several times in the Bible, with one of the more notable instances being a man who was chosen by King Solomon to serve as priest because he was loyal—see 1 Kings 1:8.

Zakkai: Hebrew, "pure, innocent"

Zale: Greek, "sea-strength"

Zayle

*Zalmon: Hebrew, "His shade, shady"

Salmon

See 2 Samuel 23:28.

Zane: English, possibly a variation of John

Zain, Zaine, Zayne

Zared: Hebrew, "trap"

*Zebadiah: Hebrew, "gift of Jehovah"

Zeb, Zebediah

This name appears several times in the Bible, including in 1 Chronicles 12:7, 26:2, 27:7.

*Zebedee: Hebrew, "the gift of God"

Zebedee was the father of James and John, two of the 12 disciples who followed Jesus (Matthew 10:2).

*Zebulun: Hebrew, "dwelling of honor"

Zebulen, Zebulon, Zevulon, Zevulun

Zebulun was the tenth son of Jacob, born to Jacob's wife Leah (Genesis 30:20).

*Zechariah: Hebrew, "God has remembered"

Zecher

Zechariah appears many times in Scripture, but the most notable instance is the minor prophet Zechariah, who prophesied of the nation of Israel's eventual restoration and redemption. His life and prophecies are recorded in the Old Testament book that bears his name.

*Zedekiah: Hebrew, "righteousness of the Lord"

Zed, Zedechiah, Zedekias

Zedekiah was the last king of the southern kingdom of Judah before it was taken captive by King Nebuchadnezzar of Babylon. See 2 Kings 24:17–25:7.

Zeke: A diminutive of Ezekiel

*Zenas: Greek, "hospitable"
Zenios, Zenon
See Titus 3:13.

*Zephaniah: Hebrew, "hidden by God"
Zeph, Zephan, Zevadia
Zephaniah appears a few times in the Bible, the most notable instance being the minor prophet Zephaniah, who wrote the Bible book that bears his name.

*Zerah: Hebrew, "morning brightness"
Zerah appears frequently in Scripture, including in Numbers 26:13, Joshua 7:1,24; 1 Chronicles 1:37,44, 6:21.

*Zereth: Hebrew, "brightness"
See 1 Chronicles 4:7.

*Zeri: Hebrew, "balm"
See 1 Chronicles 25:3.

Zev: Hebrew, "wolf"
Seff, Sif, Zeeb, Zeev

*Zichri: Hebrew, "famous, remembers"
Zichri is a popular name that appears several times in the Bible, such as in Exodus 6:21;

1 Chronicles 8:19,23,27, 2 Chronicles 17:16, Nehemiah 11:9; 12:17.

Zindel: Yiddish variation of Alexander
Zindil

Ziolo: Spanish, derived from the Greek name Zoë ("life")

Ziv: Hebrew, "brilliance, light of God"
Ziven, Zivon

> As a father has compassion on his children, so the LORD has compassion on those who fear him.
> —PSALM 103:13

Zuberi: Swahili, "he who is strong"

*Zuriel: Hebrew, "the Lord my rock"
See Numbers 3:35.

Selected Sources

Christianson, Laura. *The Adoption Decision: 15 Things You Want to Know Before Adopting*. Eugene, OR: Harvest House, 2007.

Concise Dictionary of Christianity in America. Daniel G. Reid, Robert D. Linder, Bruce L. Shelley, Harry S. Stout, Craig A. Noll, eds. Downers Grove, IL: InterVarsity Press, 1995.

Douglas, J., et.al. *Who's Who in Christian History*. Wheaton, IL: Tyndale House, 1992.

Lockyer, Herbert. *All the Men of the Bible*. Grand Rapids, MI: Zondervan, 1988.

Lockyer, Herbert. *All the Women of the Bible*. Grand Rapids, MI: Zondervan, 1988.

Tucker, Ruth A. *Guardians of the Great Commission: The Story of Women in Modern Missions*. Grand Rapids, MI: Academie Books, 1988.

Twentienth-Century Dictionary of Christian Biography, J.D. Douglas, ed. Grand Rapids, MI: Baker Books, 1995.

Willmington, Harold L. *Willmington's Complete Guide to Bible Knowledge; Volume 1, Old Testament People*. Wheaton, IL: Tyndale House, 1990.

Willmington, Harold L. *Willmington's Complete Guide to Bible Knowledge; Volume 2, New Testament People*. Wheaton, IL: Tyndale House, 1990.

Woodbridge, John. *Ambassadors for Christ*. Chicago: Moody Press, 1994.

Woodbridge, John. *More Than Conquerors*. Chicago: Moody Press, 1992.

Baby Name Worksheet

Baby Name Worksheet

_____   _____

_____   _____

_____   _____

_____   _____

_____   _____

_____   _____

_____   _____

_____   _____

_____   _____

_____   _____

_____   _____

_____   _____

_____   _____

_____   _____

Baby Name Worksheet

Baby Name Worksheet

_____   _____

_____   _____

_____   _____

_____   _____

_____   _____

_____   _____

_____   _____

_____   _____

_____   _____

_____   _____

_____   _____

_____   _____

Other Books by Nick Harrison

365 WWJD: Daily Answers to "What Would Jesus Do?"
(Harper San Francisco, 1998)

*Best of All, God Is with Us: Daily Devotions
from the Life and Ministry of John Wesley*
(Wesleyan Publishing House, 2005)

His Victorious Indwelling
(Zondervan, 1998)

*Magnificent Prayer: 366 Devotions
to Deepen Your Prayer Experience* (Zondervan, 2001)

*Promises to Keep: Daily Devotions for
Men Seeking Integrity*
(Harper San Francisco, 1996)

Survival Guide for New Dads
(Harvest House, 2003)

Other Books by Steve Miller

A Child's Garden of Prayer
(Harvest House, 1999)

C.H. Spurgeon on Spiritual Leadership
(Moody Publishers, 2003)

D.L. Moody on Spiritual Leadership
(Moody Publishers, 2004)

One-Minute Praises
(Harvest House, 2006)

One-Minute Promises
(Harvest House, 2006)

One-Minute Promises of Comfort
(Harvest House, 2007)

Survival Guide for New Dads
(Harvest House, 2003)

Other great parenting resources from Harvest House Publishers

365 THINGS EVERY NEW MOM SHOULD KNOW
A Daily Guide to Loving and Nurturing Your Child

Linda Danis

ISBN: 978-0-7369-0923-5

This daily guide to the first year of motherhood gives you prayerful, playful, and practical information to energize you in your new role. Features weekly devotionals and daily activities that help you foster your baby's physical, emotional, social, and spiritual growth.

THE POWER OF A PRAYING® PARENT
Stormie Omartian

ISBN: 978-0-7369-1925-8

After decades of raising her children along with her husband, Michael, bestselling author Stormie Omartian looks back at the trials, joys, and power found in praying for her kids. In 30 easy-to-read chapters, Stormie shares from personal experience how you can pray effectively for your children.

THE MOM I WANT TO BE
Rising Above Your Past to Give Your Kids a Great Future

T. Suzanne Eller

ISBN: 978-0-7369-1755-1

Your experience as a mother is influenced by the mothering you received. If inconsistency or neglect was a part of that upbringing, you need a healthier vision of how wonderful motherhood can be.

Suzie Eller compassionately shows how you can turn from a painful past and become the mom you want to be.

A CHILD'S GARDEN OF PRAYER
Turning Little Hearts Toward God

Steve Miller, Becky Miller
Paintings by Kathryn Andrews Fincher

ISBN: 978-0-7369-0117-8

Turn little hearts in your home toward heaven with this beautiful collection of more than 50 prayers for young children. Best-loved classic verse, original prayers, and read-along rhymes will lead your little ones to fall in love with the practice of thanksgiving. Paintings by Kathryn Andrews Fincher perfectly capture the joyous spirit of this child–friendly garden of grace.

HARVEST HOUSE
PUBLISHERS